the fish finger years

(what your mother never told you about bringing up kids)

Also by Fiona Gibson

Fiction

Babyface

Wonderboy

About the author

Fiona Gibson is a freelance journalist who has written for many publications including *The Observer*, *The Guardian*, *Red* and *Marie Claire* and has a regular column on parenting in the *Sunday Herald*. She was previously the editor of *More!* magazine. She is the mother of three small children (including twin boys) and lives in Lanarkshire. She is also the author of two novels, *Babyface* and *Wonderboy*.

fiona gibson

the fish finger years

(what your mother never told you about bringing up kids)

H

HODDER

Grateful acknowledgement is made for permission to reprint excerpt
from the following copyrighted material: Quote reproduced from *Raising Boys:
Why boys are different and how to help them become happy and well-balanced men*
by Steve Biddulph (2nd edition © 2003), is reproduced with the permission of
HarperCollins Publishers Ltd and Finch Publishing.
Extract from *Charlie and the Chocolate Factory* by Roald Dahl, published by
Jonathan Cape Ltd and Penguin Books Ltd.

First published in Great Britain in 2005 by Hodder and Stoughton
A division of Hodder Headline

A Hodder Paperback

1 3 5 7 9 10 8 6 4 2

A CIP catalogue record for this title is
available from the British Library

ISBN 0 340 83879 5

Typeset in 10.5/13.75pt Electra by Palimpsest Book Production Limited,
Polmont, Stirlingshire

Printed and bound by
Clays Ltd, St Ives plc

Hodder Headline's policy is to use papers that are natural,
renewable and recyclable products and made from wood grown
in sustainable forests. The logging and manufacturing processes
are expected to conform to the environmental regulations of the
country of origin.

Hodder and Stoughton Ltd
A division of Hodder Headline
338 Euston Road
London NW1 3BH

For Helen and Fliss,

who saved my bacon during the
Bethnal Green baby years

acknowledgments

With many thanks to:

My lovely friends who have shared their tips and experiences for this book: Jen, Kath, Cheryl, Stephen, Una, Elizabeth, Adele, Fiona, Janine, Margaret, Karen, Jacqueline, Tania, Amanda, Annwyn, Donna, Yvonne, Gavin, Julie, Deany, Sheena, Michelle, Radhika, Jane Parbury, Jane Alexander. Penny and Mink for hauling me through those ciggie cravings.

Ellie, Cathy and Wendy for huge support all along the way. Margery and Keith, as always.

My wonderful agent, Annette Green. All at Hodder especially Sara Kinsella, Emma Longhurst and Jack Dennison. Sue and Chris at Atkinson Pryce.

The many Mumsnetters who shared their tips and anecdotes on **www.mumsnet.com** (as addictive as many other leisure pursuits but without the hangovers – to any parent, an absolute godsend).

The experts: Dr Dorothy Einon, Tim Kahn, Caryn Skinner, Helena Sharpstone, Suzie Hayman, Tina Jesson, Kim Einhorn, Naomi Rawlings, Nick Fisher, Lesley Steyn, Professor Stephen Palmer, Sue Maxwell, Jennifer Smith, Steve Biddulph.

Several sections in this book were previously published in a slightly different form in the *Sunday Herald*, *The Guardian*, *Red* magazine and *Family Circle*. Reprinted with kind permission. Thanks to Jane Wright at the *Sunday Herald*, Andrea Childs at *Red*, and Hannah Pool at *Guardian Weekend*.

Jimmy and my own fish finger scoffers: Sam, Dex and Erin.

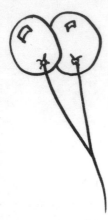

contents

introduction

Before we had kids I paid little heed to the smaller members of the species. Sure, I'd *notice* them – swiping at sweets at the M&S checkout, or thundering down from their bedrooms and hollering, 'Wanna drink!' while their parents and I attempted to enjoy a proper grown-up evening. Yes, I was aware of other people's kids, ripping off their cacky nappies in public places, and breaking free of their buggy restraints in order to catapult themselves mere inches in front of oncoming buses. Occasionally I'd wonder: why do parents slap their kids after they've prevented them from being run over? He's okay, so you smack him, then he's crying and definitely *not okay* – where's the logic? I didn't realise that logic doesn't come into it. Rarely did I consider that I might want one of these wild, unpredictable, damp-nostrilled creatures of my very own.

What I did think about was children's bedrooms: or, more precisely, the beautiful environment I'd create for the mythical being that was The Baby I Might Have One Day. Here's what I pictured: pale lilac walls, small arrangement of tasteful cuddly toys (not your battery-operated, highly-flammable acrylic pink rabbit which hops across the carpet in a sinister manner), shelf housing a neat stack of the books I'd loved as a child (*Rosie's Walk, Miffy Goes to Hospital, Where the Wild Things Are*). Like pretty much every child-free buffoon, I had less than zero idea about the realities of raising a miniature human being.

1

I thought that, when a child had finished a jigsaw, he would carefully put all the pieces back into the box and replace the lid. I didn't imagine that he would wander off to tip 762 Lego pieces out of another box, then stamp on the jigsaw box lid, before mooching off for a wee and tinkling all over the bathroom floor and failing to flush the lav, and *then* – without washing his hands – opening the fridge door, extracting an open pack of butter, licking it, and finally dropping it on to the floor to be coated by the little bits of stick and grass and soil which he'd tramped in from the garden. Then, having thoroughly trashed the house, he would swing gently on the still open fridge door and declare: 'I don't know what to *doo-hoo*.'

I'd never considered any of this, because I felt – with absolute certainty – that when I did produce kids, I would pay someone else to look after them. Someone once told me about baby hotels, where your children can go for a mini holiday without you, and I actually believed that these places exist. Sure, I was confident that I'd relish the prettier aspects of child-rearing: scampering through leafy glades, and cuddling up on the sofa with my pink-cheeked offspring – I actually thought that child-rearing would consist solely of scampering and cuddling. However, I'd definitely skip the humdrum bits (laundering bibs). In order to achieve this blissful state of affairs, I'd hire a competent, reassuringly plain-faced nanny who would present smear-free cuties on my return from the office.

Then I became pregnant, and we discovered that we were expecting twins. My partner J suggested that I take a career break. 'I'd go mental,' I retorted. My bump grew, and grew, until – at barely five foot three – I was a humungous doughball with a tiddly pimple on top. One generous friend observed, 'Your head looks like a pea on a drum.'

Our sons were born in 1997. I started to wonder whether a *brief* spell at home wasn't such an appalling idea. Maybe it was an after-effect of all those yummy pain-relieving drugs, or the mushy consistency of my brain at that time, but I thought: how hard can it be? I looked forward to lying on the grass in our East London park, acquiring a tan and flipping idly through *Heat* magazine.

And of course, it was nothing like that. Like most new parents, I was a demented, sleep-deprived wreck. Pre-babies, I'd known just two facts about our neighbourhood: that the Tube fare to work cost £1.40, and the off-licence shut at ten pm. Now I was here all the time, obsessing over what my swishy working friends might be doing. It seemed that whenever something horrible happened – vomit explosion, unsavoury nappy incident in public place – a former colleague would call to brag that she was just leaving for a conference at Babington House, or killing time between her Indian head massage and breast exfoliation treatment.

Dr Winnicott, a 1930s psychoanalyst, declared that separating young children from the home – ie, enlisting some form of childcare – could cause a kid to experience 'emotional blackout'. He failed to acknowledge the emotional blackout experienced by a previously kitten-heeled woman now stripped of her smart working wardrobe, who can no longer enter her favourite shop because the buggy's too wide. I was ridiculously envious of J's twenty-minute journey to work on the Central Line. I pictured him pondering the *Guardian* crossword when of course he was hot and fuming and wedged under a stranger's festering armpit.

Then something clicked, and I got my head around several crucial facts:

✳ Every parent should be forced, by law, to make friends with other parents. These people will save you.

✱ Parenting is unlike any other job, in that there's a distinct absence of feedback or performance reviews. No one whoops, 'Fabulous presentation!' just because you and your children have managed to emerge from the house with everyone's shoes on the right feet.

✱ Everything is a phase. Tantrums, fevers, foul nappies, bed-wetting, biting, clinginess, inter-sibling fighting, demanding ketchup sandwiches with crusts removed – all phases.

✱ When one phase subsides, another begins.

✱ There isn't a parent on this earth who hasn't calculated the precise date at which the last of their offspring will leave home.

✱ Life improves dramatically as our children grow older.

✱ In restaurants, it is perfectly normal for a child to be more enthralled by the roaring hand dryer in the toilets than anything on his plate.

✱ Every other parent is as freaked out as you are. It's just that some people are really good at pretending that they know everything, and live some perfect Boden-catalogue life.

I dearly wish that someone had shouted that last point right into my face. It would have made a big difference. And that's why I decided to write this book. Yes, parenting advice is often useful, occasionally sanity-saving – but what's really perked me up over the years is hearing about the messy, chaotic and often hugely embarrassing stuff which constitutes eighty per cent of child-rearing. I decided to collect parents' anecdotes and confessions, as well as their nuggets of advice, and piece them together with my own experience of being a very imperfect mother.

introduction

While this book doesn't claim to make parenting easy, it will at least reassure you that it's not just your kid who delights in exposing his bum, in a crowded playground, while balancing on the uppermost bar of a climbing frame.

Fiona, mother to
Sam and Dexter, aged seven, and Erin, four

1

kids in the house

Your child's bedroom: showroom or cesspit? • beating
back chaos • your pants drawer and other private places
• who wants an anally-retentive kid? • getting children
to tidy up without paying them (much) • entertaining
other people's kids (and horrible things about them) •
why your own children want to injure each other • better
things to do than fighting • our PlayStation row • how
much telly should kids watch?

Let me start by describing a bedroom. Actually, it's similar in feel to my fantasy child's bedroom, except that instead of lilac, there's white – white walls, white floorboards, white wardrobe, white chest of drawers – acres of dazzling, exhale-and-you'll-foul-it-up white. Being in this room is, I imagine, similar to finding yourself in Antarctica, minus the penguins.

In fact, there is a penguin – a cuddly penguin – nestling among a small collection of tasteful playthings. Yes, this is a child's bedroom. In fact, it belongs to a four-year-old boy – my best friend's kid.

In this room you're safe in the knowledge that you won't encounter anything disgustingly sticky and that your bare foot won't land on a slimy banana – which should be comforting but is, in fact, rather spooky. Where's the messy stack of mangled Simpsons comics, the scattering of de-robed Action Men, the billions of dried-up felt tips, the smell which I can only describe as Eau de Boy's Bedroom – a fragrant blend of festering duvet, rank socks, ancient biscuits and slowly putrefying apple cores?

Whenever I come home from Tidy Kid's house, I'm awash with revulsion at the state of my sons' shared room. Here we see not acres of hygienic whiteness, but chocolate Santas left over from Christmas, now ground into the carpet, and a lingering whiff of something which could possibly be rotting shellfish, trapped in an airing cupboard for centuries, but turns out to be an upended carton of fish food. Spend too long in this dank hovel and you start fretting that bad things are happening to your respiratory system.

I start fixating on my sons' room, blaming it for the fact that we've been invaded by small browny-grey rodents. Mouse colonies roam freely, relishing the massive soft play centre with twenty-four-hour snack bar that is my sons' boudoir. The rodent problem gets so bad that I have to call the environmental health man. When he arrives, I ask, 'What's the main reason for mice to take over a house?'

He shoots a nervous glance into my sons' room and says, 'Poor housekeeping.'

In desperation, I call my friend Lucy – Tidy Kid's mother – demanding to know how she maintains such a pristine environment. 'Children mimic their parents,' she says. 'Could you be setting a bad example?'

'It's all their stuff,' I protest. 'There's so much of it. We're drowning under seven years' worth of toys.' Actually, this is a real possibility: that my partner J and I will be found, deceased, under a 230-piece Transforming Blok Bots Ultimate Assault construction kit.

'Do they *need* so many toys?' Lucy asks.
Then it hits me. There is only one solution.

It's the toys . . . or us

Some facts to consider when poised to buy your child yet more stuff:

⭐ The average cost of raising a child is £140,000. Surely, a whopping proportion of this total is spent on toys which look pretty fabulous on the box but, once home, simply merge with the millions of other pieces of useless plastic which spear your backside as you lower yourself on to the sofa, sabotaging any hope of creating a minimalist *Elle Deco*-inspired lifestyle.

⭐ Sadly, charity shops might not want your old guff. (Gone are the days when you could dump all your old tripe in front of a sweet-faced elderly lady, and run.) Some shops will accept only toys with a BSA kite mark. Call first before depositing some enormous plaything – ie, a sixteen-floor multi-storey garage. Hospitals are unwilling to take used toys, but are grateful for as-new boxed delights. To dump the truly awful stuff that no charitable organisation would want, you can either car boot it (accepting that the real junk will follow you home) or sling it into a bin bag until the next call for jumble. Of course you could – gasp – just bin it.

⭐ Two bin liners can be filled with old dross without a child twigging that you've had a sneaky sort-out.

> ☙ In the unlikely event that your kid bleats, 'Where's that broken old biro that leaks ink and doesn't work but I really, really like?' simply reply, 'I'm sure it'll turn up eventually', or, 'I think Dad was using it.'
>
> ☙ Scary facts: by the age of three, fifty per cent of children have a CD player in their bedrooms, and forty-two per cent their own TV, according to a survey conducted by *Mother and Baby* magazine. Meanwhile, two-thirds are bought new toys at least once a month. Clearly, something must be done.

So I come up with a plan. I creep off to the Heart, Chest and Stroke shop with a heap of knackered playthings, including an infuriating 'talking' alphabet toy with only one working button ('M is for mat! M is for mat!'). Back home, I brag to J about my space-clearing endeavours. 'Great,' he says, 'they have way too much stuff – it's *disgusting*,' as if he had no part in the purchasing of these items. Truth is, he buys our kids far more of the stuff they really want – noisy weapons from Woolies, horrible neon-bright sweeties – than I do. Yet still he retorts: 'They're so spoiled, it's ridiculous. When I was their age . . .'

At this point, our children spin off to some parallel universe, where there is no tedious parent droning: 'When I was your age, I had virtually nothing. Just a tin of marbles and a second-hand Scalextric. And you know what? I thought I was the luckiest boy in the world.' J insists – rather unconvincingly – that one Christmas, his most impressive present was a packet of sparkly pipe-cleaners. One of our sons stifles a yawn. His brother jiggles a wobbly tooth and asks, 'Where is Paris?'

J is angry now. Not only do our children own more toys than any other kids in the world ('More than princes and princesses?'

our daughter asks, gleefully,) they also start humming, and spinning on our swivel chair, just as their father is reminding them that he would willingly bring in coal from the shed – at *four years old* – while holding down three separate paper rounds (total distance walked per week: twenty-one miles) and doing a weekly shop for his granny. 'Where's that Scalextric now, Dad?' one of our sons asks.

'It was passed on to another family,' he explains. 'We did that in those days – appreciated a toy's value. We didn't just throw things out.'

'Aw,' grumbles Almighty Over-Indulged One. 'I could've had that.'

Several days after dumping our surplus toys in the charity shop, I'm back in there with my kids, feeling unusually generous. I tell the children to choose one small item each. My daughter swoops on the talking alphabet toy.

'Don't we have one like this?' she asks, thumping the buttons: *M is for mat! M is for mat!*

'It's *just* like ours,' announces my son, awash with joyful nostalgia. 'Can we have it?'

£2.75 for your kids' old busted toy? That's what I'd call a bargain.

Far more effective ways to beat back chaos

Not drowning, but waving: how other parents avoid that Toys 'R' Us feeling.

I've adopted a draconian approach to mess. When James is at school, I sneak into his room and rearrange everything so he won't spot that I've taken tons of stuff. I also tell him that if anything's left lying on the floor after

tidy-up time, I'll assume it's rubbish and will bin it. Some people find this a deeply offensive approach.
Tough-talking Jane, a health writer and mother to six-year-old James

I've set ground rules – like the floor must be cleared before anyone goes to bed – so I'm not stumbling over debris in the morning. We had a 'no toys in the living room after eight pm' rule when the children were little. Recently, though, I was becoming quite depressed about Emma's room. She started pestering us for a cat. Her dad told her she could have one if she kept her room tidy for a month.

We drew up a tick box – one box for every day of the month – and inspected the room each evening to see if it came up to scratch. Emma needed twenty-eight ticks in a row before she could have her cat. Now it's been thirty-five days and we're off to the Cats' Protection League next weekend. I hope she's fallen into good habits – for good.
Tina Jesson, founder of home styling company Home Stagers and mother to Daniel, fourteen, and Emma, eleven

Ban bulky toys. Don't allow them into your house, unless you want to live in a soft play centre. My parents wanted to buy Ruby-Jane a ballpit and kept telling us, 'But it's only seven feet square!' We just said no.
Neil, a systems analyst and father to Ella, seven, and Ruby-Jane, two

Several times a year I pull a huge guilt number on James and suggest that he gives away toys he no longer wants to poor children. We end up with a tiny bag of cracked Lego but at least it's a start.
Tough Jane again

12

Brilliant ways to keep horrible
stuff out of sight

Kids are generally pretty hopeless at setting up storage systems, and so they should be: who wants to encourage a weird fascination with hanging files and those tiddly crystal tabs to hold labels? Systems are *our* job. We can help our children to decide what goes where, and label drawers/storage boxes accordingly. The idea is to con them into *thinking* they're making all the decisions, when in fact you're the one who's pulling off a fabulous organisational feat.

It doesn't really matter what you use to keep slagheaps of crap out of sight – as long as it is out of sight. We've tried stackable boxes, trays which slide under beds, enormous wicker baskets for the 8,000 cuddly toys which reside here rent-free; less successfully, we bought plastic storage bins on wheels which our offspring used to transport each other around the house at great speed, which wasn't the idea at all.

My aim now is to prevent the kids and their assorted possessions from permeating every corner of our home. Four years ago, when we'd just moved into our small Lanarkshire town and didn't know a soul, I'd invite my sons' playgroup pals around to romp about our house. I hadn't a clue about establishing rules. It didn't occur to me that not every parent allows hordes of kids to bounce on the grown-ups' bed in their wellies, or haul Mum's underwear from its drawer, and career downstairs on plastic sledges while wearing black lacy bras on top of their T-shirts. I just cowered on the sidelines, feeling helpless.

One evening it took J and me until ten-thirty to clear up. Clearly, I was being an idiot. Now the kids can play downstairs, or take their friends to their bedrooms – but there's no clambering into the walk-in cupboard where J keeps his nine guitars, or sneaking into our bedroom to snort over my pants.

My concession to having Charlotte [aged three] has been to replace our glass coffee table with a felt cube and buy two massive silver baskets from Lakeland into which her toys are stashed every night. We're moving soon, and will have a family room plus a living room just for grown-ups. I'm tempted to put high-up bolts on the doors. It's really important for us to have a child-free space to retreat to.
Pregnant, no-messing Pru

You'll find more clever storage solutions at:

❀ **Ikea:** holy grail of cheap, in loud colours. Raised beds with storage underneath, tough plastic toy boxes, bedroom shelving, cupboards and chests of drawers, every size and shape of storage basket – the whole child-sized caboodle.

❀ **www.next.co.uk** for eye-pleasing kids' bedroom furniture in non-sickly colours.

❀ **www.littledreamers.co.uk** offer a small range of simple, functional kids' furniture – zingy brights for boys, pastel pinks and lilacs for girls (ho hum . . . surely my daughter cannot be the only young female who detests pink?). Reasonably priced, but the delivery charges hoik up the cost somewhat.

❀ For nifty ideas which are almost too lovely for children try **www.theholdingcompany.co.uk**.

❀ Likewise **www.muji.co.uk** for baskets, hanging storage and clever ideas like pop-up laundry baskets which are crying out to be stuffed with soft toys.

🠊 **The Pier** for folksy appliqued toy sacks and chests of baskets (easier than hefty wooden drawers for kids to open and shut). Also shallow wicker baskets in which to bung all their gunk and kick out of sight under the bed.

🠊 If your preferred method is to fling everything into a massive chest and bang the lid shut, you'll find grown-up-looking ottomans and blanket boxes at **John Lewis** and **www.beds2go.co.uk,** or more child-pleasing toy boxes with designs ranging from the cutesy to zany at **www.just4kidz.co.uk.**

See store guide for shops' phone numbers

Tidy-up cops beware

However gorgeous your child's new storage system, please don't be too anally fixated. When you hear yourself raging, 'That's not the Lego tray, that's the *Meccano* tray, dimwit,' it's time to retreat from your kid's room, creep downstairs, and pour yourself a big fat vodka.

Two reasons not to raise an immaculate kid:

1 He'll start pointing at your knicks on the bedroom floor and shouting, 'Is that where those belong, hmmm?'

2 Your friends – at least your *normal* friends – will hate you.

Until we had Jojo my partner Matthew was a neat freak who arranged all the remote controls in a neat line. Now the baby's nine months and our flat is strewn with feeding dishes and bottles, blankets with sick all over, teddies with gunge all over . . . I'd like to be tidier, but it's not a

priority right now. It makes me laugh to think that our friends used to call our place the show home.
Mel, who can no longer find the remote

I go through phases of slinging out toys, but you do have to do it discreetly. The prospect of seeing your child scrabbling through the outside bin to retrieve Action Man's fluorescent gilet is too much to bear.
Cathy, full-time mother to Michael, nine, Caitlin, six, and Molly, four

I despise the chaos that children leave in their wake, but do allow Nina to make a mess as long as it's cleared up before anything else is brought out. I'd hate to reduce her to the tidiness equivalent of an anorexic.
Millie, self-confessed anal-retentive and mother to Nina, three, and Laura, eighteen months

A note on garden play equipment

For several years, relatives have threatened to descend upon us with enough outdoor play equipment to turn our garden into a fully-equipped amusement park on a scale not dissimilar to Chessington World of Adventures. We have managed to bat them off, knowing full well that garden playthings are destined to be ignored and will only be splattered with wet leaves and bird poo.

Judging from our friends' experiences, it seems that the only time a kid exhibits a smidge of interest in his fancy swing with boat attachment is when a chum comes to play. Then their own child hogs the swing ('It's MINE!'), yelping with delight as if to ram home what a fabulous time he's having, and ignoring the tortured sobs of his playmate.

As well as shunning swings, climbing frames and the like, we've also avoided those plastic cars which kids can sit in and 'drive'. With twins, we'd have had to buy two of the wretched contraptions or endured perpetual warfare. At a friend's house, the Little Tykes car was hoisted over the fence and placed out of sight on the canal towpath until we'd gone home.

It's bad enough that these unwieldy playthings exist in shopping centres and friends' gardens. Let's keep them there.

Kids are never too young to be put to work

We don't want pernickety children who run screaming when a parent so much as sploshes a fingernail-sized dollop of bolognaise on the wipe-able tablecloth. ('Mess! Boo-hoo! Wipe it away!') However nor do we wish to raise pampered princes/princesses who leave a trail of litter in their wake.

Children should, of course, help around the home: we owe it to ourselves, and their future life partners, to encourage, cajole and bribe them into learning basic domestic skills. Boy children especially. Research commissioned by the EOC indicates that daughters are willing to get stuck into the laundry and washing up – ie, tasks usually tackled by Mum – and nearly half keep their rooms tidy. According to the survey, boys are more inclined to assist Dad with DIY and gardening and just a piddling third of them regularly tidy their rooms.

There is, of course, no reason for this to be so – in fact, it's ludicrous to assume that little Chloe will delight in pairing up the socks from the laundry basket, while Danny will only acquaint himself with heavy-duty welding-type activities taking place in the garage.

Some parents have wangled a helping hand from both sexes:

Everyone loads their own plates and cutlery into the dish-washer. I made this a rule as soon as Ben was capable of carrying a plate without smashing it. Gone are the days when everyone zooms away from the table, leaving me with a crime scene.
Mary-Ann, teaching assistant and mother to Timothy, ten, and Ben, seven

Emma sets the table, Daniel clears it, and each child does a 'scrap-and-swill', scraping leftovers into the bin and rinsing the plate before loading the dishwasher.
Home Stagers' Tina again

I realised I was treating my daughter as a 'mother's little helper' while the boys got away with occasionally picking up Lego. Now everyone has their jobs – Hoovering, washing up, polishing shoes, stacking up the videos neatly. I've had to learn not to be a perfectionist and let them tackle tasks in their own chaotic but well-meaning way.
Eleanor, self-employed management consultant and mother to Adam, eleven, Charlie, ten, and Emily, seven

Actually, it only occurred to me that children are capable of simple domestic tasks when my sons' friend Cameron, aged six, came round for tea. A cheery, well-mannered boy, he wolfed his meal, placed his knife and fork tidily on the plate – then carried it across the kitchen and deposited it beside the sink. 'Wow,' I said. 'Thank you, Cameron.'

My own kids have yet to follow his example. The boys are supposed to receive a quid a week's pocket money for keeping their room in reasonable shape, but we have yet to witness much effort being made on the decluttering front. Trouble is, pocket money is so often forgotten – resulting in a parent being hit with a final-payment demand of seventy-two quid – or a child cottons on to the 'labour = reward' concept and starts demanding fair remuneration for picking up a dropped teaspoon. However, after Cameron's visit – and reading a report in parenting magazine *Junior* which claims that, in helping around the house, children are learning valuable life skills – I decided to put my children to work. *Junior* magazine reckons that, by six or seven years old, children should be capable of sorting laundry, setting the table, keeping their rooms tidy, weeding the garden and helping to wash and dry dishes. Here's how my children fare with a variety of tasks.

Packing a suitcase. I suggest that my daughter (aged four) helps to choose her clothes for our forthcoming holiday. She selects a manky, washed-out pair of orange shorts, around 35 soft toys and several damp, fungal-smelling towels. 'All done,' she says proudly, slamming the case shut.

Putting away an enormous heap of videos. *Son one*: But I didn't mess them up! It's not fair. (I explain that no videos will be watched until the pile has been put away tidily in the cupboard.)
Son two: Look! *Star Wars*. I wanna watch *Star Wars*.
Daughter: No, *Bambi*!
Son one: It's not fair. She always chooses.
Daughter: *Bambi*! Whaaa!
Me: If you don't stop this, it'll go to the charity shop.
Son two: What will?
Me: Er – everything!
Daughter: Not my toys! Whaaa . . .
Voice in my head: *You want a cigarette. You want a cigarette. Go on – just one little ciggie won't hurt you.*
J: Why don't I flip a coin? (He does this. Daughter wins.)

Son two: That's not fair! Do eeny-meeny-miney-mo. (*Bambi* is put on.)
Voice in my head: Yummy, yummy cigarettes.
Daughter: Don't want *Bambi*. Want *Finding Nemo*.

Sweeping up. Although my children view this as way down in the hierarchy of chores, the brush now becomes highly desirable and is fought over with gusto. Son one: 'You never let me brush up! It's not fair!' The brush is confiscated, and I do the sweeping up while they're all watching *Finding Nemo*.

Cleaning the bathroom floor. With my favourite FCUK jumper. Actually, this doesn't count as a chore. The frantic mopping of lino is my sons' attempt to avoid a PlayStation ban (standard penalty for flooding the floor during bathtime).

'Improving' the kitchen wall. Throwing himself into the spirit of enhancing our home, one of my sons starts to pick bubbly paint off the kitchen wall. J joins in, and by the time they've finished, the wall boasts an enormous mottled grey bare patch, and there's a pile of paint flakes on the floor. 'That's better,' J says. Then he walks away and sidles up next to our daughter to watch *Finding Nemo*.

Tidying bedrooms. This amounts to my sons ramming filthy clothing into their drawers. I am then obliged to sniff each garment before re-sorting it into a 'clean' or 'dirty' pile as appropriate.

Packing lunchboxes. Rather than being genuinely useful – ie, swilling out yesterday's slurry of orange juice and tuna-mayo – one son chooses a Blue Riband chocolate biscuit plus a handful of chocolate coins from the goodie tin, gleefully announcing, 'I'll do this every day for extra pocket money.'

Cleaning out the car. There's so much fun stuff to do in your average vehicle – turning on indicators and lights, beeping the horn, trying to climb out of the sun roof – that it's hard for my kids to concentrate on the valeting service which our car so urgently requires. A son retches at the unidentifiable decomposed fruit or vegetable matter in the hand recess of the door. There's sand on the floor from last year's Cornish holiday. From under a seat my daughter discovers a horrible stiff black thing, like a withered hand, which is later identified as a banana skin. She then monopolises the Dyson for so long that it overheats, cuts out, and refuses to rouse itself for the rest of the day.

So can kids really be useful around the home? Of course they can, with supervision and the promise of hard cash. However, the above experiment has also made me realise that, although they may be perfectly capable of undertaking simple tasks, young children tackle the more tedious chores in such a cack-handed manner that you're tempted to give up and do everything yourself.

Which is, of course, precisely what the little buggers want.

I reward special jobs like cleaning out the car or a serious stint of helping in the garden. Maybe 50p or a pound if they've spent all afternoon doing something. But not everyday jobs. You can't get to the point where you're doling out cash just because they've remembered to flush the toilet.
Tom, furniture-maker and full-time father to Lauren, seven, and Charlie, five

Other people's kids in your house

When you think about it, there's zero point in aiming for a squeaky clean home. Even if your own children are impeccably neat, and bark, 'Wipe that up!' if you so much as smear jam on a worktop, chances are that other people's kids regularly invade your home. And they will mess it up, big style.

Other people's kids are so much harder to handle than our own. While we're familiar with our offspring's bodily functions – their toileting habits, the rich odours they produce – having to wipe the bum of a child to whom we're not directly related is most unpleasant, and has, on one occasion, caused my lunch to bubble up into my throat. Are you really obliged to change a visiting kid's nappy or can you possibly pretend, when his parent picks him up, that he's *only just* soiled himself? I'd say that any non-liquid emissions which occur less than thirty minutes before pick-up time count as 'just done'.

Even more frightful are their runny noses. The sight of two quivering columns of mucus really makes me want to puke. I've wiped my own kids' streaming noses a billion times without flinching – yet, when a friend popped round, and urged her three-year-old son to 'give Fiona a kiss', a mere glimpse of his dribbling nostrils triggered me to emit a loud barfing sound, to which the child enquired, 'Is you sick?'

My sons' mates, who are around six and seven years old, have at least mastered the art of cleaning their own orifices. Yet it still amazes me how different these kids are from each other, and how misleading appearances can be. The tough cookie, who looks like he feasts on entire lambs and could happily gnaw a chunk out of the Forth Rail Bridge, quietly studies a Ladybird book entitled *Let's Study Seashells*. The seemingly meek child, whom I've invited for tea in the hope that he'll teach my kids some manners, stampedes through our house, ripping open new boxes of cereal in order to access the free gizmos, and teaches my daughter to respond to any question with: 'Arse.'

Other people's kids have behaved appallingly in our house, even with one of their parents present. One neighbour – whom I have since stopped inviting round – would just sit there, wearing a faraway smile, as her child repeatedly slammed a miniature double-decker bus into the glass panel of our front door. His mother would prattle on about her new sofa, and her forthcoming holiday to Sardinia, oblivious to the fact that the kid had now thundered upstairs to vandalise my sons' bedroom and run himself a bath.

At least boisterous kids keep you so occupied that time flashes by. Before you can catch a breath, they're clattering off home, having 'borrowed' your child's favourite possession and left a tangle of loo roll on the bathroom floor. When the morose visitor comes for tea, time grinds to a halt. You sense your life slipping away, and worry that your blood might be curdling. You examine your reflection and see that you have aged since the guest's arrival. New wrinkles have formed. Your skin is pallid, your mouth dry from firing questions: 'Do you like steak pie?' 'No.' 'Spaghetti?' 'No.' 'Tuna pasta?' 'No.' 'What would you like then?' 'Anything.'

It feels like the kid's been here for weeks, yet it's still only half past three. I have done my utmost to ensure that a shy visitor has a fabulous time – letting the kids make ice-cream sundaes, and bring worms into the house – only to have the guest murmur in a teeny voice: 'I want my mum.'

However, it's more common for other children to take a shine to our home and become regular visitors. At our last house, a seven-year-old boy used to show up and force entry. As my sons were only three, I hadn't a clue how to interact with a massive specimen like Billy. Would he be offended if I offered him Duplo? Should I tell him to blow on his food, or was he mature enough to cope with hot fish fingers without setting his throat on fire? Billy took to calling at eight-thirty am on a Sunday. I'd tell him to come back later. At eight-forty-five he'd be trying to kick the door in. As I let him in, he'd announce, 'Mum says I've got to be home before it gets dark.'

Such a child can force you to behave in a weird shifty manner:

keeping the curtains drawn, and wearing a coat at all times so you can pretend you're about to go out. Billy started calling when my kids were at nursery and I was working from home. 'I'll help you,' he'd insist, wedging our door open with his walloping trainered foot.

The child stalker would while away hours by swinging on our gate. I'd be skulking at our back door, chuffing a quick Silk Cut, and spy his eyeball glinting through a gap in the fence. I felt sorry for Billy because his dad had scarpered and he seemed to spend the entire summer holidays poking around the bins at the back of a Chinese restaurant. I'd have bad thoughts about this boy, wishing he'd find another family, then feel guilty and take him to Edinburgh Zoo. We only managed to shake him off by moving house.

These days, our house reverberates with the shrieks of small people. It's hosting a children's party three times a week. As they hare around the house, fizzing with artificial colorants and complaining that our toilet's dirty, I mentally spirit myself away to a calmer place – like a spa, with top-to-toe massage on offer. However, I was forced to intervene when I caught my sons' school friend attacking our crumbling outhouse with a claw hammer. What's the etiquette of telling off other people's children? They're not yours, so you can't send them upstairs or take their favourite toy away. You can't yell at them, unless they're engaged in a high-risk activity involving mains electricity and water. This time, though, I really let rip. I loomed over the boy as he hacked at the bricks, glad that J and I had produced our own delightful children and not this destructive beast. 'Never mind, Simon,' I growled. 'I expect it was an accident.'

More horrible things about other people's kids:

✿ Their fondness for squirting your Crabtree & Evelyn lavender bath foam (£8.99) down the plughole.

❧ The way they scowl at the meal that you've slaved over, and say, 'Ew.'

❧ Their nits (see page 197 for the only effective way to eradicate unwelcome wildlife).

❧ Their lurid sweets which send my sons into a hyperactive whirl, and trigger my daughter's eczema.

❧ Their advanced sexual knowledge.

However, there is one very good – in fact, *essential* – reason to welcome other people's kids into your home. When they have friends around to play, your own children are less likely to fight.

Q: why do siblings hate each other's guts?

It kicks off at seven-forty-six am. 'Get out!' one son roars. 'I hate you.'

'Hate *you*,' my daughter yells back. Something heavy is thrown, and my daughter is crying, and my son (who looks spectacularly guilty) turns on me, saying: 'You! It's all your fault. You let her get away with anything. I wish she'd never been born!'

To illustrate blatant favouritism, his brother chips in: 'You sent me to school yesterday with gym shoes that hurt my feet. Now I've got a fer-oo-ka.'

I'm thinking: *bugger off to an orphanage then*. I say: 'I'm so sorry, darling', and count the seconds until the next fight breaks out. Over the years, my children's bust-ups have resulted in: one son stabbing his brother in the cheek with the scissors I had left on the stairs after wrapping Christmas presents; me storming away from a dinner-table fracas and eating my meal while perched on the edge of our bed (normal!); J driving away with our kids' spare-clothes bags on the roof of our car after a spectacular three-way brawl on exiting nursery (cause: who got to press the button which unlocked the front door).

As an only child, I find inter-sibling fighting extremely disturbing. When I was a kid, there was no one to snatch my favourite toy, or whack me with a cutlass, or slam the garage door on top of my head. J and I might snap at each other, and have the occasional full-scale row, but we don't yell, 'You're so *schoopid*,' or jab each other's stomachs with a plastic devil's pitchfork. Common areas of inter-sibling conflict are: what to watch on TV, who gets to use the toilet first, and one child perceiving that he has been allowed 1.2 seconds less than his sibling on the computer/PlayStation.

Interestingly, kids tend to fight only on home turf, and rarely on holidays or outings. Yet no family can spend 365 days a year at safari parks or Legoland. We have tried splitting up the kids: J takes one or two for a swim, while the remaining child does something equally thrilling with me. However, our children – like most youngsters, who spend vast portions of their life in the company of women – are disgusted not to be with their father. The 'left with Mum' kid gazes mournfully at the gate and keeps asking, 'When are they coming back?'

Most childcare experts would have it that ignoring the fighting is – unless real injury is likely – the best measure. Of course they'll still scrap. At least you're not shouting and dragging them apart and working yourself up into an extremely unphotogenic, purple-faced fury. You can also award yourself one glittery parenting star for – cue rapturous applause – Not Losing Your Rag.

What the experts say we should do about war on the home front

Say positive things like, 'It's brilliant that you played so nicely when I was on the phone.' Show that you notice the good stuff as well as the squabbling.
Caryn Skinner, spokesperson for The Parent Company who run parenting seminars in London

With minor squabbles, stay within earshot but don't watch. Children love an audience. Only intervene in a ganging-up situation or if there's an imbalance of power. It's not helpful to say, 'He's only a baby,' or, 'Be a big, grown-up boy.' Sometimes the elder one deserves to be babied, and the younger can be encouraged to be responsible and think of others' feelings.
Helena Sharpstone, also from The Parent Company

I don't understand why your children fight so much. You never did that.
My dad (yes, but I'm an only child . . .)

What parents do

Once, when Shona and Holly were ripping into each other, I calmly walked away, stepped into my wardrobe and shut the door. It freaked them out so much that they stopped fighting immediately.
Cheryl, occupational therapist and mother to sparring partners of seven and five

*I think you have to remember that there's this period
when the older one is maybe six or seven – not mature
enough to make allowances for a younger sibling – and
the little one's still at the stage when they'll snatch
anything their elder sibling has, and wreck all their
games. Ours are six and nine now and co-exist reasonably
happily.*
Simon, a sports coach, on his eerily feud-free family

*I call a friend on the cordless phone and storm off to a
different bit of the house. I'll only run to see what's
happening if I hear glass breaking, or if there's blood loss.*
**Sophie, a nurse with two and a half children (Thomas, five,
Morvern, three, plus one-on-the-way who can't join
in the fights . . . yet)**

*I try not to get involved, but there are times when some-
one's going to get hurt and you have to step in. Then it's
a TV and Gameboy ban for that day, no matter how
brief the outburst, or who started it.*
**David, IT manager and dad to Louie, seven, Dan, five
and Finn, fourteen months**

Other parents say that the following measures can bring peace
and goodwill to the family home – at least for as long as it takes
to hoik the cork out of a bottle of wine.

When kids are brawling over a toy. Bear in mind that the youngest
only wants the darn toy simply because his sibling is playing
with it. If it's a shared toy, allow each child five minutes with it
– but ask the child who has the toy to find something else for
his sibling. Or try to distract the little one by offering something
far more alluring than the bent plastic teaspoon he so desires. *Or*

28

involve them all in an activity (like cooking) so everyone has a different role and the ruddy plaything is forgotten.

One child refusing to share his favourite thing in the world. Everyone has their special things. These are theirs and not for sharing. As one friend pointed out, when I berated one of my sons (then four) for not 'sharing' his Peter Pan dressing-up outfit: 'He loves that costume. He goes to bed in it. Please don't make him share it. How would you feel if someone stormed into your house and demanded to borrow your wedding dress?'

Younger child wrecking older kid's game by being bloody annoying. Stress to the older child that his brother/sister is only curious, and wants to be just like him (flattery, flattery). If it gets too much, whisk the younger one away. Every child deserves a smidge of space without a little one clambering on his back and demanding that he's a 'donkey like on the beach at Scarborough'.

Perpetual non-specific bickering. It sounds barmy, but invite more children round to play. This can alter dynamics and diffuse tensions. Or, if it's humanly possible, arrange for each of your children to have time alone with you. My friend Meg, who has five-year-old twin sons and a seven-year-old daughter, told me about the day when one of the twins plucked a dried pea from his nursery's 'touch and feel' table and – rather helpfully – shoved it into his ear: 'The GP couldn't get it out, so Josh's dad took him to Monklands hospital in Glasgow where he had a general anaesthetic and the pea was removed. He had a lovely day – not with the whole brawling family, but just him and Dad. They had lunch out and chose some books in Borders. No fighting, no bickering. It was probably the best day of Josh's life.' (Note: please do not resort to inserting a pea into your child's ear in order to wangle a day alone with him.)

What doesn't stop the fighting. Expecting your child's teacher to have any effect on his/her behaviour. Recently, after a bout of appalling conduct in the classroom, one of my sons was sent for a stern telling-off from his head teacher. When I heard about this, and demanded an explanation from my son, he said, 'Yeah, I was invited into Mr X's office. It was great fun!' So it worked, then.

And one miscellaneous useless fact. Same-sex children, three years or closer in age, are prime candidates for perpetual brawling as they're most likely to be constantly compared by their parents and friends and tend to feel horribly hard done by, the little buggers.

A note about the only child

Please don't give the parent of an only child a withering glance, thinking, 'You don't know how stressful it is, having children who fight all the time. You, parent of singleton, have *no idea*.' As Sean, father to seven-year-old Poppy points out: 'An only child doesn't have any siblings to fight with. What she does is direct all her anger and spite on to her parents.'

Tons of stuff your children can do instead of fighting

Between them, these parents have twenty-seven children. Here's what they pull out of the bag on those tense days when it feels like it's been raining for seventeen years.

kids in the house

When you really can't be arsed:

Tania: *When my two [Isobel, eight, and Evie, three] are roaring at each other, I've stuck on Channel 4 racing and divvied up the big jar of coppers which we keep in the kitchen, and we've played betting. Get them into gambling as early as possible, I say.*

Elizabeth: *Planning an event, like a picnic or party, provides a diversion. It involves lots of talking, making lists, even drawing the food they'd like to have. It's often more fun than the actual event, and doesn't mess up the house at all.*

Peter: *Loud music's essential to drown out the constant bicker-bicker-bicker. What I've done – and this is a bit mean – is play hide and seek and sent them off all over the house, but not bothered going to find them.*

A modicum of effort required:

Una: *We make a pirate ship by pulling two sofas together and piling them with 'cargo' – toys, books, whatever keeps them occupied. Away they go to an island – the rug – where there's treasure, like a packet of biscuits to share.*

Sheena: *We pull out the clothes that Ruby [aged six] hasn't worn for yonks, setting aside a few things for charity. She'll try on the rest, prancing around, doing catwalk wiggles. We've also discovered the most compulsive game ever – a dance mat with a Tetris game on it from the Next Directory. Totally compulsive – plus it's exercise.*

Kath: *Gracie [four] loves making potions with the manky, out-of-date bags of flour and spices from the back of our pantry.*

Amanda: *My kids [aged twelve, seven and four] love defacing newspaper pictures, drawing on glasses, hair, foul teeth. Big rolls of paper [from Early Learning Centre and Ikea, or use cheaper-than-cheap lining paper from DIY shops] are great for hand prints, drawing round each other, and mass painting sessions.*

Peter: *I take the kids to the Pound Shop, give them a quid each, and let them choose whatever bit of tat they want.*

Una: *My Aussie friend Bron has sessions called 'munchie, duvet, movie'. At the end of the day – or when you want the kids to calm down – rent a vid, gather together some treats, make a bed area with duvets in the living room, and close the curtains.*

Slightly messier pursuits:

Helen: *We crush up white chalk and charcoal in small pots and add water and soil from the garden to make cave paint. The boys [aged three, seven and nine] slap it on to sugar paper or any absorbent paper to make prehistoric artwork.*

Sheena: *I make (or buy) a batch of cup cakes and Ruby ices them and sprinkles multi-coloured bits on top. Or you can use icing pens to draw pictures.*

Warning: I once let my sons do this. They iced digestive biscuits, scoffed them, then launched into a whirl of E-additive-fuelled mayhem – slamming doors, clanging their sister on the head with a sword, and retiring to their room, sobbing, because I'd confiscated their PlayStation handsets. Just thought I'd mention the peril of icing pens – fg.

Elizabeth: *I once let my three loose with the Argos cata-*

logue and glue. They made collages which I had laminated to make placemats. I felt like a completely fabulous mother for the whole afternoon.

Not for the faint-hearted:

Amanda: *Very messy, this. We squirt shaving foam on to a plastic tray, adding cornflour to make it more malleable.*

Jen: *My pal Kelly puts a gigantic piece of paper on the floor and lets her girls do body painting – bums, feet, hands, whatever. I have to say, I'd die if this happened in our house.*

Jimmy: *If it's foul weather we give into it and go out to splash in puddles.*

Craig: *My kids love making potions with mud, grass and flowers. And it does calm them down. A bit . . .*

Kath: *Gracie has brilliant all-in-one waterproofs from Muddy Puddles [www.muddlepuddles.com]. Buy them miles too big and they'll last for years.*

Craig: *A yearly pass to a nearby castle or other historic building is worth the expense. Looking at the same old suits of armour is better than everyone scrapping in the living room.*

Jimmy: *Anything is better than them scrapping in the living room . . .*

The great thing about board games . . .

. . . is that, when your kids reach a certain age (around five or six) they'll love nothing better than playing with you, as it's a nifty means of gaining your undivided attention.

My kids' favourites include:

- Junior Monopoly
- Ker-Plunk
- Frustration
- Mousetrap
- Tumblin' Monkeys
- Junior Pictionary
- Connect 4
- Snakes and Ladders

All of which trigger a pleasing wave of wholesome good-old-days nostalgia in the parent.

More ridiculously simple things my kids like doing

- Washing up (or making a ham-fisted attempt at it). Problematic only when more than one child demands to stand at the sink, and starts washing wine glasses.

- Going anywhere on the bus.

- Tying each other to trees.

- Sword fights. ('Stop that! You'll put someone's eye out.')

- Finding woodlice under flowerpots to examine through a magnifying glass.

⟡ Making spectacular snacks from digestives heaped with bits of fruit and covered in jam. ('Let's keep it for Dad when he gets home.')

⟡ Seeing how many pairs of pants they can put on.

⟡ Storytapes: keeps the darlings quiet, right? And it's not the telly or PlayStation. In fact it's *literature*. One gigantic gold star to you.

Our PlayStation and telly rows

J [reading what I'm writing]: You're doing it again.
Me: What?
J: Slagging off PlayStation. What do you expect them to do after school? Play cat's cradle?
Me: Don't be bloody facetious.
J: You've got a *thing* about it.
Me: No I haven't! It's fine!
One of my sons: Want a go, Mum?
Me: No, thank you.
J: Why are you pulling that sort of face?
Me: What sort of face? It's just my *face*, all right?
J: Oh, for Christ's sake . . .

Before I became a mother, I was confident that I'd never 'plonk' my children in front of a flickering screen. The language employed – in particular the verb 'to plonk' – hardly implies that playing PlayStation, or watching TV, offer a worthwhile learning experience. We don't say, 'I am allowing my child valuable quiet time after a hard day's lessons.' We say, 'I've plonked him in front of the box. That'll shut him up for an hour.' Interestingly, we never 'plonk' him in front of a jigsaw.

I reckoned that, if I did plonk my kids, they'd be watching *Blue Peter*, a nature documentary, or something about the Romans. Not any old twaddle. Not cartoons. Certainly not *Robot Wars: Arenas of Destruction*. I thought my friend Sophie was being really clever when she told her son: 'Cartoons are only on at Granny's', and he believed her (at least until he was six). And I vowed that I'd never let my children eat in front of the TV, but did think one friend had lost it when she banned the picture book *Not Now Bernard* just because it shows Bernard eating his tea in front of the telly.

However, I soon discovered that TV – and playing games which involve gawking at a flickering screen – is a child's first love. They adore it: sitting way too close, with their mouths lolling open, while gripping the remote control or handset. It would be easy to use telly/PS2 as a bargain babysitter who won't drink our beer or snog boys on the sofa. And even now I cannot stop myself from charging in the moment the credits roll, or they've completed a new stage in their game, and announcing, 'All done!' They troop miserably back to their colouring books, despising me. J says it's more my problem than theirs. Kids and telly, he says – it's a love thing.

Josie can identify Downy in the supermarket and once shouted, 'That stops clothes from creasing.' Her class had been writing about themselves under the heading 'My favourite thing'. Other children had listed ballet or their kitten. Josie had written Sky TV.
Suzie, mother to Jack, ten, and Josie, seven

Two hours a day is Holly's max – I prefer Disney vids to TV programmes so I know what she's seeing. How

hypocritical would I be to insist that she spends all her time making clay models when, the minute I've put her to bed, I flop out in front of some vacuous docu-soap?
Ellie, mother to Holly, seven

As parents, we think that nostalgic programmes like Top Cat *are okay, but* Batman of the Future *is bad. Who are we to judge what's good or bad? We should just let our children chill out.*
Matthew, team manager and dad to Fergus, nine, and Cal, seven

Two hours of TV per day is fine as long as it's not in one clump and is broken up with other activities. One hour at a time should be the absolute max. Let's be realistic – adults need to get on with things, and no parent can or should feel obliged to entertain their child every minute of the day.
Child psychologist Dr Dorothy Einon

Of course they should watch what they want, within reason. They live here! It's their house!
My partner J

2
what kids want

'He always gets more than me!' • running your home like
the army • 'We always have Coco Pops for dinner' and
other dastardly fibs • Rebel Dad and his foul foodstuffs •
pester power (just say no?) • kiddie crazes and their
detrimental effect on the adult brain • can I have a pet?
• no you bloody can't • our bad fish day • why we can't
make our kids want what we want

Kids want so much stuff. If we gave them everything they
wanted, we'd be forced to remove all furniture and adult
possessions from the family home in order to accommodate their
loot. Eventually we, too, would have to move out and reside in
the garage or shed or under a bush, thus allowing the house to
be transformed into Woolworth's toy aisle x 100.

Of course this cannot happen. We must limit treats and toy
purchases, shutting our ears to tortured pleas that 'It's not fair',
because – and of this we can be a hundred per cent certain –
it *is* fair, and we are right. In any case, whatever we buy for
them, and however we endeavour to share out our time and
attention in equal measures, our children will still conclude that
they're victims of Gross Unfairness.

what kids want

Recently, while babysitting my friend Kate's four-year-old twin boys and six-year-old daughter, I found myself idly scanning the charts and rotas Blutacked haphazardly around her kitchen. I wasn't snooping exactly; how else is the adult babysitter supposed to while away an evening in someone else's house, other than by prowling around in their kitchen? I'm too old and craggy to have a boyfriend come over and fumble about with me on the sofa. It's been decades since anything exciting like that has happened to me.

So I perused the bed-time story rota (which ensures that each child gets to choose a book at least twice a week); a star chart for the efficient cleaning of teeth and getting ready for school/nursery without a fuss; and, oddest of all, a stern-looking list entitled Who Picks TV Prog.

When Kate and her boyfriend returned, I admitted that I was intrigued by the TV chart. She said, 'You wouldn't believe the screaming matches we have over what they're going to watch. You try to remember who chose yesterday and the day before that, but they're convinced you're favouring someone. The only programme they all agree on is Scooby Doo. So it's simpler to write it all down.'

Rotas and charts have never worked in our house. They've been meticulously filled in for three days, then fallen off the wall and ended up being swept under the cooker along with a sinister-looking black pellet which looked like the dropping of a terrifying super-rodent, but was more likely a meatball, flicked from a highchair when my sons (now seven) were toddlers. Also, rotas make me feel rather sergeant-like. Occasionally, I catch myself trying to run our household like the army – barking orders, shepherding everyone into the car while shouting, 'Hurry up! Seat belts on! Sit up straight! Stop poking each other NOW!', like we're on some critical mission and not on our way to their favourite swimming pool with the bubbly Jacuzzi bit. I don't like being like this. Rotas make me feel too military.

Yet for some parents, like Kate, they're the most effective means of achieving some semblance of fairness. Children are obsessed with detecting a mere hint of injustice. It's their life's work. Recently, one of my sons roared, 'It's not fair!' because the pair of pants I'd put out for his brother were slightly less war-torn than the pair I'd selected for him. (Don't ask me why I 'put out' my sons' pants; okay, if I don't, the entire contents of their drawers are flung over shoulders, like chicken bones in a medieval banqueting hall.)

It's NOT FAIR that they have to go to after-school club occasionally. It's NOT FAIR that they can't go to after-school club any more. (They warmed to the club after discovering that it has better PS2 games than we have at home.) One morning, one of my boys roared, 'You like him [his brother] better than me!' Well, sorry – but sometimes they're right. A parent does temporarily prefer the child who has completed his homework without drama or incident, and played patiently with his sister, to his sibling who has managed to get butter all over his school reading book, *and* filled the bath with cold water into which he has deposited every towel in the house. Under these circumstances, it's hard to dish out equal helpings of affection. Unfair, yes – but human.

My sons certainly felt that life was hideously unfair when J and I were selfish enough to produce another child. Clearly, we should have held a family meeting to discover whether a third infant might be accommodated without bitterness. I can vividly recall the day when, three years after our daughter's arrival, one of my sons remarked, 'Remember when Erin was born and you weren't interested in us any more?'

I wanted to yell that she needed me to feed, dress and change her – *because babies can't do these things for themselves*. I wanted to remind him that Grandma had stayed for a whole month, to ensure that he and his brother didn't feel neglected and enjoyed lots of fun days out. I even bought him a bloody talking robot. I was seized by a desire to jump up and down; to yell, 'How can you *say* that? Did you really think I wasn't interested? That I no longer loved you?' I didn't do that, as we were pushing seventy on the M74. Besides, it would have been pointless. That's how my poor, neglected firstborn perceived our family pecking order.

I know parents who bend over backwards to ensure that fairness pervades the family home. They feel that, in praising one child ('You got a housepoint? That's brilliant!') they must also applaud his sibling(s): 'And you're fantastic too, and I'm sure you'll get loads of housepoints tomorrow, because you're *so* clever . . .' I have caught myself doing this. The housepoint child has mooched away, as if thinking: 'But it was me who got the housepoint. Why does he get all the attention?'

Meanwhile, his brother has glared at me, as if to say: 'How does she know what will happen tomorrow? She's just trying to make me feel better. She's a twerp.'

What my children don't realise is that, within reasonable limits, J and I are willing to do most things they ask of us. If they've been reasonably cooperative during a shopping trip, we may buy them a Twix, or a 49p clear rubber ball with an veiny eyeball inside. While we might not really *want* to build a Lego Tornado Racer right now, as the last dozen pages of our book are pretty gripping, we'll set the novel down, and – in an act of selfless devotion – start fixing little wheels on to axles. Do we bang our fists? Do we start crying and shout, 'It's not fair'? Er, yes. Sometimes we do.

Some not-fair things my kids say I've done:

- 'You let him have ages and ages on Gameboy and I've had . . . one second' (a side effect of living in a one-Gameboy home).

- 'I hate Baby Bel! You always make me have it!' (Baby Bel cheese has been my daughter's preferred snack for as long as I can remember.)

- 'His trainers are dry. Mine are soaking wet!' (My son forgets that, despite being instructed not to, he plunged into the stream on the way home from school yesterday, and trainers take around six months to dry.)

- 'He *always* gets the best boiled egg.'

- 'She gets sweets every day' (on spying his sister chomping an ancient Quality Street toffee which she'd sniffed out from under a sofa cushion).

Coco Pops, Fruit Winders and food poncery

. . . And it's not fair that we're not taking them to my friend Kath's wedding. Well, would you? We've been told that the party room will be illuminated by hundreds of candles. So my dad agrees to look after our kids, single-handedly, for the very first time ever.

When we return from the wedding, I ask Dad, 'What did they have for dinner tonight?'

'Coco Pops,' he replies.

'Really? Just Coco Pops?'

'Yes,' Dad says. 'The boys told me they often have cereal in place of proper meals.' Later, I learn that my dastardly sons took my gullible father on a shopping trip 'to buy the things we always have'. The bolognaise I'd cooked and left in the fridge – untouched by human hand. They'd filled a trolley with jelly snakes, peelable cheese, chocolate cereal; in fact, my dear boys had exhibited such zeal in the aisles that Dad was astounded by their helpfulness.

Refined sugar plus nasty chemicals are what children want, and they'll go to any lengths to scoff them. From the first day of primary school, I was informed by my sons that 'everyone has sweets for their playpiece' (the Scottish term for playtime snack). Obediently, I purchased humungous quantities of nutritional delights such as Starbursts and Refreshers so that my offspring would not be ridiculed by their peers, develop an aversion to school, and grow up illiterate.

For five years, I had done such a great PR job on the humble rice cake that my sons viewed the dreary circular slabs as acceptable snacks. And now I'd crumbled. All that effort – wasted. Those treks to health shops for 'sweets' made from yoghurt or slabs of pressed fruit – down the pan. My sons would no longer tolerate tangerines, dried apricots, the humble apple.

Now they're just starting their third year of school. We have arrived at the point at which certain snacks are deemed cool ('mix-ups' – a paper bag of horrible things like cola bottle sweets and chewy rings) and others irredeemably naff (raisins). They want those sticky green strip things. ('Yeah,' says one son, 'Fruit Winders. They're great!') How can they live like this? They see living examples of what happens when bodies are mistreated, in the form of their parents. I have opened my mouth and made them examine its interior: all those fillings, requiring injections and gas and a rough dentist's pokey fingers. Did they want a mouth like that? They merely said, 'Urgh,' and carried on sucking their Chupa-Chups.

Of course I don't give in to every demand. Yet the Coco Pops incident did make made me wonder if I should loosen up on the food front (my kids did seem in extremely good spirits after being looked after by my dad), and so I came up with these five foodie commandments:

Thou shalt not freak out over Granny's nasty pink wafers.
My in-laws hail from North Lanarkshire, Scotland – confectionery capital of Europe. Sweetie giants test new lines in this area, figuring that, if it doesn't take off in North Lanarkshire, it certainly won't sell anywhere else. As soon as they were capable of holding small objects in their sticky hands, my sons were greeted by a gigantic Rover biscuit tin on each visit to Gran's, and offered so many alluring goodies – pink wafers, chocolate fingers, minty biscuits wrapped in green foil – that I'd be muttering to J through my teeth: 'They've had enough, can't you say something? Do something! Stop them!'

As parents, we should be in charge of our children's nutrition. However, on these occasions I wish I'd just clamped my gob shut and let my mother-in-law get on with it, instead of sitting there, all red-faced and trembly. After all, small mouths are clean-able; our infants never woke up to discover their teeny milk teeth scattered all over their pillows. And as J's lovely, seventy-something Aunt Chrissie once said: 'Chocolate's good for them. It's got milk in it.'

Thou shalt give good picnic.
Children want popcorn and Jaffa Cakes, not ham rolls or your tedious fruit. But we can aim for a balance. Setting out little dishes of grapes, cherries, strawberries, melon slices, tangerines, cucumber sticks and raw baby carrots at least counteracts the white-trashy effect of the Quavers, Dairylea Lunchables and Friij chocolate milk which are stashed out of sight in your bag.

Thou shalt pay no heed to thy parents' wifflings.
Take zero notice when they crow that you always cleared your plate, never whined for chocolate, and consumed only Good Things, always. I vividly recall that my Ski yoghurt was liberally sprinkled with sugar, and that Vesta curries (with sultanas in)

were a firm favourite. When I was a kid – 'in the olden days', as my kids refer to those long-ago times – bottled water was unheard of, dandelion and burdock and Tizer slugged with enthusiasm, and no one gave a stuff whether babies were breast-fed or weaned straight onto Spam fritters and those papery flying saucers with sherbet inside. When my dad observes my picky children peeling the crumb coating from their fish fingers, and says, 'You never behaved like that at the table', I remind him that, while I might have eaten like a starved buffalo, I was also a total horrorbox who ran away to Blackpool at the age of fifteen.

Thou shalt not be a withered old hypocrite.
During my first two years of parenthood, I encountered mean-ness on a major scale. During coffee mornings, mothers would palm off their kids with breadsticks and slices of apple. Then – without shame, in full view of these children – the parents would stuff their faces with brownies and Kit Kats until their mouths sloshed with molten chocolate. One mother I knew would hog finger upon finger of Twix, explaining, 'I've been up half the night, so I need an energy fix.' Then, from her pocket, she'd pull out a little bag of Shreddies, which she'd offer to her child as 'sweets'.

Since James [aged four] started school he's been exposed to phenomenal peer pressure. If he's offered Ribena or Smarties or Cheese Strings at friends' houses, I don't make a fuss. But we never have them at home. That's the joy of Internet shopping. I just say that this stuff's not available at Ocado.
Marina, James' crafty mum

Snack foods are okay if they don't pretend to be fruity or healthy. What I object to are so-called children's foods

intended for mealtime consumption: chicken nuggets, children's yoghurts – why? – and Alphabites. I only buy them when other children are coming to tea. I just want them to have a nice time, and Mia gets upset if her friends think our house is 'funny'.
Rhona, full-time mother to Mia, six, and Thomas, four, whose playdate compromise is to offer 'choosing plates' of sliced chicken, cherry tomatoes, red pepper, pizzas and one sweet thing, like cupcakes

My pet hates are boiled sweet lollies which I'm scared they'll get rammed down their throats. But a banned food list just makes them crave these things even more.
Carla, teacher and mum to Sophie, four, and Adam, two

They're allowed Jammy Dodgers and Iced Gems at Granny's but never at home. With party bags, I have a quick rifle through and bin anything unsuitable – unless they've been super-fast and scoffed it before I've managed to nab it.
Rosie, mother of three (she refers to this process as 'editing' a party bag, rather than blatant theft)

James often has Organix Cheese Puffs, Hugh Rock black-currant squash and Green & Black chocolate, so his life's not totally miserable.
Marina softens up

Clearly, there's no definite rule here. The sweet-deprived child makes an almighty show of himself at other kids' houses, piling in as many goodies as his small gob can accommodate. Not pretty. The alternative – sweeties on tap – results in no teeth. After seven years I've come to the conclusion that the occasional bag of the sweets they really want – Jelly Tots, Chewits, Dolly Mixtures, and not some yoghurt-coated-raisin alternative – will cause no harm at all. And in the time it takes to scoff them, you will be elevated to the lofty position of Top Mum.

Rebel Dad and his foul foodstuffs

My best friend is having a fortieth birthday party. I'm primed for a weekend away by myself. 'I want to come!' one of my sons bleats. His eyes are all moist and his bottom lip's thrust out. I know he's faking because, in truth, life with J is so much better than being with me.

Though I hate to generalise, of all the families I know, it is, without fail, the dad who's more lax on the telly-viewing, sweetie-scoffing, Coke-guzzling front. Why? Because women still tend to be the buyers and readers of childcare manuals. We devour Steve Biddulph and Penelope Leach; we parp, 'What's that he's drinking? Irn Bru?' Goodie purchaser doesn't care. He is Rebel Dad, and proud of it. Whenever mother (buyer of tedious mini boxes of Sunmaid raisins) goes away, *abandoning* her loved ones, Rebel Dad fills the house with forbidden goodies and everyone sniggers over how mad Mum would be if she knew.

Although I hate to admit that we've fallen into such stereo-typical roles, all this goes on in our house. For instance, for months now, J has been chundering on that we really 'need' a chip pan. While this is not quite as alarming as him saying that he 'needs' a new girlfriend, or even a Doberman Pincher, I still feel uneasy because it illustrates how differently we view children's nutrition. He's been saying this – 'We NEED a chip pan!' – for about five years now, and I've always feigned deafness or muttered, 'Uh-huh, we'll get one ... eventually.' But this time, without any debate, without my *permission* being sought, it's arrived. Seventeen quids' worth of aluminium plus a ruddy great two-litre bottle of oil and piles of potatoes for CHIPS.

The children won't help to pick lettuce from the garden because they're busy cutting potatoes – for chips. Our daughter, who has been let loose with a knife for the first time in her life, sternly reminds everyone that this is 'MY chip'. She waggles a strip of raw spud, which looks pretty much like the mounds of soon-to-be chips which are littering every kitchen surface. No one wants to help me wash all this rocket or pick chives.

J reckons I'd rather our children snacked only on dried prunes while listening to Elgar, which isn't remotely true. He says, 'Stop being a ponce, for God's sake! We'll only have them occasionally.' But my head's saturated with alarming statistics: about obesity in children, and chip pan fires. Less worrying, but still irksome, is the fact that a chip pan counts as a kitchen implement and will wind up being stashed in the pantry along with a vast range of dust-covered gizmos: the juicer, the thingie for sizzling meat at the table (never used), the white plastic bucket for steaming rice in the microwave (also never used). Despite J's reassurance that the oil will 'never go rancid' (just as the fish tank would 'never get dirty'), I fear we'll stumble upon the long-forgotten chip pan while having a clear-out as our children prepare to leave home. We'll lift its lid, and peer inside, and it'll be truly horrible: a thick opaque gloop containing one scrap of festering potato. My towering teenage daughter will loom over my shoulder and growl: 'That's MY chip.'

As I plan my trip, I know that my kids are anticipating chips with everything; I'm aware, too, that a walk 'up the street' will result in at least one toy and a comic each, then loads of telly and Nutella on toast and no discernible bed time.

My departure day comes. And something's wrong. Our daughter thunders into our bedroom – the kid who's never suffered anything worse than a stuffed-up nose – and I can hardly make out her features for the simmering mass of chicken pox. Child-free break for me? Chips and toy-shop trolley dash for them? Not this weekend, I fear.

Shop-bought goodies: how much should kids have?

As her son's birthday approached last year, my friend Jane confessed how stressed out she was feeling over her twelve-year-old son Danny's wish list. He wanted a Blind skateboard, which he reckoned has the best graphics, plus an extensive array of skate-related clothing. As a budding DJ, he wanted his own set of decks. He 'needed' several Xbox games and an entire rack of DVDs.

Jane, a single parent, couldn't afford to buy everything he wanted; he would have to save up for the skateboard and decks himself. Sounds reasonable? Danny stomped around the house, complaining that the battered skateboard he'd had for all of two years would make him the laughing stock.

I'm convinced that the want-too-much kid is just trying it on. Do children really expect us to say, 'Yes, of course you can have that!' every time something catches their eye? Recently, when my daughter swooned over a little net bag of plastic ice-cream cones in John Lewis, she almost fainted with shock when I said she could have it. She didn't realise that, in sitting patiently while I tried on nine different tops in Gap, she had earned the pretend ice-creams, and that our extremely pleasing shopping day had made me unusually benevolent. Normally, though, I find that, if I keep saying yes, and let them select bits of tat from whichever shop we happen to be in, then their demands escalate. Then I can't even pop in to pay our paper bill without the three of them grabbing at any old crud ('Mum always says yes!') and slamming it on to the counter.

We can curb the must-haves by:

◎ Having a sly word with the parents of our kids' friends (particularly pre-Christmas) to find out how much loot they're really getting.

◎ Being honest when we really can't afford it.

◎ And, even if we can afford it, saying we can't. On short, non-shopping trips – ie, the walk home from school, or en route to the park – I've simply stopped bringing my purse (then felt mighty hacked off when I've fancied an ice lolly).

◎ Never crumbling beneath a barrage of whingeing and moaning.

I was strict with the boys when they were little because we couldn't afford much. These days we're more likely to buy them little treats and it's opened the floodgates. Even in Tesco they're after videos, CDs and toys. Sometimes I wonder how I've managed to bring up such a couple of spoiled boys.
Carrie, mother of Stephen, eight, and Laurence, six

I always buy my step-daughter a small souvenir from a gift shop – maybe a notebook or pencil case. Now she gets pocket money she can top up with her own cash. To her, the browsing is as much fun as the buying.
Allie, mother to Zach, eighteen months, and step-mum to six-year-old Jess

When we're on a day out, I point out that it's a treat in itself, and rarely buy presents. I can't get fleeced in the gift shop on every day trip. We often take our kids'

*friends, and they make it clear that they're usually bought
something, but we still don't budge.*
**Matt, auctioneer and father to Benjamin, nine, Thomas, five,
and Daisy, three**

*The only places I always say yes is in charity shops. They
bring home the most disgusting tat: an onyx sphinx, a
vile furry puppy in a pink plastic basket. When they're
sick of these things I sneak them back to the shop. I look
upon it as recycling.*
Toni, mother to Charlotte, seven, and Miles, five

What the experts say about pester power

The last decade has seen children become increasingly
aware of what's available. They have far greater access to
the media and, like adults, vie with each other in terms of
what they have. It's society that's become more consumer-
orientated, not just children.
**Suzie Hayman, a counsellor and spokesperson for parents'
advisory service Parentline Plus**

We need to educate our children into becoming responsible consumers. If you're letting your child choose something for five pounds, let him look around and choose,
then ask him, 'How long do you think this will last? You
have another quite like it at home – wouldn't you rather
pick something else?' Remember, too, that human beings
are, by nature, pretty demanding. If we were let loose in a
clothes shop, we might just go crazy too.
Caryn Skinner, Director of The Parent Company

Children are smarter and more acute than we give them credit for, and we shouldn't pour scorn on what they want. Even if we can't understand why something's so important, to them, it clearly is.
Suzie again

I fell into the habit of bringing my son a toy each time I'd been away. If I hadn't managed to get to a toyshop, he'd be bitterly disappointed. Now, if I come back empty-handed, I change the subject by chatting about what he's been doing at school, or we read a book together.
How Caryn deals with the 'where's my present?' issue

Kiddie crazes: a bluffer's guide

I'm wary of writing too much about kids' crazes because, by the time this book is in the shops, Yu-gi-yo cards will be as covetable as discarded lolly wrappers and kids will have moved swiftly onwards to some new, highly desirable thing. However, I do think it's worth bearing in mind that crazes are, by their very nature, pretty short-lived so, while we want our children to be able to join in, and not be several decades behind their peers with a clapped-out Ninja Turtle or malfunctioning Furbee, we don't have to remortgage our property in order to furnish the little dears with the biggest and best. To my shame, I once spent a ridiculous amount of cash, and three hours of my time, bidding madly for 400 Pokemon cards – including many rare shinies! – on eBay. The experience left me feeling rather silly, and also red-faced and panting.

My friend Johnny reminds me of the year when his son Louie was given a heap of Bob merchandise for his birthday – Bob rucksack, Bob sponge painting kit, Bob umbrella, the lot. Just because he liked Bob on TV didn't mean he wanted or needed Bob pyjamas. He just stared at it all, as if thinking, 'What *is* this stuff? Why does everything have Bob on it?'

I do sympathise. Bob is pretty smug and unlikeable, and wears terrible dungarees. As for *Thomas the Tank Engine*? You've reached the really nail-biting bit when a clapped-out engine is shunted into a siding. And you're not only forced to read the books. Caring Parent is obliged to learn the trains' names – there are loads of them – or have some angry tot retorting, 'That's not Gordon! That's *Henry*!'

Postman Pat makes Thomas seem positively thrilling. What's it about? Some elderly lady trundling about on a bicycle with fruit on her hat, and those Pat vans craftily positioned outside supermarkets. Negotiating Safeways with a pair of brawling toddlers was testing enough. Just when I thought I was on the home strait, with wine bottles clanking in their carrier bags, my sons would throw themselves to the ground because some other fortunate child happened to be 'driving' the van.

Children's characters are carefully designed to a) not look very nice and b) do parents' heads in. Take *The Teletubbies*. Like Louie's deluge of Bob the Builder gifts, I only had to murmur that our sons 'quite liked' that vile Tubby Custard machine for a hail of *Teletubby*-related paraphernalia to clatter into our house.

There was no such onslaught when I was a kid. Telly took three years for its valves to warm up, and *Vision On* was as good as it got. Yes, we had crazes: bulldog charge, a fine example of creative play involving the entire primary school splitting into two teams and smacking headfirst into each other. But we didn't have the Official Bulldog Charge chocolate bar. There wasn't even a website.

A couple of years ago, I could barely fight my way to my PC for small children clustered around the Action Man site. What's that all about? He doesn't even have proper hair. Now Action Man has lost all his clothes and been kicked behind the wardrobe. The Bey Blades lie forgotten in a mangled shoebox, the Bionicles reside in a dusty tray beneath a son's bed. Yet when I suggest passing them on to a younger child 'to make so much more space in your bedroom', I'm met with one fiery response: 'But they're MINE . . .'

'I want a pet!'

Ah, children. They fill the house with their debris and shouting, systematically destroy it and, when you think that they really cannot impact upon your home environment any further, start demanding real, live animals with whom to share their bedrooms. Over the years, each of my children has requested a pet. If I won't agree to a creature as high maintenance as an adorable spaniel pup, they'll lower expectations and accept a small rodent. 'Everybody has a pet,' one of my sons informs me, just as *everybody* takes packets of Chewits to school every day, and is allowed to have sleepovers on week nights.

Overhearing this, J chips in: 'Well, it would be quite sweet. Imagine a scruffy, lovable dog, padding about the house.' He forgets that dogs don't merely 'pad'. Just like small children, they mar every surface with mysterious stains, gnaw things they're not meant to, wolf evil-smelling food and foul up your house with their bad breath and farts.

Oh, I've read the studies which claim that pet-owning is hugely beneficial to children. Children can tell animals their problems, and find them comforting. Well, of course kids are drawn to small mammals. A cat doesn't care about a messy bedroom, and won't harangue a child to finish his broccoli. J argues that having a pet 'teaches children to care about something other than themselves'. Then he sighs and says, 'Sorry, kids – Mum won't allow it.'

Let's look at the true picture. Every weekday, J is out of the house for around eleven hours. I'm either working from home, or looking after the children at home. Who could possibly find themselves lumbered with the additional task of nurturing Towser? Even hamsters, though small enough to be ignored most of the time, require cleaning out and feeding, or they stink to high heaven, or die. While children embrace the fun aspects of pet ownership – the handling and holding, the choosing of names – show me the kid who relishes the prospect of shovelling out poo.

Deprived of their own creature to care for (except for the blasted fish – see page 56), my kids are reasonably satisfied by bringing our friends' Labradors on walks. (Their real owners' kids exhibit zero interest in their own animals, reinforcing the point that, once a pet's been around for a couple of weeks, no one wants anything to do with it.) We also visit a horse which lives close to our house, and most of our day trips involve close examination of some kind of creature at Edinburgh Zoo or Deep Sea World. I'm also quite happy to point out ants and slugs in the garden.

So here, in case you're wavering on the pet issue, are reasons to Just Say No:

◎ **Winter.** Pity the poor dog-owner on a drizzly January evening: slumping through parks, picking up doggie deposits with carrier bag-covered hands, freezing their backsides off while they wait for Dasher to widdle on the grass.

- **Their smelly deposits.** Much of pet ownership revolves around the animal's toileting habits, necessitating either a 'walk' at eleven-thirty pm in the battering rain, or cleaning a cage, litter tray or garden. (Although your child might be the animal's official 'owner', you can hardly force him to de-poo the lawn.) Dogs bark in the night, waking the entire household. They have to be toilet trained just like children do. And how are you rewarded for your efforts? At least kids do grow into fine, upstanding adults who'll be willing to lift your heavy furniture when you move house (allegedly).

- **Their bladders.** Mice dribble wee constantly. They are incapable of holding on for one second. Why invite a creature with such shoddy muscle control into your life?

- **Their mating habits.** Fancy a couple of pet rats? These creatures multiply like crazy, copulating at least twenty times a day. Who wants that kind of excessive behaviour going on in their own home?

- **Pet mice are no different to the creepy, scrabbling kind which invade our homes.** Nothing is surer to put you off small creatures than the vile sight of something slithering in the pasta bowl which you didn't wash up. Dark flashes, nocturnal scratchings: at one point, J and I thought we were losing our minds. The only way of ridding ourselves of our 'infestation' was to move house.

- **They die.** Unless your children have hearts of ice, they'll be devastated when their pet corks it. It's bad enough when a friend's pet dies while in your care. When I was a kid, my parents were obliged to inform the Pickles family that dear Tiger, an overweight tabby, had uttered its last yowl in the back of our Mini Van en route to the vet. All the owners said was, 'Oh well.' Maybe they had hearts of ice too.

⊚ **They don't die.** I've seen friends fall out of love with their pets, usually once a baby has arrived. They've attempted to drive them out of the home, as if they're an unwanted lover, by being all aloof and not stroking them any more. One friend said of his puss: 'He stinks and he's so bloody neurotic. I wish he'd go to live somewhere else.' As in the human world, the unwanted party rarely takes the hint, preferring to prolong the agony by squirming around your thighs, licking your face, and refusing point-blank to move on.

The guinea-pigs are fine because they live in the garage and Rosie does all the feeding and cleaning out. But the cat was a pain. He scratched Hannah – she had to have a tetanus – then got into a fight and cost us £75 to have his jaw mended. Three weeks after we'd paid the vet's bill he had the cheek to walk out on us.
Vicki, mother to animal-mad girls of eleven and five

Don't let your kids have stick insects. As they don't actually do anything, they're incredibly poor value as pets. Plus, it took five years for the last of ours to die off.
Helen, mother to Patrick, seven

Dad! I WANT that chameleon!
Sour-faced girl of around eight years old, overheard by one of my sons at Butterfly and Insect World, near Edinburgh

When are you going to collect Champion?
My mother, circa 1983, lumbered with a rabbit after I'd flown the nest

Our horrible fish tank

Trying to get on the kids' good side and earn a Good Cop medal, J presented our children with a fish tank and two delicate, peppery-coloured creatures. These fish now reside in putrid water. As the children can't actually see them, they've forgotten there's anything living in the tank. It's just a stinky glass box full of gravel and slime.

One crucial aspect of pet ownership is that, once you've crumbled, there's no going back. I'm not so cold-hearted that I can bring myself to give the fish away, or feign some 'tank falling off the table' tragedy in which all lives are lost. But at least the fish serve as a constant reminder that my family is unable to care for any creature lower down the food chain than ourselves.

Our pets are, however, elevated to Favourite Possession status when their tank is smashed by my sons during an energetic roll-the-jam-jar game. Water seeps out all over the boys' desk. The fish, which no one cares about, are scooped out by brave, brave Daddy amidst rivers of tears, and are plopped into my favourite lime green Habitat salad bowl. The same bowl in which I intended to wow visitors with Jamie Oliver's Mixed Leaf Salad With Mozzarella, Mint and Prosciutto.

J barks that the fish will go back to the shop and we'll never have another pet, ever. Our sons' punishment amounts to a fancy new tank (£35) and the realisation that adults are soft idiots with Switch cards, which don't count as real money anyway. J even lets the kids choose new accessories for the tank. In the pet shop our daughter spies a chinchilla. 'Oooh!' she says. 'Can we have it?'

'You can have one,' I tell her, 'when you're grown up and have your own house.'

'I'm not your friend,' she whispers.

We can't force our kids to want what we want

Before my daughter was born, I imagined that raising a girl would involve lots of low-stress activity: painting, drawing, and shopping for nail polish and Crayola craft kits. My third child, Thug Girl, is now four, and plays with tanks and Action Man's hideous opponent, Doctor X, whose veins burst from an upper arm. I gave her my very own doll's house, planning to chuck out the late sixties/early seventies furnishings, and create a pared-down, contemporary style fit to be featured in *Wallpaper** magazine. I'm so glad I didn't waste weeks of my life sanding wood and cutting out fabric for carpets, as my daughter declared that the house was 'horrible', and should be put somewhere else, like the garage.

One summer's day, Thug Girl and I go clothes shopping to H&M. She has specified black for her capsule autumn wardrobe. We see a family with three remarkably pretty girls, all dressed in lilac and clutching Bratz dolls. I once bought Thug Girl a doll, and last saw it stripped of its pretty pink dress, tightly bound with pipe cleaners, and attached to the inside of a cupboard with Sellotape.

Keen to observe girlie-girl families, and glimpse their feminine world, I take my daughter to the tiara emporium that is Girl Heaven. Little princesses in glittery platform boots and pink feather boas are trying on fairy wings and having their lips painted by make-up girls in the

Princess Studio. Actually, it's quite disconcerting. In such a sugary world, I feel like a gigantic heifer. When the staff launch into a song and dance routine outside the shop, we have to leave Girl Heaven. And I think: do I really want a pink fairy for a daughter? A Tinkerbell, rather than a Captain Hook?

That evening, Thug Girl is being hosed down in the bath by her dad and bragging about her new black capsule wardrobe. Surely there's a gap in the market for a shop selling pre-ripped clothing, scar/wound tattoos and a wide range of daggers and miniature power tools. A high-pitched alarm would go off if anyone wearing pink tried to enter the shop.

It's not quite the mother/daughter shopping experience I'd envisaged. But I guess that kids want what they want, and not what *we* think they should want.

3
kids in public places

When your kid goes plank-rigid in public • the horror of
children in supermarkets • visiting grown-up places (nice
shops, galleries, Ikea) *en famille* • losing it (the adult
tantrum) • the day our son split his head on a table leg
• eating out without embarrassment or injury • clever
stuff to have stashed in your bag

I used to think that kids fell into two camps: those who behaved
impeccably in public (known as 'playing a good away match'),
attracting admiring glances and making a parent's heart swell to
ridiculous proportions – and The Other Sort. This child – devil
spawn, whom no one would want for their own – would storm
through shopping malls, slapping at sleeping babies in their
prams, and roaring for a £39.99 toy, his face distorted and purple
like a chewed-up blackcurrant sweet.

On the day we'd moved from London to our temporary new
home in an unlovely Scottish new town, I witnessed The Other
Sort in the gloomy shopping precinct. The kid was making a
terrible tantrummy noise – 'RAAAAAAA!' – as his dad thundered
along behind him, flapping a gigantic smacky-hand and shouting, 'Fookin' cum*eer*, Nathan.' As the dad blundered on after
the boy, aiming for the backside but just smacking thin air, I

looked down at my own sons (who were eerily stain-free, and asleep in their double buggy). And I thought: *I am so lucky because neither of you will ever behave like that.*

What a head-up-the-backside idiot I was. Oh, and I was wrong about the two types of kid. Every child – even the little girl who trots daintily around department stores without even attempting to topple a precarious display of Nigella Lawson cookware – has the potential for the almighty horror that is . . .

. . . the public tantrum

I'm not going to bother mentioning the at-home tantrum, apart from saying: every single child-rearing expert I've ever read advises a parent to turn a blind eye, and simply waltz out of the room. As long as no one's likely to be hurt, and a neighbour's not about to pop round and twitter, 'Oh dear, Bethany never does that – isn't there a helpline you can call?' there is nothing wrong with vacating the room in which the tantrum is taking place, and calmly sitting down with the newspaper. (You won't be able to read, of course; it's enough to show that the tantrum isn't bothering you one bit.)

But the public tantrum is a different matter. You can't just walk away, shut a door, and flip nonchalantly through the recipes in *Guardian Weekend*. People are watching. Strangers are thinking either, 'Poor, poor parent', or, 'Imagine – allowing a child to behave like that! It would never have happened in my day. What we need is a war etc etc.' Some of these strangers even have the damn nerve to stomp over and *tell you off* for shouting at your kid, or having dared to produce such a foul-natured infant.

Just to make you feel better, here's our worst tantrum ever. We're in one of those soulless retail outlet villages. I'm hoping to find some cheap-yet-lovely shoes. J and I have allowed one of our sons [then aged two] a go in a Little Tykes car in the play area. After about twenty minutes, another child wants to climb in. Our son sits tight. We plead, cajole, talk in stern deep voices, offer bribes, but still he refuses to exit the vehicle. Eventually, we have to prise his coiled fingers from the steering wheel and literally drag him out of the car by his feet. He is inconsolable – kicking, trying to bite us, and potentially triggering a dramatic rise in vasectomies. I'm in tears. We're hauling our kid towards the car park when a colleague from J's new workplace glides by, checks my streaky wet face and hurries away.

Our son screams all the way home. I run upstairs and bang my own head against the bedroom wall. Then I blunder out of the house, drive away, and go shopping.

We pulled up in Safeways carpark. As soon as Claire clocked the building – she detests Safeways – she started yelling, 'No!' I managed to feed one of her legs into the trolley but the other was rigid, so I carted her along semi-horizontally and squawking. I felt terrible – embarrassed and stressed – until an elderly lady turned to me and said, 'Don't worry, dear, you're doing fine.'
Karen, full-time mother to daughters aged eight, six and three, on the kindness of strangers

Frankie's tantrums became easier to ignore once I realised she was actually enjoying them. I'd see her straining to check out her teary reflection in shop windows and mirrors, actually fixing her pigtail bobbles at the same time.
Kelly, solicitor and mother to five-year-old twins Harry and Francesca

I heard that Bach Rescue Remedy is good for mellowing children out and bought some for Claire, but ended up slugging it myself.
Karen again, hitting the bottle

We were having a lovely day at the fairground until Sophia [then three] started stropping because I wouldn't buy her a massive foam hammer to hit people with. I tried to distract her with hook-a-duck but she was fixated on this hammer. She hurled herself on to the ground and a woman came up and said, 'Excuse me, are you this little girl's father?' I carried Sophia – she was stiff with rage – over my shoulder, with this wretched woman scuttling after us, obviously thinking of calling the police.
Sophie's dad David, who still refused to buy the bloody foam hammer

Sam had fallen into a pattern of having a tantrum every time we passed the baker's. He'd cling on to the door handle, screaming for cake. Eventually he grew too big to pull off the door handle so we simply changed our usual route until the baker's shut down and turned into a dry-cleaning place.
Penny, who's eternally grateful that Sam now prefers sitting quietly with his Gameboy and doesn't even like cake

These facts won't stop tantrums . . .

. . . but they might act as a small consolation when your child goes plank-rigid:

- Rather unfairly, children rarely have tantrums at play-group, nursery or with a childminder. During the peak of my daughter's tantrum phase – between age two-and-a-half and three – it drove me bonkers that no one but her immediate family ever witnessed her spectacular displays. Unfortunately, a kid tends to reserve tantrums for the person she's most deeply attached to, simply because there's so much more at stake. So, when strangers stare, open-mouthed, at your abominably behaved child, you can reassure yourself that she's only making an almighty din because she really loves you.

- It's a rare parent who hasn't experienced the super-market screamer. Naturally, kids don't want to be there, and so they'll make the whole process as horrific as possible, ensuring that you emerge with a mishmash of random snacks and none of the nutritious, *real* food (ie, items which, when combined, produce a meal) that you'd gone in for. They also knock things over, get lost on purpose, nag for strawberry laces, ricochet wildly in the wine aisle and shout, 'Are you an alcoholic?' if you stash more than two bottles in your trolley. My sons also enjoy blundering around the Co-op in a pretend-drunk fashion. Even though they've never actually seen me drunk, other shoppers no doubt assume I'm plastered out of my brain every night of the week.

❀ Most parents would agree that smacking has zero effect, apart from prolonging the tantrum and making you feel the size of a garden pea. In fact research has shown that children who are forgiven readily tend to outgrow the tizzy phase sooner than those who are severely reprimanded and have all their toys taken away.

❀ Just as we fret that our children will still be encased in stinking Pampers at the age of thirteen, they become dry and fragrant and horrible dollops no longer roll out of their trouser legs. Likewise, tantrums. They tend to kick off at around twenty months, the point at which a child begins to recognise himself in a mirror (and sees himself as a separate being, with wants and needs of his own). But between two and four the vast majority of children make exhibitions of themselves occasionally – as do many seemingly well-functioning adults in positions of authority. From four onwards they'll tend to happen far less frequently.

❀ When they do kick off, just ignore them, yawn, stare into the middle distance, yawn some more, gaze at your watch.

❀ Please pay no heed to disapproving onlookers. They're not really disapproving anyway – just fascinated by your child's antics and thanking their lucky stars that they're not required to intervene. So, in some ways, your kid has made their day a bit brighter.

The tantrum is an instant way of grabbing your attention when you're involved in something else. It's a survival mechanism from way back when we were hunter-gathers,

2,000 years ago. A child simply had to gain his parent's attention – otherwise he might not have survived.
Child psychologist Dr Dorothy Einon

Personally, I suspect that a healthy dose of realism helps to minimise those tense, nervous moments. For instance, you wouldn't expect a three-year-old (or even his seven-year-old big brother) to sit through a ninety-minute wedding ceremony, with lots of adults reading from boring big books, without making the occasional squawk.

Here are some pointers on handling a range of sometimes-fun, sometimes-tedious, everyday outings without tears. Just *life*, basically.

Public transport

My children can cope with (and actually enjoy) bus or train journeys of up to forty minutes or so. Recently my daughter entertained a bus-load of strangers on such a journey by firing questions about the emergency door. What was it for? What would happen if the bus tipped right over? Would the emergency door then be on the roof? So how would we get out? In fact, her line of questioning was so brain-melting that I actually fell asleep, effectively leaving three vulnerable children unattended and capable of alighting the bus by themselves or being kidnapped or anything. I was finally woken by a worried-looking man, shouting, 'Are you *all right*?', which suggested that I'd been making some untoward noises, or maybe dribbling.

Taking them on the bus has become easier since we've ditched the buggy. My kids still love to travel this way. It pains me to remember that, during our year in the Scottish new town, my toddler sons loved nothing better than being taken by bus to the shopping precinct, where we would sit in a dismal café and eat yellow cakes.

Try to keep luggage to a rucksack so your hands are free. When my children were younger I'd keep them on reins at bus or train stations. Use only an umbrella-folding buggy, take small toys, sticker books and a personal stereo for older children. On trains, don't be afraid to ask a stranger to get you a coffee from the buffet car – no one expects you to struggle along the length of the train with your children. And always reserve seats in advance on trains for longer journeys, even for a baby – you'll need the space.
Non-driver Rosie, mother to Theo, six, and Iris, five

If you're travelling by bus and have to fold the buggy and carry your child, ask the driver not to pull off until you've sat down. Or get on first so there's a queue behind you.
Stella, who has been caught by the look-lady-I'm-in-a-hurry driver, and is mother to two-year-old Nina

Small toys, colouring books, storybooks, felt pens and paper are all handy on trains. Reading might make them feel sick on bus journeys, but you can read to them. The downside of bus travel is them constantly dinging the bell, swapping seats and needing the toilet. It really helps if you have a storybook to read aloud which appeals to all of them.
Victoria, receptionist and mother to Ruby, seven, Grace, five, and Finlay, four

On buses we try to play I Spy but one of them usually starts making things up, like E for elephant, or A for America, and the others are furious, going, 'But we can't

see America!' I find it's easier just to ignore them and gawp out of the window.
Gabrielle, full-time mother to Felix, eight, Laura, four, and two-year-old Samuel

Doctor's waiting room

Do-able if you take along books/comics, and even if you don't: most children delight in stuffing all your spare change into the charity collection boxes and poking the horrible gnarled toys, which is fortunate, as our kids are the only reason we frequent these places. I didn't see a doc for fourteen years until I had children. Occasional hazards: your child roaring, 'What's wrong with that man?'; displaying an unnatural interest in the water dispenser; rapping on the receptionist's little window, causing her to pull her sucked-in-lips face and requiring you to bluster, 'It wasn't me. It was ... er ... him.'

The library

You'd think all children would love the library. After all, it's just like shopping, except you say 'yes' all the time. (At ours the kids are allowed a whopping ten books each.) However, while my daughter loves browsing the shelves, my sons and the library just don't click. Once they've been to the toilet a couple of times (requiring us to request the key from the stern library lady), twiddled with the magnetic thingies which keep the enormous heavy doors open (and been told off for doing so by stern library lady), then they just want to go home.

We leave, with me staggering beneath the weight of the books they've chosen. Months later, I spend an entire morning rounding up the books and realise that, although no one's read any of them, we've still accrued a £25 fine.

When Oliver was little I dreaded going to the library. He'd run up and down these terrifying stone steps, pull handfuls of books from the shelves and spill crisps all over the carpet. Now he's older and a very keen reader, and can happily pore over a science or nature book while I browse the adult section. It's his favourite place. It was hell at the time but I'm glad I persevered with the library. **Debbie, counsellor and mother to a six-year-old bookworm**

Lovely shops

Of course children should be forced to come grocery shopping, or to buy tedious items like a bucket or can of WD40 occasionally. That's just reality, which cannot consist solely of 24/7 soft play centres with steady supplies of those fishy whale things which are grey inside and smell of sour dishcloth. For that, let us be thankful. However, as for *pleasurable* shopping with one's youngsters in tow, this takes some planning. After all, in the likes of Oasis and Jigsaw there's precious little to amuse children apart from plunging into rails of delicate garments, or sneaking into changing rooms, or wiping their noses on an embroidered Karen Millen shift dress. (Actually, I'd never act with such lunacy as to haul my infants into Karen Millen or, for that matter, Hobbs; these shops are just too *hushed* for small people.)

It is possible to go clothes shopping with children. First, warn your kids in advance that you'll be doing some shopping for yourself. On your shopping trip, take them

70

into a shop or two of their choice – Woolies, the Gadget Shop, whatever they fancy – to emphasise your generosity. Promise another shop of their choice but only after you've had the chance to buy something. Impress on them the need to take turns and share the fun. Warn them that, if you're not having fun, then they'll have no more fun either and you'll all go home.

Once in the shop of your choice, deposit the oldest in a safe yet tucked-away place with his Gameboy. Take the youngest one with you and whiz round collecting anything you vaguely like. Round up your children and take them with you into the changing room. They might lie on the floor and whine a bit. With luck, they'll tell you how lovely you look.

Tiger, graphic designer and mother to Jake, ten, and Rory, four

Galleries and exhibitions

The one time J and I hauled our then-toddler twins around an exhibition – at the Royal Academy, if I recall – the lofty crowd looked so appalled by the foul nappy aromas wafting up from the buggy that we hurried out, and didn't glimpse the inside of a gallery for another five years.

Some parents brag that they all spent three hours at the Tate and everyone had a lovely time. I think it's only do-able with extremely docile (or fast asleep) children, or if there's an extra adult on hand to take the kids outside when they start to experience art overload. Other hazards: the wires around exhibits which trigger alarms when touched (set off by my kids *five times* during one brief visit to GOMA in Glasgow); the general echoey-ness which serves to amplify every sound made by your child; stern staff (one friend tried to plug her child's mouth with a bottle, but was told off, as a dropped bottle might splatter its contents on to the paintings); the distinct feeling that you are disturbing someone's peaceful cultural afternoon.

I took Shannon [ten] and Lara [four] to the Turner Prize exhibition. There was a sign clearly stating that the show might not be appropriate for children under sixteen, but I thought, 'It's art, it can't be all that bad.' First thing we saw was a blow-up man and woman doing a sixty-nine, his oversized penis in her mouth. I didn't even see what was happening at the other end. It was very brightly coloured and looked a bit like they were lying on an airbed, so it was very attractive for small children.

The other piece in the same room was a gruesome sculpture of a couple of decaying human bodies hanging from a tree, covered with worms and bugs. Lara is quite fascinated by gore, and wanted to look more closely at this. I dragged them through to the next room to find those beautiful ceramic pots. From a distance, lovely; up close, images of child abuse. Great! And Lara, tugging at my sleeve, roaring, 'I want to go back and look at the man and lady in the boat.' I got the kids out as quickly as I could. Then we went and looked at some nice Victorian paintings of children with lanterns.
Della, an art lover who now visits galleries on her own

Try to do art exhibitions in shifts. Outside the Tate St Ives, the beach is glorious. The kids and I paddled while the other adults went in. Then they took over the children, and I went into the gallery by myself. Very satisfying.
Jo, administrator and mother to Jessica, eight, and Sophie, three

John Lewis's china department

Advisable only if you feel your life's lacking excitement and drama.

A fireplace shop

J and I take Erin, our youngest, to look at new fireplaces to replace the 1960s beige tiled monstrosity in our living room. The showroom is wall-to-wall 'real' fires. We take it in turns to restrain Erin in a vice-like grip to prevent her from setting herself on fire. Result? We spend £950 on a totally unsuitable fireplace which we hate, and which cracked when the builders installed it.

Ikea

Me, J, and the three kids. So far, so good. We're up the stairs and no one's shouting or crying. J is actually smiling, albeit in a strained way. In the main furniture bit, he speeds up to an impatient trot, announcing, 'We're getting a bed and that's it.'

The bed is selected, plus mattress and mattress pad – something we didn't even know existed, let alone that we need one. 'It refines the feeling of the mattress,' says the sales guy, 'and, of course, offers protection.' We must look like the sort of people who have unfortunate accidents during the night. Shopping done, I am banned from glancing at – and certainly purchasing – the things I really want: candles, textiles, *essential* brightly coloured circular boxes which fit into each other. J ploughs onwards to the warehouse and starts barking, 'It's not here, you've written down the wrong number', and glares at me as if I should be able to locate a Sultan Molt Matt Pad as easily as my own eyebrows.

We finally make it to the checkout where a woman repeatedly bounces her trolley against J's backside. I take our children – who are now pirouetting wildly due to extreme boredom – to the hot dog area where the ice-cream 'doesn't taste right'. Our daughter pumps the mustard dispenser with no hotdog beneath it. One of our sons is announcing: 'I am going to tell Miss X [his teacher] that all we did this weekend was go to Ikea and I never want to come here again.'

Sadly, my children are unimpressed with the ballpit, the hot dogs and even the bouncy beds. But the real Ikea problem lies squarely with J and me. I assume that, when we first met, he imagined that we might spend languid mornings in bed, perhaps venturing out to markets offering copious quantities of cheap, rare vinyl. He didn't bargain for an Ikea sort of life. But hang on. Neither did I.

Ikea is a dream as long as you take just one child. Put them in the crèche, do a quick whiz round, then wolf a Danish and bottomless coffee. If they're not keen on the crèche, go at ten am on a Sunday. They're open but aren't allowed to sell anything until eleven am. Let your kids climb over the sofas and play with the toys until, by the time the crowds flood in, they're docile enough to sit in the buggy.
Sally, training officer and mother to Louisa, three, and Imogen, two

Kids in restaurants: a piece of cake?

Our bad café day #1.
We've stopped off for a quick lunch at a café called Well Bred (clearly, something which our children are not). We hope to

wallop down the glamorous delicacy that is the baked potato with baked beans and cheese. Our sons (then aged three) clamber all over their seats until one topples right off, plummeting floorwards and clanging his head against the table support which happens to be one of those old-fashioned cast-iron sewing machines.

He's screaming, his brother's screaming, I'm screaming. We have wrecked the peaceful ambience of the Well Bred Café. Blood oozes from the back of my kid's head. We hurry out, pressing a wet paper napkin to the wound, and drive at great speed to hospital, with the uninjured son complaining, 'Where's my baked potato? I want it. I'm starving. It's not *fair*.'

Our bad café day #2.

Four years have passed since the aforementioned incident. I've been lulled into believing that, as a family, we can manage to eat in cafés without drama or incident. This time we're in central Glasgow, our favourite shopping location. Rain starts belting down so we dive into a nondescript café. I park the three children at a table while I determine whether the sandwiches on offer will be acceptable to my pernickety offspring. My eyes have barely skimmed a label which reads 'chicken and swee—' when they're off, shoving each other and bickering over I don't know what – a broken toothpick, or a biscuit crumb left by the table's previous occupants.

I swing round from the sandwich display and, like Basil Fawlty at his most demented, shout: 'Right! Right! Put your coats on. We are *leaving*.'

Rather harsh, you might think, considering that my kids haven't eaten for four hours. *Mean trout*, you might say, overreacting like that, when a few stern words would have sufficed. Miserable hag then hauls her (now droopy-faced) children back out into the rain, past a sympathetic-looking elderly lady who looks like she'd dearly love to press barley sugars and shiny new coins into their palms. Seconds later, I'm awash with remorse. But too late. We can hardly troop back in, past the boiled-sweet lady, and sit down at the same table.

Actually, our café incident is unusual. Normally, I tend to adopt a rather eerie, Stepford-Wife-Meets-Mary-Poppins demeanour when we're out. It's a reaction against the terrible day when I bawled at my daughter outside Mothercare – some almighty row over being allowed a fifth go on the Thomas Tank ride, if I recall. A passer-by glimpsed my hideous twisted features and muttered, 'Look at the face on that.' Later, at home, I wondered what the woman had meant, and tried to recreate the vile expression in our bathroom mirror. She was right – it was truly grotesque. A terrible gargoyle made flesh. So, from that day, I vowed to be smiley *at all times* and, when that proved impossible, at least to adhere to a firm-but-fair approach.

Back to our fun day out in Glasgow. My kids and I slump onwards through the driving rain. One of my sons asks, 'If your body runs out of food, do you die?'

We meet up with J, who has spent several hours wafting around Virgin Megastore. 'I feel like I've ruined their day,' I tell him. 'I'm a bad, bad mother.'

'Hmm,' he says. And so we steer them up to the café in Borders where they're allowed one curious lolly with a pink and gooey interior, a whopping slice of cake, and a chocolate chip cookie the size of my daughter's head.

Our bad café days illustrate that we have yet to master the art of eating out with children attached. Yes, things are getting easier; like many parents, we use Pizza Express as a pretty fail-safe option – so often, in fact, that by the time the children leave home I won't wish to encounter another doughball, or that weird ice-cream that's just *too white*, for the rest of my life.

It has also taken me nearly seven years to conclude that it's unreasonable to expect children to remain static and silent for thirty minutes, while waiting for their food. Duh.

Here's what some rather more clued-up parents have figured out.

Liz: *The main thing is, bring something for them to do. Pens, paper, whatever keeps them happy. We make sure Emily [aged three] sits where she can watch what's going on – no one likes gawping at a blank wall. Sometimes we'll ask for her dessert early so we can finish our meal in peace.*

Sue: *Staff are more amenable at lunchtimes or early evenings when it's quieter. Far better to have bored staff, who are happy to amuse your kids, than waitresses who are run off their feet. Service will be faster too. If you're going later, persuade your child to nap during the day. Maybe feed them something light beforehand so they don't end up starving if service is slow. Bring a plastic beaker for a toddler, wet wipes and, if possible, back-up adults – we often eat out with my sister and brother-in-law, so there are more of us to keep the kids happy.*

Felicity: *Go for buzzy places with a reasonable level of background noise so you don't feel too conspicuous.*

Millie: *I think the most hair-raising period is between eighteen months and two-and-a-half, so that's only a year . . . We find non-British restaurants more child-friendly – not just Asian or Italian, but tapas bars and Turkish places, where extremely butch waiters have gushed adoringly over our children.*

Hazel: *In Italian restaurants Ailsa [aged two] is usually happy with a bowl of pasta with butter and Parmesan –*

some places only charge a quid for that. Having your favourite place where the staff know your child by name makes things so much easier.

Millie: *A glass of wine for the adults makes everything easier.*

Liz: *And chips, of course . . .*

Becky: *Chips! Last time we ate out, the baby was screaming with hunger so I gave him a chip from my plate. I didn't realise it was boiling hot, and carried on feeding him – next morning I notice there's a blister on his thumb . . .*

Millie: *See – chips are very, very bad.*

Cate: *Sometimes you have to admit that eating out with kids is a pain in the arse. With mine [three boys under five] it's too stressful.*

Allie: *I'd feel trapped and depressed if I couldn't go to restaurants. I'll often take Charlie [aged two] to Café Rouge. One time he fell off his chair and banged his head, but I soon cheered him up with jellybeans from the machine.*

Clever things to take to restaurants

I'm not suggesting that it's necessary to bring Playmobil Pirate Ship with five billion components, but a few small unobtrusive items plucked from your bag can make all the difference to everyone's peace of mind. Plus, any other parents watching will think you're incredibly clever and resourceful. Some ideas:

- A tiny storybook that fits in your bag. My daughter loves *Harry The Dirty Dog* and *No Roses For Harry* (both titchy, handbag-sized books from the Red Fox Mini Treasures series). Unfortunately, she's also partial to the *Mr Men* series – also pocket-sized – and will insist, solely to torture me, that I name off all the wretched characters pictured on the back cover, even though she blinking well knows them all.

- Small pack of felt tips, crayons and a tiny notebook for scribbling, drawing, or games.

- It's not very earth-mommyish, but our boys adore the very basic games on our mobile phones (they don't make any beep-beep noises to irritate other diners).

- Carly advises: 'Take a rare treat, like chocolate buttons, in case your child has "a moment".' However she avoids restaurants which are intolerant of 'moments', saying, 'Where's the pleasure in spending loads of money just to get filthy looks?'

- Small doll, toy car, teeny Lego model or puzzle. One of our favourite lunch places, the Sunflower Café in Peebles, Scotland, has a box of wooden puzzles and small toys which has kept our three (who veer towards the challenging end of the behaviour-in-restaurant spectrum) spookily quiet until their food arrived.

I'm not bragging, but I just had to squeeze in here . . .

Our lovely café day

For a parent, there are few things more pleasing than having your children admired by a stranger. In the absence of praise from a boss, and pay rises – actually, any pay at all – it's the surest way to feel that we're doing a decent job of child-rearing, and that our kids are unlikely to grow into malfunctioning adults, requiring intensive therapy. Honestly, having a stranger praise my children gets me ridiculously damp-eyed and trembly-lipped. It's quite a pathetic sight.

So one afternoon, we're in a dainty teashop – a quick pitstop after the library – and an elderly lady wearing a pull-on woolly hat (not *just* a pull-on woolly hat, but that's what sticks in my mind) gazes fondly at my kids and says, 'What delightful children.'

They look up from their slabs of chocolate cake and beam at her. What I'd give for the necessary equipment to tape the lady's kind comment and replay it at home 6,000 times. I only just manage to stop myself from saying, 'Well, they're not usually like this, they're *usually* –' Instead, I just thank her, as if strangers say nice things about my children all the time.

In truth, though, such moments are as rare and special as a total eclipse.

4

where are we going today?

Parents who do too much • making your day adult- and child-friendly • 'We don't do that!': can you stomach an outing with a perfect family? • day trips to make your kids love you for ever • dark moments on canal boats and helter-skelters • our lovely shiny new motor • which I am gonna puke all over • scrapping, snacking and other in-car irritations • journey's friends: making car trips less painful • storytape heaven (and hell) * staying in is the new going out

I spent the first couple of years of parenthood in East London where the emphasis was firmly on 'doing things' with your children. There were dance workshops for toddlers, even painting classes for babies, at which my sons would scuttle about on the floor, always managing to locate something treacherous, like a drawing pin.

My week would be scheduled to the hilt. If I wasn't attending local groups, I'd feel obliged to take the boys to some children's farm in Hertfordshire with a few polluted-looking llamas. I'd screech into a pub carpark on the way home, and beg the barmaid to warm the kids' milk. There were so many events to remember, so much stimulation to squeeze into the week, that the calendar buzzed with reminders. I could barely remember where we lived.

Why do we put ourselves through this? Left to their own devices, young children don't ask for much. Show them a churning washing machine, or rain streaking down a window, and they'll gawp at it for hours. In packing kids' lives with experiences, it's easy to forget what small people enjoy most: taking one bite from each item in the fruit bowl, and seeing what happens when they hold a Clinique powder compact under a running tap. Those simple pleasures – discovering whether the remote control sinks or swims when dropped into the toilet – are being lost. Take a kid to a shopping centre and he expects to be wheeled about in a red plastic vehicle and have his face painted by a clown. How many treats do children really need?

My friend Liz, mother to three sons, says all she can recall from her childhood is dismantling dry-stone walls to grind into fine powder, yet regularly takes the boys to Legoland, or for a spin on the London Eye. I wonder if the youngest (aged three) appreciates her efforts. The first time I brought my sons home from the zoo, their fleeces adorned with I WENT WILD AT EDINBURGH ZOO stickers, they asked, 'What are we doing today?'

'You've just been to the zoo!' I roared.

Of course, day trips are worth all the effort and expense – sometimes. For one thing, there's too much for your kids to look at and take in to even think about punching each other in the stomach. There's no Action Man's husky to grapple over, no kitchen drawers in which to trap each other's fingers. On those long, long days at home, when one of my kids has tried to impale a sibling on a long-handled barbecue fork, an impromptu trip has saved our bacon. I've found that the pleasure factor (for the adults, that is) is increased 300-fold if I've been sorted enough to:

* Present the day out as a fait accompli. No discussion about where to go – zero consultation. If you have more than one child, they'll disagree on where to go just to spite each other. If you ask anyone of pre-school age where they'd like to go, answers range from 'Africa' to 'the kitchen'. You know best. You can, of course, disguise an adult-oriented outing as a 'mystery tour', then watch their crestfallen faces as you pull up at Ikea, or a country house with magnificent gardens, when they thought they were heading for an adventure playground the size of Manchester.

* Choose destinations no more than an hour's drive from home. Any further and the yowling and howling, the stops for nappy change/toilet/snacks/puking episodes cancel out any fun derived from the trip.

* Bring a picnic (even if it's bucketing down). Most food on offer at child-friendly attractions is overpriced crap, lumps of frozen stuff flung into the frier that you'd feel bad flinging in the path of a starving stray dog. Kids, of course, adore this junk.

* Avoid buffeting crowds by going mid-week if possible.

* Swerve past the ubiquitous gift shop. If you're forced in there, at least have a pound coin handy for each of the kids so they can choose a tiny souvenir and not some whopping soft toy to join the eight million other soft toys you have at home. If they bray for plastic tat, and

you give in, console yourself that the particularly nasty item will be wrecked by the time you get home.

* Let them bring toys to play with in the car, but *leave* them in the car. (Many a day out has been ruined by having to perform a speedy U-turn because ratty old Biscuit – a matted dog that smells kind of cheesy – has been left behind in a castle dungeon.) Do avoid bringing anything that really matters to your child or you'll discover that, on arriving back home, it's still in the tearoom in Cromer.

* Ditto, let them bring a friend. Resign yourself to the fact that he'll have brought no money of his own, and will say very little apart from, 'I'm thirsty.'

* Bribe an adult friend to keep you company and share the responsibility. Choose carefully, though, as the wrong grown-up companion can utterly wreck your day. One friend watched, horrorstruck, as my kids clambered all over a ruined abbey. 'Wanna get on that wall,' her son muttered. 'No, Charlie,' said his mother. 'But they're on the wall. She lets them climb.' 'Fine, but *we* don't do that.'

Some fellow parents offer more direct criticism. They think that, being a vague acquaintance of yours and having produced kids themselves, they are therefore Boss of All Children and allowed to reprimand anyone under the age of sixteen for so much as flicking pebbles into a river.

On a walk in the woods, my sons picked up sticks to waggle about. (What else are woods/sticks for?) 'Hold that stick lower,' warned the other child's mother. 'You'll have someone's eye out.'

My sons continued to brandish twigs, sabre-style. 'Point your stick at the ground,' thundered the woman. My sons were in bother for *carrying sticks at the wrong angle.*

Days out to make your kids love you forever

If your child loves:

Animals

* The zoos in **Colchester** (www.colchester-zoo.co.uk), **Paignton** (www.paignton.org.uk), **Whipsnade** (www.whipsnade.co.uk) and **Blackpool** (www.blackpoolzoo.org.uk) are lovely: well-kept with plenty of picnicking spots and a lack of bored-looking, pitiful animals.

* For the whole Noah experience **Noah's Ark Zoo Farm** (www.noahsarkzoofarm.co.uk) in Wraxhall near Bristol will keep everyone happy for a whole afternoon; however you will be bombarded with so many 'Is Noah/God real?' and 'Weren't we apes?'-type questions that your head will be rotating by the end of your visit.

* For a more farmy atmosphere head for **Almond Valley Heritage Centre** (www.almondvalley.co.uk) in Livingston, West Lothian. With tractor and train rides, adventure playgrounds and lambs in springtime, it's been a big hit with my kids since they were toddlers.

* My brood also love deep-sea-type places, especially those with touch pools where you're allowed to prod rays and get your sleeves soaked. A big favourite is **Deep Sea World** (www.deepseaworld.com) in North Queensferry, Fife.

Things with wheels

✱ For all manner of trams and buses to clamber all over, head for Glasgow's **Museum of Transport** (www.glasgowmuseums.com), then stop off at the nearby Botanic Gardens for a picnic.

✱ The **National Railway Museum** (www.nrm.org.uk) in York offers a day's exploring for your Thomas-mad kid.

✱ Okay, no wheels, but my kids loved the remote-control sailing boats and being able to see beneath the water-line of Falmouth Harbour at the **National Maritime Museum Cornwall** (www.nmmc.co.uk).

✱ Let's face it: steam engines do have the edge on your contemporary Virgin Rail experience. Hop on to the **Keighley and Worth Valley Railway** (Keighley-Oxenhope, West Yorkshire, tel 01535 645214 www.kwvr.co.uk) which features in the original *Railway Children* film; I grew up near here, and was thrilled that the waving-red-petticoats scene was filmed just down the road from my granny's. Also: the **North York Moors Railway** (Pickering-Grosmont, North Yorkshire, nymr.demon.co.uk); **Ffestiniog Railway** through Snowdonia National Park (www.festrail.co.uk). Do keep journey times short enough to avoid an 'I wanna get off now!' crisis.

Bloody battles

✱ Your *Horrible Histories* fan will relish the authentic smells (my kids *love* stinky places) at York's **Jorvik Viking Centre** (www.jorvik-viking-centre.co.uk). The reconstructed Viking villages might even remind the little dears of their bedrooms at home.

* Castles thrill kids, but you may need nerves of steel when faced with the small child/twisty stone staircase/ unexpected hole in the ground combination. My kids are happy to kick around any old ruin so long as there's a dungeon attached, but you can't better the whole medieval experience of **Warwick Castle** (www.warwick-castle.co.uk).

Twiddling buttons and knobs

* At **Glasgow Science Centre** (www. glasgowsciencecentre. org) there's tons of on-screen stuff your kids can do (like morph their face with a celebrity's) plus Imax cinema; the **Observatory Science Centre** (www.the-observatory. org) at Herstmonceux, East Sussex, also offers a whole day's worth of interactive twiddling with telescopes and craft activities. Science museums are generally geared towards primary-school age and upwards, but toddlers can still amuse themselves with lots of random button-pushing and charging about.

* **Eureka** (www.eureka.org.uk) is an exception: designed for kids and packed with 'how it works' exhibits (everything from a toilet to the human tongue). Grown-ups may need a lie down and cold flannel on the forehead afterwards.

Pelting around

* **Leeds Castle** (www.leeds-castle.com) near Maidstone, Kent, is breathtaking but it's the fabulous hedge maze, which leads to a shell-studded cave, that delights my kids. In fact I've shoved them in, then disappeared to the pub for three hours (that's a joke, social services lady).

* A favourite tearing-around place of ours is **River Dart Adventures** (www.riverdart.co.uk) on Dartmoor, South Devon. The vast park has flumes, forests, natural-looking lakes to swim in – kiddie heaven (lovely for adults too).

* **Harewood House** (www.harewood.org) near Leeds, West Yorkshire is a stunning stately home – but stuff posh houses, it's the excellent adventure playground which will boost your fabulous parent rating.

Beware: not all outings go swimmingly . . .

Our disaster day out #1: the canal trip

A narrowboat trip may not be your idea of heaven (perhaps you're thinking: canals = stagnant water, plus rats). However, I'm pretty fond of the soupy-coloured urban canal with its suspect scum on top. An ex-partner and I lived on a narrowboat in North London for a couple of years; how loafy life was then, especially as we were too idle to use the boat to actually go anywhere. With a cruising speed of three to five miles per hour, even the sanitary station at King's Cross seemed a continent away so – rather cleverly, we thought – we took to emptying the chemical lav down a friend's domestic toilet whenever he was away (shame how friendships can end so abruptly).

So my mother, kids and I are on holiday in Yorkshire with an afternoon to kill. Why not take a boat trip? And they love it, until the point at which the boat is unleashed from its mooring. 'When does it speed up?' asks my son, anticipating the thrilling moment when this dreary branch of canal joins the M1 of inland waterways.

88

My mother explains how to distinguish the male mallard duck from the female. But my sons are not listening. They are jumping on the seats, spraying Ribena at each other. How foolish I feel now, having forgotten that a narrowboat is no different from any other small, enclosed space. A need for space is the sole reason why we exchanged our two-bedroomed terrace for a crumbling home with mysterious parts called 'the breakfast room' and 'the outhouse'. A big old house may surprise you with its potentially fatal circuit boards, but at least it's *big*.

Which a narrowboat isn't. My daughter is crying because she wants to get off. I check my arm to make sure my nicotine patch is still in place. Finally, fifteen years later, we arrive back at the canal basin. My mother climbs off, making a mental note to embark on boat trips only with fully-formed adults. 'Look,' she says weakly, 'that's a cygnet.'

'I know that,' rages my son.

Our disaster day out #2: the fairground

'Last time I was at a fairground,' says the man before us in the big wheel queue, 'I went on one of those chair-o-plane rides. I looked down and saw the guys who worked the thing, smashing the machinery with hammers, trying to make it stop.'

I glance up at the big wheel. Although it rotates quite slowly, it is, as you'd expect, bloody big. I'm not fond of heights, not one of those people who insists on haring to the top of famous buildings – the Eiffel Tower or Sagrada Familla – just so they can brag that they've done it. I'm even less keen to find myself elevated to a ridiculous height in a swingy metal basket.

'That chair-o-plane,' the man chunders on, 'went on spinning for half an hour. I thought my guts would explode. When they finally managed to stop it, everyone staggered off,

89

throwing up all over the grass. Ambulances were waiting,' he adds cheerfully.

At such moments, it strikes me how very different our lives would be had we not produced children. Digimon, Pokemon and Jackie Chan would remain as unfamiliar and confusing as the Cyrillic alphabet. If we were childless – or child*free*, as we're supposed to say now – J and I would not be spending this Sunday afternoon in the relentless drizzle, preparing to shout, 'Stop jiggling the basket!' for the duration of the ride.

'Ever been on a log flume?' the man in front asks his companion. 'No? Don't even think about it. My sister went on one in Florida. You know the bit when the log reaches the very top, just before it plunges down at a hundred miles an hour? It stopped there. Jammed. Fire brigade came, helped them all down on a ladder. Log flumes are bad news.'

Our kids are unconcerned by these horror stories. Yet there's a certain age at which being whirled around on a creaky machine stops being fun. For me, the turning point was clambering from a ghost train carriage to discover that I'd been sitting in a puddle of someone else's wee. 'I used to love rides,' J agrees, as our damp family edges closer to the big wheel. 'But now I'm not so keen on being . . . catapulted.'

As it turns out, the big wheel is totally un-scary as long as you keep your eyes firmly fixed on your shoes. Hook a duck is more worrying. For £2 – 'Pick any prize you like,' the stall guy announces – our children are rewarded with swords and a plastic eye patch, playthings of dubious quality which actually cost 9p each. We're about to head home when my daughter demands a go on the helter-skelter. J suggests that I accompany her up the spiral stairs. Generously, he offers to wait at the bottom.

We reach the top, and are so high up that the moon looks bigger than usual. Daughter climbs on to her mat. I give her a shove. She slithers a bit, then stops. She can't slide, it's too wet. 'Get off your mat,' I urge her, 'and crawl back to me.'

Normally she's a fearless kid who'll punch anyone in the jaw, no matter how big and ferocious they are. But I'm scared witless and she can sense my fear. Terrified adult = terrified kid. It's like the horrible moment on New Year's day when smoke started to belch from the bonnet of our ritzy Citroën AX. Despite the fact that it hadn't been driven for a week, the car appeared to be trying to barbecue itself. J and I freaked out – no smoke without fire, right? – and our children, who had regarded the smouldering vehicle with bubbling excitement, were soon clutching each other in terror just because we were in panic. Only the arrival of the firemen – who propped open the bonnet with a skateboard, and calmly removed the car's battery – could convince them that everything was under control.

Now my daughter is rigid with fear, and I can't crawl towards her, I just can't. I'm sweating and can't bear to look over the sides of the helter skelter where the people are so, so far down below. 'Crawl back up,' I yell, 'like a baby.'

She edges towards me and, by the time we arrive at the bottom, is yowling furiously. 'Were you scared, darling?' J asks her.

'No,' she rages, 'Mum said crawl like a baby. I'm not a baby. I'm *four*.'

Children often don't appreciate how special and interesting things are. I took our sons to a vintage motor show, and they had a lovely time, annoying the vehicles' owners by honking horns and trying to climb into the cars. But when we returned home they told their dad, 'Mum took us to a carpark.'
Patricia, community education worker and mother to Aaron, five, and Jacob, three

We'd had a great time at Drumlanrig Castle – three mums, seven children – until we finished up at the café where a small group of elderly ladies were enjoying their tea and cakes. The kids went wild, barging back and forth to the counter, spilling drinks, crawling under the table. We were aware of the elderly ladies' disgust, and headed home, our spirits deflated.
Anne, full-time mother to Josephine, six, and three-year-old Alex, who now avoids the tearoom experience

Our day touring the Glasgow museums would have been perfect had we not stopped at Abington service station on the way home, where Clemmie spotted a gimmicky miniature toilet that made a farty noise. When we wouldn't buy it, she sobbed the whole drive home, ruining any good feelings we'd had about enjoying a day out together.
Rose, accountant and mother to Clemmie, seven, and Ella, three

I lost Jack at a country fête. He'd snuck off the bouncy castle and wandered off. I was running around the field, dragging his twin brother along, yelling his name. People kept asking, 'What does he look like?' and I'd point at Max and say, 'Him!' The police were alerted and checked every car as it left the field. We found him, twenty minutes later, smugly sitting astride a tractor and going, 'What?'
Trisha, wedding co-ordinator and mother to five-year-old twins

At four and five, Joey and Cait were far too young to stand in a queue for forty minutes, waiting to get into a Neolithic tomb in County Cork. Inside were long, dark passages. Just as the guide started to talk about ancient

Celts, the wailing started. We had to hurry the kids out to the daylight. They would have been far happier rolling down the hill.
Dad David, who has postponed his plans to visit more ancient monuments until the children leave home

Our lovely shiny new motor

The children have departed for flats scattered across the country. We have exchanged our ravaged Rover with its evil-smelling interior for a saucy number, that's so blatantly rude-looking that passers-by stop to stare, take video footage and occasionally lick it.

And then I wake up, and realise that our youngest child will not live independently for at least fourteen years. (In fact, grown-up offspring are finding life with the parents so cushy – with agreeable twenty-four-hour room and maid service – that they're skipping the lifestage at which they used to move out.) And the new car? An MPV. A car which says: big family. A lawn-mowing, food processor-owning family.

Actually, I'm pretty delighted with this new acquisition. It has seven seats, which means we could feasibly produce two more children – ha ha – without upgrading to a minibus. There's a remote control central locking device – which most car owners have had for decades – but my children find so enthralling that the car is locked and unlocked several hundred times, and the alarm set off twice, attracting the attention of the permanently-vexed neighbour who's forever accusing me of stealing her bin and causing her electricity to go off.

This car is an automatic, which provides an entertaining diversion when I slam my foot on the accelerator instead of the brake and the vehicle hurtles forward. More worryingly, J informs me that this car will ensure that we'll never need to go on an abroad holiday again.

Still, let's enjoy this new driving experience. Its lack of rattles and belches is extremely restful. I take the kids on a day out to a spectacular-sounding castle and glance back to see if they're enjoying the ride. They're unusually quiet. No one is fiddling with window controls or the little tray with a hole in which to put your drink.

'I feel sick,' a son announces. I slow down to twenty-five miles per hour – in open countryside – and open all the windows. I worry that the smoothness of the ride is having a nauseating effect.

'It's coming up,' my son declares. I wish I had something – plastic bag, sandwich box, even my new beaded shoulder bag – into which he could vomit. In our old car it wouldn't matter. In this new thing I can't bear the thought of second-hand lunch hitting the unblemished upholstery. This is the first time we've owned a car which does not smell (apart from in a clean, Hoovered way) or make a crunching noise when you step into it. Now it's about to be ruined, forever whiffing of stomach lining.

I thought they'd grown out of being car sick. At the peak of their pukey phase my kids would reserve dramatic explosions for journeys when we'd been joined by a friend, who'd flown up to Scotland from London, and was looking forward to gentle meanders through the fishing villages of Fife. This friend would, perhaps, be considering starting a family of her own. She'd watch bravely as car seats were stripped and children mopped down and say, 'Honestly, it's okay – the smell doesn't bother me at all.'

Our children would reach the point of no return only when we were without spare clothes. We'd screech to a halt at a cripplingly expensive kiddie boutique selling only Baby Dior, Oshkosh and Young Versace. Until then, I had wondered who decked out their children in such finery. It seemed like asking for trouble: rips, immovable stains, and incidents involving livestock dung. Surely things are a little askew if your kids are better dressed than you are. Then I figured that toddler 'boutiques' rely on emergency visits from the ill-prepared parents of motion-sick kids.

The solution, of course, is to fill the car with towels, hose-down clothing and vicious disinfectants. Then encourage the sweating, pasty-faced child to look outside instead of playing with his Gameboy, or reading. As long as he's 'properly restrained' (as an AA spokesman put it), he can have a spell in the front seat to combat nausea. This becomes problematic, however, when he wants to 'help' you drive, and repeatedly lurches for the gearstick.

Increasingly, I'm growing more fond of train travel.

More in-car irritations:

* The distraction of kids sprawling and brawling in the back of the car is as dangerous as blethering on your mobile while driving. Road safety charity Drive reports that, in taking your eye off the road for two seconds while driving at fifty mph, you'll have travelled the length of a football pitch. Eek. The trick is to keep the wee blighters occupied with visual games which encourage them to look out of the windows. (This also helps to combat car sickness.)

* If there's more than one person under sixteen in the car, you can guarantee that they'll need to go to the toilet at different times. You can make them hold on, fibbing that there are toilets just around the corner, or shepherd everyone into a service station loo and loom

over them, forcing them to pee. Naturally, children feel the urge just as you've passed the service station. However, pulling over on the motorway hard shoulder could gain you a fixed penalty charge. Oh, joy.

* Regarding in-car snacks, please bear in mind that certain foodstuffs will be nibbled at, then cast aside to rot and stink your car out. Best to ban excessively crumbly or mushy foods, chocolate and vividly-coloured drinks unless your car is soon to be destined for the scrapyard. Reasonably non-messy (and non-pukey) snacks: dried fruit, Twiglets, oatcakes and grapes. (Once, for some bonkers reason, I let my sons take sole charge of a large box of Shreddies in the car. It was like a blizzard, but with little brown squares in place of soft snowflakes.)

* If you're losing your rag, please bear in mind that, at some point, our offspring will no longer wish to go on day trips with us. Then we'll come over all moist-eyed and yearn for those days when we stood there at two degrees below zero, sipping brown, tasteless liquid while our children fed bedraggled goats fragments of mouldering cabbage from a plastic cup.

* Having slept during the homeward journey, your children will now be fully refreshed and bounding with energy. When they finally crash out at eleven-thirty pm you can get down to cleaning the car out.

The best things we've bought are a travel tray from Britax for Jemma [aged five] and a lap tray from Blooming Marvellous for her little sister Grace [two]. Jemma can

have her colouring books, drinks and snacks to hand without us constantly reaching back. And Grace can pick at raisins and cereal from her tray.
Pam, a scarily well-sorted mother

I've grown to like certain song tapes – we have a favourite featuring a Stax version of 'Old Macdonald's Farm' which keeps everyone in good spirits when we head off on day trips.
So says Allie (not a killjoy who insists that the in-car stereo system is 'broken')

They need something to play with, but not so much stuff that they keep dropping it all, and demanding that you reach back and find some twiddly little toy on the floor of the car while you're driving. Favourites of ours are magic slates for drawing on, and those horrible bendy smiley men which they can fiddle with for ages.
Lina, speech therapist and mother to Matthew, six, and Conor, four

Film soundtracks are a good alternative to song tapes. The Shrek soundtrack is much appreciated in our car. You might find that you can work sideways to other music by featured musicians – like Nina will ask for 'the uh huh, uh song, Mummy', by the Proclaimers.
Millie, mum to a couple of music-loving starlets

Yes, tapes can keep the kids happy but please heed . . .

Our storytape hell

'In a small wooden house,' begins the storytape, 'on the edge of a great town, there was a big bed. And in this bed there were four old people.'

Roald Dahl: King Child Pleaser. I glance over my shoulder and witness happy youngsters tucking into Butter Puff crackers (perhaps not the wisest car snack available, but you can't get everything right). We're heading down the M74 towards Keswick when the storytape – *Charlie and the Chocolate Factory*, a great favourite – ends. 'Enjoy that?' asks J.

'I want it again,' one son mutters.

'No you don't,' I inform him. Slowly, rhythmically, he starts to kick the back of the driver's seat. The tape is replaced with the devil's own sound that is Radio 1. There is whimpering in the back. Soon the children are crying relentlessly. It's that non-specific-boredom crying: '*Uh*-uh. *Uh*-uh. I want . . . *something.*' You can't help but sympathise. I recall the symptoms of overwhelming tedium during my last proper office job: watery eyes. Perpetual coffee drinking. No amount of 'popping out to the bank' could save me so I resorted to producing children instead. There must be less drastic ways to entertain yourself. I could have just sneaked out to the occasional matinee, or mooched around FCUK in Covent Garden.

By the time we leave the motorway the storytape is on its second playing. In a terribly juvenile fashion, J has substituted a vowel in Willy Wonka's name. 'I want to go to a chocolate factory,' announces one son. J is racking his brain for thrilling in-car games. 'Let's see how long a mile is!' he cries.

Finally we reach the lovely Keswick hotel where we're staying for the night. Our other son just yawns and says, 'I've been here before.'

'No, you haven't,' I snap. 'Look – isn't it gorgeous? Aren't you lucky that we bring you to places like this?'

'I want to go home,' says our son.

For this reason, I don't believe that every non-school day must consist of a trip to a safari park or a quick hop in a private jet to Disneyland Paris, or even a drive to the country. Wall-to-wall day trips would result in financial ruin and spoiled brats incapable of amusing themselves for one minute. No – home is where we live. Even looming school holidays shouldn't have us cramming the calendar with a terrifying scrawl of so many trips that you're forced to carry a clipboard with cast-iron schedule attached.

I just don't think we need to force them to gymnastics and Beavers when they make it quite clear that they'd rather lie on the sofa and inform us that Golden Grahams now come in cinnamon flavour. We worry: am I stimulating them enough? Shouldn't we be admiring Egyptian artefacts at a museum, or at least making a pterodactyl outfit from an old velvet curtain? Shall we go to the circus, the bowling alley, a dry ski slope?

Whenever I experience guilt at not doing enough, I remind myself that . . .

Staying in is the new going out

When you really can't be fagged chivvying everyone into the car, direct your little dear to the PC and the following London Museum websites. (Lazy? Certainly not. This is *educational*.)

* **British Museum** (www.britishmuseum.ac.uk): Brilliant site incorporating a Kids' Compass section chock-full of

competitions and print-and-do pages. On the main site, loads of gruesome mummified objects to ogle. My sons lap this stuff up.

Science Museum (www.sciencemuseum.org.uk): No kids' section as such when we visited, but a whizzy interactive Launch Pad section with games and science shows for your budding nutty professor.

Natural History Museum (www.nhm.ac.uk): Jazzy site with kids' section, inviting children to investigate wildlife (woodlice, at the time of writing) and send in their findings. My kids were thrilled at the idea of delving into dank, murky places, until I told them to leave our laundry basket alone.

5

kids on holiday

**Head wound, car crash, arse-smelling sofa:
our challenging first holiday-with-infants • are package
holidays just a cop-out? • are kids' clubs all they're
cracked up to be? • the camping 'adventure' • is it
possible to do it in a tent? • how to destroy a
holiday cottage • the two-family holiday: survivors' tales
• the big family suitcase**

I know parents who go on holiday as if they have no children at all. On their return, they insist that their kids 'coped wonderfully' in India and Guatemala, implying that if travelling with infants is even slightly stressful, then it's due to the parents being uptight and unwilling to expose their offspring to new and varied experiences.

Curiously, though, such families often scale down their plans for the following year – opting for Corsica, say, or Cornwall. Personally, I believe that long-haul travel with kids is all well and good – brave, actually, as our children have been no further than Europe – but that there's no point in planning the kind of holiday you had pre-children simply to prove that 'kids haven't changed anything' and 'we can go wherever we like'.

We were guilty of over-challenging ourselves as we planned our first holiday since having the boys. They were six months old. We decided – because *nothing had changed* – to drive from London to Belgium to see friends, then to J's sister's place near Constance, Germany, then through Switzerland, to finally arrive at a 'beautifully furnished holiday apartment in a converted grain mill'. We'd salivated over the brochure, reading: 'This stunning property is surrounded by rolling hills. While away the evenings at our charming courtyard restaurant.' That clinched it: a restaurant, mere inches from the apartment. We'll plug in the baby listener, eat food cooked by someone else, quaff alcohol, and behave like normal adults.

We arrived at the apartment shell-shocked and requiring heavy-duty medication after our marathon drive. The old mill looked so promising, nestling deep in a valley. The stresses of driving with six-month-old twins in the back, screeching for milk, just melted away. We were greeted by a dishevelled man who'd swapped his Holland Park townhouse for this glorious property. He was purple faced, very sweaty, and pissed out of his brain. After allowing his Alsatians to lick the untainted faces of our children, he slugged rosé wine from a plastic carton – the kind that usually contains car oil – and, for some unfathomable reason, called me a 'slapper'.

I'm not so ill-humoured that I can't take a little light-hearted ribbing, but was hardly in the mood for such banter after spending several years in a car stuffed with mangled ham rolls and hollering babies. Wine Man introduced us to his elderly mother. The weeping scab on her forehead was, he explained, the result of a recent incident involving lots of gin and a wooden pillar. Our spirits sank further when the 'beautifully furnished apartment' contained little more than three damp beds, a sofa whiffing of other people's backsides, and a shower tray smattered with toenail clippings. 'It's not too bad,' J said, bravely. 'Anyway, we'll be spending most of our time at that restaurant.'

Which didn't exist. There was just a filthy kitchen milling with dogs and cats and a vast chest freezer which belched a mouldering veg stench each time it was opened. The deal is, Wine Man explained, guests can cook a meal if they feel like it. Or – he rubbed his blackened hands together – he'd cook for us.

He started to yank partially-frozen chicken thighs apart. His hands had encountered neither water nor soap since patting his mother's horse. The horse which appeared to live in the old lady's apartment. We'd seen it, looming out of the top half of the barn door; later, J spied the beast lying down in her living room.

So how do you cope when your holiday accommodation falls way short of the brochure description? You can tell yourself that people keep all kinds of interesting pets in their homes – newts, snakes – so why not a horse? Perhaps the elderly lady was infirm after the gin incident. Maybe she rode the horse to the bathroom. You can view the whole deal as an experience, even though the French authorities had clearly shut this place down, which explained why we'd been asked to send payment to a mysterious account in Ireland. You can tell yourself you're lucky because your partner only wrote off your six-week-old Renault Espace – thankfully not injuring himself – due to chronic sleep deprivation caused by lumpy wet beds. You can view Wine Man as a lovable eccentric and feel quite flattered when he calls you at home, checking that you had a safe return journey. 'Sorry about the crash,' he slurred.

'That's okay,' I said, 'no one was hurt.'

'No bad feelings?'

'No bad feelings.'

'Great!' he said. 'See you next summer, slapper!'

In praise of package holidays with kids' club attached

I should never have been so snooty about package holidays offering kids' clubs. Three years after our disaster in France, we popped into a travel agent's in Sauchihall Street, Glasgow. I was massively pregnant. Our sons crashed about the place, yanking brochures off desks and throwing them into the air. 'Do you want somewhere with a kids' club?' asked the young sweet-faced travel agent.

We glanced at our sons, who were now trying to scorch themselves with the coffee machine. And we shouted: 'YES!'

Other parents praise the package deal:

We only started to enjoy family holidays when we accepted that they'd never be the same and scaled down our expectations. Previously, we'd been to places like Mexico and China. We did take Elliott to Thailand and I spent the whole flight walking him up and down the aisle with everyone hating me. You learn to make things easier for yourself, and not to bother packing fifteen paperbacks.
Sally, full-time mother to Elliott, six, and Natasha, two

I'd always poured scorn on package holidays, thinking they were all about clubbing and shagging. But we're converts now, at least to the family-type resort. You think about what makes kids happy – the pool, beach, other children to play with – and know you'll have the chance to relax.
Sylvia, teaching assistant and mother to four-year-old Rory

You don't have to succumb to the whole resort experi-

*ence, like joining in with activities. We just use the apart-
ment as a base, and find restaurants in town, to lessen
that tourists-as-cattle feeling.*

**Ruby, mother to Stella, three, and Ailsa, one (who adds that
there's no point in walking endless miles with your child in
her buggy, trying to get her to go to sleep so you can go to a
restaurant in peace: 'Accept that the kids will be very much
there, or pack a babysitter.')**

Are kids' clubs all they're cracked up to be?

I think it depends on the quality of the club, and whether
your child is the type to strut happily into new places, or flips
out if you so much as visit the toilet without him. Our club
experience, in Majorca, was pretty cruddy; the children spent
most of their time indoors, which seemed ludicrous, and most
of the staff mooched around with their heads down, emitting
can't-be-arsed vibes. There was a box of Lego and some battered
picture books. The one time we used it, we were summonsed
over the Tannoy to pick up one of our sons, as he was 'extremely
distressed'.

Next year was more successful. We'd accepted that our sons
would rather be with us, and used the (much better) club only
occasionally. Great kids' clubs are a godsend. But ones run by
dull, droopy staff only serve to crank up the parental guilt, should
you use them.

If you're desperate for a breather:

☆ Use the club for short periods only so your child has less chance of becoming mightily peed off.

☆ A reluctant child can be persuaded to go to the club if you stash a few deeply unsuitable (and normally banned) sweets in his pocket.

☆ Some clubs do day trips. Even my club-shy boys have loved their visits to theme parks and zoos.

☆ Supply him with plenty of drinks. We once picked up two very hot, miserable boys; we'd forgotten to give them their bottled water, and the staff hadn't provided any (deep shame).

We went camping and lived to tell the tale

The tent arrived. A guy from the outdoor shop flung it into our porch with a thump. I stared at the enormous black holdall containing something constructed from breathable nylon and polyester (PU-coated). I hoped I wasn't going to be expected to wear it, at least not in public. 'It's your tent,' the man said helpfully.

'*My* tent?' I said. 'I don't have a tent.'

He told me that J had ordered it the previous week – when I was safely out of the way at my mother's – but neglected to pay for it, so a sizeable cheque was now required. As a sweetener, he added, 'It can comfortably sleep six adults, so your kids could invite a couple of their friends on your trip.'

This was happening too fast. What trip exactly? I hadn't realised that we had progressed from hazy discussions of 'Wouldn't it be fun to go camping one day?' to actually buying a tent, and inviting half the damn town to sleep in it, rather than pitching it on the lawn for the kids to eat biscuits in. When I confronted J, he just said, 'We agreed, don't you remember? Weren't you listening?' I must have shut down my hearing mechanism, trying to blot out the horror of it all. 'Think of the money we'll save,' he added. 'It's an investment.'

I have never been big on investment shopping. In fashion terms, it means purchasing something boring and hideously expensive, like a plain grey skirt, as opposed to something frivolous that actually makes you feel attractive. Worse still, the tent's arrival coincided with my friend Fliss's return from her debut camping trip on a large 'lively' site. 'Awful,' she said, shuddering. 'The evening entertainment got Dylan [her three-year-old] so overexcited that he un-toilet trained himself and spent the weekend soaked in pee.

'Don't expect the children to go to bed,' she continued. 'You might think you'll be able to zip them into their compartments and drink wine outside, but they'll be pelting around until *you* go to bed. The only good thing is, they'll be knackered when you get home.'

To counter her negativity, I called my friend Johnny, who's experienced most things, to ask for tips on making our trip a success. All he could think of was a dodgy video he once watched, called *Camping With Big Roger In Copenhagen*, which wasn't what I had in mind at all.

As a trial run, we put up the tent in the garden. I worried that our neighbours might spy the vast nylon construction and conclude that J and I were conducting some 'sleeping apart' experiment. As he'd also bought five – five! – sleeping bags (without prior consultation) this was becoming quite tempting.

We set off, with the sun splitting the sky, and me telling myself: *loosen up, this could be quite fun.* I tried to conjure up an image of a picturesque field, populated by nothing but sheep, which would have the good manners to leave us alone and not baa at unsociable hours. 'Are we there yet?' the kids kept chirping. J explained that this was a motorway, not a campsite; that's why fast-moving cars were on it.

4 pm. So here we are, at a campsite in Bamburgh, Northumberland. 'Imagine,' J says, striding around, 'waking up with the grass still wet with dew, the aroma of bacon, drifting through the air . . .'

Into our laundry basket he has packed an unlikely selection of 'essentials': strawberry jam, can of tuna, Jacob's Cream Crackers, bacon. I hope that he is not planning some *Ready Steady Cook* scenario, resulting in confit of tuna and bacon with crumbled Cream Cracker topping and strawberry 'jus'. As well as the tent and five sleeping bags, it seems that we have also acquired a camping stove, whistling kettle, five torches ('we need one each'), plus five thin mats which look like they're intended for yoga but are, alarmingly, our 'mattresses'. We have spent so much money that I suspect the outdoor shop's owner is considering the purchase of an open-top Porsche.

The campsite, we discover, doesn't allow 'single sex groups'. Regarding this as a positive sign is a sure indicator that you're ageing rapidly and should consider wearing support hose. We also discover that the site has recently experienced 'water problems'. There are signs warning ALL WATER MUST BE BOILED!!!

This is almost as alarming as the fruity language which is spilling from J's lips as he attempts to erect the tent. Our 'pitch', which is sloping and spiked with protruding rocks, is littered with bundles of nylon, pegs and guy ropes. 'Jesus wept,' retorts our daughter.

4.45 pm. J now requires my assistance, even though I was instructed to 'keep the children occupied' to stop them tangling guy ropes or having a shot with the hammer. We attempt to pull the tent into a semi-upright position; it billows wildly, like gigantic out-of-control knickers.

5.15 pm. A kind German family grabs various corners of the tent, hauls it to the ground, and finally tames it.

6 pm. The children are starving and keen for evidence of outdoor cooking, but J still has to fix all the inner pods of the tent, a rather optimistic set-up to ensure that everyone sleeps in separate bedrooms. I walk the kids around the site to marvel at caravan gardens littered with plaster puppies and hedgehogs. 'Has Dad got it up yet?' my daughter shouts, too loudly. Trouble is, when you're 'sent away' so an important task can be undertaken, you're never away for long enough. We return forty minutes later to discover that none of the bedrooms has been put into place. What had J been doing? I check his breath for evidence of alcohol or fag consumption. He says he's 'been trying to figure it out'.

7 pm. A couple around seventy-five years old arrive at the site and start pitching their tent.

7.45 pm. The elderly couple have pitched their tent and are now cooking something that smells like lamb cutlets infused with rosemary. A camping know-all bounds over to inform us that our guy ropes are too long. 'You shorten them by sliding these' – he waggles a plastic thing – 'along the ropes. Then they'll be nice and tidy, like ours.' I whack him on the head with our frying pan. No I don't. I pass on the information to J. 'Our guy ropes are fine,' he snaps, 'as they are.'

8 pm. Our tent is up and actually tent-shaped. Exhausted, we lumber towards the restaurant and gorge deep-fried delights.

9 pm. The children spend at least an hour zipping and unzipping their doors and turning torches on and off.

10 pm. This is possibly the earliest I have crawled into bed since childhood.

11 pm. I'm wide awake, feeling like I'm lying on a bare rock face, with blood surging to my head. I'm aware of each of my internal organs, and all are twitching nervously. I think about reading, but don't want to disturb anyone with my torch. I wonder what the heck to do now. 'Do you think,' I whisper to J, 'it's possible to do it in a tent?'

'Definitely,' he says. 'But not in this tent.'

Camping is great fun but raincoats and wellies are essential – you may as well be realistic. Also liners for sleeping bags, and airbeds rather than those skinny roll-out mats – much more comfy. Check kids' sleeping bags for foul underwear. We noticed a horrible whiff all the way back from France to Scotland. Turned out Finn had been hoarding all his dirty socks and pants in there.
Laura, sales manager, hardy traveller and mother to Johnny, seven, and Finn, four

My boyfriend went to the Isle of Wight festival recently with his mates. They camped and had a great time. Now he wants to take the kids camping. He's bought all the gear. I'm not keen at all, although I'd agree to meet them for a barbecue in the morning. I am a woman who stays in a hotel when she goes to Glastonbury.
Kim, mother to Lily, four, and Freddie, twenty months

Amanda and her kids Rosie, eleven, Joseph, eight, and Hazel, five, all love the sleeping under canvas malarkey. A pharma-

cist by profession, Amanda dispenses advice:
Fold little kids' sleeping bags under so they don't disappear down them – no need to buy special infant sleeping bags. Take some form of night light as it gets surprisingly dark, and we've had lots of piercing night terrors at two am. It's usually wet underfoot in the morning, so for early toilet dashes make sure pyjamas are short and wellies are long.

Amanda reckons her Beano Pie recipe is so speedy to cook (ten minutes of Camping Gaz) that you don't have to change canisters every meal:
Boil a kettle and make up Smash (three mins). Fry an onion (one min) and chuck in a tin of chopped hotdog sausages (one min), plus a tin of beans. Put the potato on top with some grated cheese and heat (four mins). Keep the lid on to melt the cheese. (Amanda also recommends three-minute spaghetti with stir-in sauce which is ready in, er, three minutes.)

We love camping and going for trips in our campervan. I have a laminated list of everything we take with us, which we tick off and wipe clean. I know, it sounds terribly sad. The only disaster we've had is when Nicholas, then aged three, peed through his sleeping bag and fabric-type bunk on to me and his dad, who were sitting directly below.
Lorna, assistant manager of a day nursery, who couldn't understand why the rain was coming in

The case for self-catering

(The following is written on my laptop in a holiday house near Padstow, Cornwall. The house is very old and beautiful, surrounded by lilac bushes, and I want to live here.)

Pre-parenthood, I avoided self-catering holidays. The fact that the word 'catering' featured at all – implying hours spent slaving over bubbling pots – was enough to have me craving hotel delights such as fluffy towels and skinny sachets of Nescafé.

Then the kids came along and hotel living became less about wallowing in free Molton Brown foam bath and more a matter of preventing the junior members of my family from breakfasting on pistachios and Coke from the mini bar. Self-catering saved our bacon and the gorgeous house we're in now, near the north Cornish coast, makes me realise that there are millions of reasons never to stay in a hotel again:

✩ **The owner.** Ridiculously, I assumed that Mr Rose would hand over the keys, give directions to a golden cove no one has heard of, and melt away. However he appears to spend all his waking hours in his workshop next to 'our' house. His mysterious bangings enthral our children so much – 'Mr Rose! What are you doing in there, Mr Rose?' – that we needn't have come armed with an additional suitcase stuffed with *Scooby* vids. Mr Rose develops a nervous demeanour, as if he's being stalked.

✩ **Pretending we really live here.** I can't help thinking that, if we bolted Mr Rose in his workshop and made this our real home, we'd morph into nineteen-year-old surf gods/goddesses with taut backsides and fancy wetsuits. When I mull over getting a tattoo, I have to slap myself and remember that I was born when 'Help!' was number one, and not in the Culture Club era.

✩ **Finding nothing slimy in Mr Rose's fridge.** And therefore being able to open said fridge without retching.

☆ **The challenge of guarding precious items.** This house contains spindly standard lamps and antique French display cabinets filled with delicate glass. Although I'm tempted to tie our children to the pear tree in the adjoining orchard, it seems kinder to ensure that maximum hours are spent on the beach, at least five miles from Mr Rose's crystal decanter.

☆ **Inviting friends to stay.** Our mates – two adults, plus their two kids – are coming for the weekend. We haven't asked Mr Rose's permission. The tactic is to be so inconspicuous that he doesn't notice a second car parked in front of the house. I'm hoping he'll fail to notice that our three children have become five, or assume that his vision has gone blurry. Anyway, are five children more problematic than three? It's the kind of question I ask myself when mulling over whether to have more babies. The answer is always a deafening OH MY GOD, YES, followed by a swift visit to the friendly lady doctor.

☆ **New-found obedience.** When I find three children teetering on an antique pedestal table, I only have to roar, 'That's Mr Rose's table!' for them to leap off, trembling. I wonder if our surly owner might agree to come back to Scotland with us, and assist with behavioural 'issues'.

☆ **Observing the gradual deterioration of the house.** We arrived to find a clutter-free haven. Slowly, though, the detritus of family life creeps through the house, like a rash. It's amazing. Soon the cottage is as untidy and manky as our real home.

☆ **Two baths.** And four toilets. This means you can go about your business without anyone lolling against your thigh, because the kids are hammering on the door of the bathroom you're not in.

✡ **Reading books left by previous guests.** A particular gem is *How To Clean Everything*, first published in 1952, 'for women who dislike housework but like nice homes'. There are tips for cleansing Formica (do NOT use steel wool!) and even the lawn. I'm amazed that anyone was so obsessive as to vacuum their grass, then discover that lawn is 'a fine material made from cotton and/or polyester', and should be ironed while damp.

✡ **Seeing real joy on the owner's face as we pack up to leave.** We've rebuilt the rockery dismantled by our children and slung out the lamb we forgot to cook. Mr Rose hovers at our car as we load everyone into it, perhaps to reassure himself that we really are leaving. 'We'd love to come back next year,' I tell him.

'This is my last year of letting,' he says firmly. 'Guests are becoming too . . . demanding.'

He hurries back into his workshop. 'Mr Rose!' bawls a son as we drive away. 'What do you *do* in there?'

It took a while to figure out that self-catering is much easier than staying in hotels. I never felt comfortable perching on the end of the hotel bed, whispering to my husband and watching rubbish TV while the kids tried to sleep.
Sophie, full-time mother of three under-sixes

Renting a cottage or apartment is the only way you can sit outside in the evening, drinking wine, before falling into bed.
Deborah, bookshop manager and mother to Hannah, aged three, getting her priorities right

We've rented cottages in Devon and Cornwall for the past three years. It gives you space which is essential with children, especially if it rains. If the house is full of delicate objects we do a quick mine-sweep as soon as we arrive, hiding any breakables. The best places have been where a few cottages are grouped together, so the boys have had other children to play with.

Deena, mother to house-wreckers George, six, Daniel, four, and newborn Natasha

Two-family holidays: for or against?

For:

☆ Babysitters on tap.

☆ Other children to keep yours entertained, so you're required only to lob kid-pleasing snacks in the general direction of their mouths.

☆ Extra adults to share the practical stuff.

☆ More people to get drunk and have a laugh with.

☆ Badly behaved children to make yours appear impeccably behaved; little angels (hopefully) set a fine example to your kids.

Against:

☆ Discovering that, actually, your lovely friends are a gigantic pain in the pants.

☆ The other couple doing it, very noisily, at two-thirty am.

☆ The children deciding they hate each other.

☆ Competitive cleaning syndrome: the other adults constantly mopping and sweeping your holiday house, thus implying that you're a slovenly oaf.

After considering the previous points, we decide to hook up with another family. Oh, I know such set-ups can go belly-up; we made the mistake of heading off into the yonder with our thriftiest mates, not realising that this would entail a ban on eating out, and seven days spent miserably sucking on sandwiches which had been marinated in split Ribena during the short walk to the beach.

Even worse was our weekend in the Lake District with the feuding couple. I'm not averse to the occasional row; flinging stuff at J – our daughter's vest, or a son's sock – can liven up a rainy Sunday afternoon. But there's no fun to be had with other people's rows. They're not your own, so you can't join in. Unfortunately, though, you are expected to take sides: the woman usually ranting to me, as a fellow female, about her lazy/drunk/unhygienic partner. I've been pumped with so much anti-men propaganda that I've started to view J in a less favourable light. (Hell, yes! He lay in till nine-thirty-three this morning. That's thirty-three minutes over the legal limit.)

Even seemingly perfect friends can become irritating when you're on holiday together. We thought we'd have a rare old time with Neil and Caroline – great friends who came with the added advantage of being sensational cooks. And yes, they beavered away in the kitchen, filling the holiday apartment with mouthwatering aromas. Tragically, though, a rota system was quickly established. We'd cook on alternate nights. How do

you follow glazed pork accompanied by red pepper marmalade?
You freeze up, unable to operate the oven.

I soon figured that Neil and Caroline were au fait with fresh
herbs and marinades due to their idyllic child-free existence. I hate
the way I behave around such friends: explaining the workings of
young people as if they've never been in the company of persons
under fifteen years old. There's also a tendency to over-praise –
'You read *Green Eggs and Ham* with such feeling! You're so
good with children!' – which comes out as horribly patronising.

The truth is, though, that I can't help finding child-free friends
glamorous and alluring. I forget that their lives involve jobs and
blocked toilets and picture them lying in bed until three pm,
nibbling at pepper-flavoured Green & Black chocolate (which
most kids hate). Their fridges can, if they so desire, house only
vodka and a lump of Parmesan. The make-up bag of a child-free
woman is a glorious thing: here we find lip balm containing
extract of orchid and real gold particles in gorgeous, bash-free
packaging. No one's jammed a thumb into her blusher.

And their carefree lifestyle! Our friends had recently relo-
cated from London to Northumberland and were often found
strolling along its glorious beaches with Floss, their black Lab.
They'd brought Floss to the holiday cottage. She sat in a corner,
quietly licking herself. 'Can we have a dog?' my children wittered.
'Can we have a dog just like Floss?'

A couple of days into the holiday, I started to feel mildly
jealous. It wasn't that I didn't want my kids or my life; more that
I was seduced by this notion of kicking off your weekend with
a stroll along the beach, rather than negotiating a minefield of
breakfast demands and no one liking any of the eighteen cereals
currently turning stale and cardboardy in our pantry. The fact
that we have a pantry at all astounded our friends. Why would
anyone want a weird little room stuffed with sprouting potatoes
and jumbo packs of thirty-six toilet rolls?

I noticed, too, that our children were doing their utmost to dissuade our friends from ever producing a child of their own. I set out the kids' pens and paper; they wrote 'poo' and 'dire-ear' in massive letters. Our friends were now looking quite frightened and volunteered, with suspicious enthusiasm, to pop out to the off-licence for piles of booze. They returned two hours later, whiffing of pub. Our kids greeted their reappearance with a spectacular three-way fight, culminating in slamming a door so hard that the handle cracked a hole in the wall. 'I hope they're not doing your head in,' I said.

'Don't worry – everyone has their off days,' mumbled Caroline.

I worried that our kids had disturbed them during the night as our friends were up at six am next morning, stomping around the kitchen. But no – Floss had been up several times, pooping and being sick in the garden.

A few days after our return home, we received an email to apologise for Floss's behaviour. They couldn't understand it. She wasn't normally like this. They were having her checked over by the vet.

On questioning our kids, I learned that the hound had been drip-fed an unsuitable range of confectionery over the entire long weekend. And I emailed back: 'Don't worry. Everyone has their off days.'

So this year, I'm hunting for friends with children, plus a fondness for eating out, and who like each other (though not too much – I don't want to be shamed by their nocturnal rompings). Their children must be pleasing to have around, and adhere to a rigid bed time (seven-thirty pm), though not be so well behaved that they make ours look like uncontrollable wildebeest. Trickiest of all, they must be liked by our kids. And this is where our plans may come unstuck. My sons are incredibly picky, dismissing the hordes of children I arrange to come round and play with them with a steely gaze and a muttered, 'When are they going home?'

I'd always assumed that kids were drawn to other small people – that they'd love nothing better than a week of charging around in a pack. It seems my sons would prefer to holiday just with Mum and Dad. And it's just as well. When I call our favourite friends – those who remain as pathetically milky under the Mediterranean sun as we do – they reply that they're sorry, they had their holiday sorted out months ago.

Our good friends Katie and Tom were planning to stay at Tom's brother's house in Normandy, and kindly asked us to join them for a week. They don't have children but have always seemed very fond of ours, and have known them since birth. But in France the kids were far more demanding than usual – probably due to the long journey, and being in unfamiliar surroundings. The girls' tantrums grew worse. Katie and Tom became withdrawn. One evening I walked into the living room to find Tom sitting there with his head in his hands. I said, 'Do you just want us to go?' He replied, 'Yes.'
Beverly, full-time mother to Ella, seven, and Chloe, four

What to take to make everything easier

☆ With an absence of TV/PlayStation, a stack of paper and the world's biggest pack of felt tips keeps kids occupied in the apartment or holiday cottage. (They can make and decorate paper planes, draw maps, play word games and quizzes, write letters home, cut things out, devise codes, draw pictures of each other covered in warts and boils, etc.)

☆ A disposable camera each. Yes, they'll take pictures of their ankles and bits of rock. It's art, okay?

☆ A diary or scrapbook (plus Pritt Stick) for them to scribble notes and stick souvenirs in.

☆ A small toy – ie, one Lego model each to make on the journey – but nothing with billions of tiny components (Playmobil, Hama bead kits) which will get lost and require an extensive search of the apartment/tent/hotel room before you're allowed to go home.

☆ Magnifying glasses for examining sea creatures, ants etc.

☆ Their beloved cuddly thing of the moment.

☆ Plus, everyone can pack their own small bag (ours look like those old-fashioned gym kit bags) with stuff they can't possibly live without – but don't touch for the entire holiday.

☆ You can bring inflatable beach toys (boats, rubber rings etc) but they're so cheap and it's nice to pass them on to another family when you leave. Ditto buckets and spades etc. Peanuts to buy, and we experience a pleasing flush of generosity as we pass them on, all cracked and knackered, at end of the hol.

Thoughts on packing a suitcase

'You've packed too much,' says J, with the smug air of one who travels with a toothbrush rattling around in a minuscule rucksack. 'What's in there, anyway?'

What's *in* there? Three children's plus my clothes for every possible climatic condition; vast assortment of toiletries and medical kit, books, notebooks, toys, guidebooks, CDs, CD player, make-up, some space-saving dual-purpose products (including a sunscreen which miraculously 'firms' the body), beach towels, sunscreens in five different factors, plus aftersun; various footwear – sandals, heels for evening, boots, trainers for early-morning jogs (ha!), sunhats, sunglasses, camera, laptop . . .

J watches me, trying to jam the case shut. 'Do you really need all this?' he asks.

'Of course we do. It's all the kids' – '

'You should travel light, like me,' he says. He does indeed seem to need very little. In fact, you'd be forgiven for believing that he doesn't have any children at all.

J aside, most parents come to accept that it's impossible to merrily book your hols with zero regard for the junior members of the family. Our holidays these days are very different to the piffling two we enjoyed pre-kiddies. We no longer get piddled on sangria (at least not in the day). We might pack fourteen novels between us, but feel strangely gratified if we manage to plough through one each.

I'd say that, at this slightly easier stage – no walloping buggy to haul on to the plane, no worries about sterilising, or tracking down acceptable foodstuffs for babies – our trips have become a whole lot more fun and are certainly worth all the planning required. I can even cope with our daughter moaning the entire ferry journey to France, just because no one will tell her what the f-word is.

6

kids v work

Tears or cheers? How mums felt about returning to work • nurseries: from scruffy to swanky • nannies and childminders • are grandparents all they're cracked up to be? • working from home (dangerously close to the biscuit tin) • the school holiday/working mum juggling act • why working mothers need wives • or at least a cleaner • why family life goes belly-up at weekend • so is it all worth it? Oh yes . . .

I'd been at home, looking after our sons full-time for several months, when a glamorous former colleague showed up unexpectedly. 'I popped round earlier,' she said. 'You must have been out at one of those coffee morning things or whatever it is you get up to.'

Coffee morning? So that's how my former colleague thought I filled my days. While she click-clicked from meeting to meeting, swinging her Prada handbag, I lolled on splattered sofas, stuffing cake and waggling rattles. Stay-at-home mum: she can identify Milo from the other Tweenies. She sports a wilting perm, a gravy-stained housecoat and finds herself being horribly flirtatious when the man comes round to fix her leaky guttering.

At least, that was my friend's view. Jill (not her real name) works on a glossy magazine and is therefore a regular fixture on the front row of fashion shows. She has her hair cut weekly and owns about eighty-five handbags. When your life is dominated by bot-wiping and measuring out scoopfuls of formula for bottles, it can be rather disarming to be in the company of such a rarified being. Jill mentioned a mutual acquaintance who had also just had her first child: 'She's bored out of her box,' she said. 'She's so clever – it's such a waste.'

I wasn't surprised by Jill's assumption that full-time child-rearing is only fit for porridge-brains. The term 'stay at home mother' hardly gives one an air of pizzazz. In fact, it implies that you never actually leave the house, apart from an occasional excursion to a mother and toddler group to witness twenty-five kids all attempting to straddle one plastic vehicle. As for house-wife: mercy! This implies certain talents in the food preparation and home-cleansing arena. If housewife was my job these days, I was thundering towards a written warning.

By the time the boys reached their first birthday, I could no longer hack it as a full-time mother. When asked to be involved in a short-term project at my former workplace, I trawled round East London nurseries – one had peeling-off wallpaper and, with-out exaggeration, every single child was crying – and finally found a place I was happy with. The boys howled when I left them. I phoned my friend Jen, barely able to speak for the tears and snot streaking my face, and announced: 'They think we don't love them any more.'

The boys did settle, and I returned to the office, realising, with horror, that the only footwear I possessed were Birkenstocks and mud-caked flat boots. My workplace's endearingly clunky PCs had been replaced by whizzy new models with too many functions. I felt like a ninety-eight-year-old lady encountering an answerphone for the first time.

Going back to work is never easy – but neither is staying at home with a delightful yet extremely demanding individual who only comes up to your hip. You'd think that we might have reached a point at which full-time parents are not written off as having tapioca for brains, and working mums are neither pitied nor loaded with guilt.

My gut-wrenching guilty moment

I'm heading off to pick up my daughter from her nursery trip to a museum. Lots of parents have gone on the trip but, as this was a work day, I'd declined to put my name on the 'parent helpers' list. A neighbour, who went on another group's museum trip two days previously, spies me and says, 'Ah, didn't you go with her? The day I went, there were only two children whose mums didn't go. The poor little things stuck out like sore thumbs.'

I'm tempted to shout, 'But I've been working!' The voice in my head hisses: *you don't have to justify yourself.* Yet I still turn up ten minutes early to meet my girl from the coach. And let her choose her own tea from the deli.

How other mothers feel about kids v work . . .

The first time I left Joely with her childminder I just felt glorious relief. Quite a disturbing level of relief, looking back on it. She was four months old and took to her childminder amazingly well. Second time around, leaving Jack with the same childminder, I felt more wobbly, and I do miss them in the daytime. My neighbour thinks I'm the bride of Satan for

preferring to work than be with my cherubs all the time.
Zara, freelance illustrator and mum to Joely, three, and Jack, fifteen months

The nursery staff had to peel Poppy off me on her first day. I waited outside the door, in tears, thinking: what kind of mum am I to put her through this? There was a big box of tissues on the table for mothers like me. Things didn't improve and I'd often drive to work with tears streaming down my face. We were relying on my in-laws to pick up our elder child from school, supervise his home-work and cook his tea – I felt like they were taking over our home, doing things their way. After a few months it was a relief to resign from my job and be at home instead of feeling torn all the time.
Cheryl, former IT tester and currently full-time mother to Kyle, seven and Poppy, three

Clare [aged four] is fiercely independent and loves Alice, her childminder. There's a whole room of toys at Alice's – it's an Aladdin's cave. Clare cries when I come to pick her up, and shouts, 'No! You're too early!' I couldn't stand being at home all the time. I'd be deranged.
Elizabeth, human resources manager

Being with the children is what I've chosen to do, but I know it's not for everybody. There are days when I feel hugely unchallenged. Small children can be boring, frustrating, maddening. One afternoon I looked into the living room where Liv and her friend had been quietly playing. They'd shaken glitter all over every surface. It

*looked like a grotto. At times like this I think: can I really
stand this until they're all at school?*
**Samia, full-time mother to Liv, four, Helena, two, and expect-
ing her third**

*We'd found a lovely nanny but I still felt awful about
leaving Eve. A colleague stuck a Post-It note which read,
'SHE'S FINE!' to my phone.*
**Nancy, mother to three-year-old Eve, who did, finally, redis-
cover the joy of having desk drawers to which no small
person can gain access**

**Beth, a teacher, was living with her partner in Liege, Belgium,
when their daughter was born five years ago:**
*I put Eloise into nursery at three months and went back to
work full-time. I had no qualms about putting her there.
Nursery staff often do a better job than parents do. They
can focus on the children, rather than trying to do ten other
tasks at once, and have at least had a good night's sleep.*

*We returned to Yorkshire, had a second child, and
decided that I'd take a career break rather than see my
salary go on childcare.*

*Disaster! Constantly clearing up was the worst part –
doing it over and over with no visible result. I explained to
my partner that it would be like him going into the office
and finding the previous day's work wiped off his computer.
I'm now in a part-time teaching post and it's wonderful. I
shout less, and have more patience. I'm even reading stories
and plaiting hair, whereas, a few months ago, I would
have shoved on a video to keep them out of my way.*

*Lots of women don't seem to mind the relentlessness
of looking after babies. But from the night our eldest*

daughter was born, I was hit with a feeling of: so I have to do all this myself? I knew I'd have to work, at least part-time, for my sanity's sake, and would do whatever it took to find childcare we were happy with.
Louise, production assistant and mother of three

Nurseries: from squat-like to scarily posh

A friend has just enrolled her child in a swanky Edinburgh nursery. We're talking top-notch kiddie care here: if you're detained at your meeting in Zurich, a member of staff will take your child home and stay the night at your place. Personally, I have always been wary of super-posh childcare options. I'd worry that, should our children become accustomed to such luscious surroundings, they would register the shabby condition of their own home and refuse to park their dainty rears on our clapped-out sofa.

And what about food? It's all organic at my friend's kid's place. Coming home to some cobbled-together pasta offering would be such a come-down that I can imagine my daughter demanding to be driven back to her nursery, even at weekends.

The whole nursery issue is so tricky to get right. When we lived in East London, we looked around gleaming, show-roomy places where parents would be fined £90 if they dared to be five minutes late. Other establishments were basically rank stinking living rooms which you'd never guess were nurseries, apart from the presence of fifteen children, all bleating for their mums. One place seemed ideal – brightly painted with a welcoming atmosphere and well stocked with toys, plus a large photo montage showing the nursery children out on a trip. The staff were all merrily puffing away on their fags. Yes, I've choked down a speedy Silk Cut while my kids' backs have been turned; I'm their mother, so it's allowed (in fact *they* drive me to smoke).

127

But a professional carer topping up her nicotine level while surrounded by small children? It just didn't seem right.

Oddly enough, the poshest nursery our kids ever attended turned out to be the worst. Each time I went to collect them, I'd be informed that my sons were 'very disobedient. Maybe they're hyperactive?' their carer would suggest. 'Could it be triggered by all that cheese you put in their lunchboxes?'

One afternoon, after running amok with a xylophone hammer in some Cheddar-induced frenzy, my son, then three, was parked in The Naughty Chair. When I complained to the nursery boss, she admitted that the carer in question 'finds young children difficult to manage'. Well, of course they're difficult. We don't know this before we produce them; we reckon parenting amounts to some hazy round of sandcastle building and being creative with face paint. Then real babies arrive, four hours are shaved from our nightly sleep quota and, by some weird quirk of nature, we start looking craggier than our own parents. So I took the kids out of Naughty Chair nursery and found a lovely place which our three children have now all been through. It may not boast super-whizzy technology (unlike Swanky Nursery, where children can email their parents at work), but the carers put me to shame with their kindness.

I think a parent knows when she's walked into the right nursery for her child. The carers are interacting with the children in a relaxed way, rather than bursting into a manic rendition of 'Wheels on the bus' on spying a visiting parent. Most of the children seem happy to be there, and the surroundings are reasonably clean and tidy, but not anally so.

For us, finding a wonderful nursery has been like acquiring a caring and ever-willing branch of the family who – rather than grumbling about 'hyperactivity' and the wrong sort of cheese – have never uttered one negative word about my rather challenging children.

The downside of nurseries is that they are, understandably, very particular about not taking children when they're ill. One morning I took the twisty road to nursery a bit too fast. By the time we got there, Laura was feeling sick and actually retched in the carpark. I felt terrible, shovelling her in through the door and legging it before the staff could stop me.
Tricia, stage manager and mother to four-year-old Laura

I've recently dropped from five work days a week to three. The boys enjoy nursery but they've reached a point where they've had a heck of a lot of sand and water play and resent spending so much time with little ones. They've unplugged the nursery water tray and flooded the floor umpteen times. I think nursery is wonderful in the early years but boys especially start to kick against the rules.
Simi, occupational therapist and mother to Tim, four, and Joe, three

Nannies, au pairs and childminders: the good, bad and sanity-saving

I'm a big fan of male au pairs. There's less disco-diva behaviour. We've had lots of boys working for us and they've tended to be confident and fit in easily as part of the family. A boy can balance things out, especially for single mothers. It's only dads who can be iffy about having another guy about the place. They might be jealous of a man doing dad-type activities with their kids.
Naomi Rawlings, managing director of nanny agency 3 to 4 in Bristol, who has seven children ranging from ten to twenty

Sheila, our nanny, has been with us for five years and does far more than we do with the kids. She takes them to museums, the cinema, even to Chelsea matches. Now they're both at school, Sheila has more free time. She's more like an older friend to them these days.
Cara, director of a publishing company and mother to Nat, nine, and Marcus, six

If you opt for a nanny or childminder make sure they take your child to toddler groups so they're mixing with other children, and not just friends of the nanny.
Bryony, midwife and mum to twins Robyn and Jessica, two

Amy's first childminder had a moment of madness and left three children alone in the playground while she hurried off to fetch her car. She was reported by one of the other mums whose son had told her what had happened. Amy loved her childminder but she wasn't allowed to look after children any more. I have an hour-long commute to work, and this episode made me feel even more dreadful about being away from Amy for long hours. But I'm a single parent – if I didn't work we'd lose our house. Our new childminder has been brilliant, and I trust her completely.
Lori, psychologist and mother to four-year-old Amy

Lucy used to go to a day nursery but when we had another baby I realised it would be easier to have a nanny who came to our house. Luckily, one of Lucy's nursery carers was leaving and she's been working for us for over a year. The kids adore her. And Lucy, who can be a real handful, has improved loads since she's had more individual attention, rather than fighting her corner at nursery.
Katya, mother to four-year-old Lucy and Casper, one

Grandparents as carers: blessing or curse?

Loving, trustworthy, part of the family. Who better to bridge the childcare gap than Granny and Grandad? A family member is often willing to care for your child, even when he's running a temperature and capable only of sweating and bleating for drinks in front of a video. They'll accommodate unsociable working hours, tolerate your child's whims (milk on the side, not on the Frosties), never fine you for being late – plus, they simply cannot be younger or more fresh faced than you are, which is always a bonus.

And yet, weirdly enough, not every grandparent is willing to sacrifice even small chunks of their limitless free time in order to have small people stuff melting ice lollies into their pockets. Some actually enjoy living hundreds of miles from their 'energetic' grandchildren. Birthday and Christmas presents are your lot. They might visit occasionally, but perch nervously on the edge of the sofa, and regard your kids' antics with a 'Haha ... aren't children *different* these days?' Some grandparents barely register the children's names. One friend complained that her mother-in-law insisted on calling her three- and four-year-old grandsons 'this one' and 'the other one'.

Here's what a clutch of parents had to say about grandparents as gallant life-saving knights:

Helene: *My mum's great – totally spoils our son Jackson [aged four] and is happy to look after him as a back-up, like if he's under the weather and can't go to nursery or has a contagious condition like conjunctivitis. My husband's family is different – they rarely visit, so Jackson barely knows them. I tell myself that it's their loss.*

Miranda: *I can't help feeling jealous of friends who have Granny living round the corner.*

Millie: *But the downside of having rellies nearby is . . . having them nearby.*

Miranda: *My in-laws do help us. They've had Miles for two weekends in the two years we've had him – we've been to Paris and Rome, which was wonderful. It's geography that's the problem, not willingness. We live in Newcastle, my mum's in Nottingham – runs her own business, very much has her own life – and the in-laws are in Essex. So they're not available for regular child-care, and I'd rather pay for it anyway, so I'm more in control.*

Yvonne: *I work the equivalent of four days a week from home. My in-laws look after Alasdair [four] and Stuart [eighteen months] two days a week; I make up the rest in the evenings and at weekends. Having family help gives me flexibility if I'm held up. It's not the end of the world if I'm stuck in traffic – grandparents are understanding, whereas a childminder expects you, quite rightly, to pick up your children on time.*

Ava: *I hated relying on my parents for childcare. Mum would point out that I'd sent Niall to her in a grubby T-shirt, and was really shocked when he was wearing some temporary tattoos. You can't get into a dispute because you need them too much.*

Cath: *My mother-in-law used to present my baby daughter back to me with the comment, 'We've bathed and changed her. I think she's fine now.'*

Ava: *I was so relieved when we found a good local childminder and Mum just had Niall on an occasional informal basis.*

kids v work

Sara: *Granny Joan, my mother-in-law, had looked after Mia four days a week since she was four months old. She won't accept payment and does enjoy it, although I think she was quite relieved when Mia started playgroup, then nursery, and she had some time back for herself. The downside is that Granny Joan makes a lot of the day-to-day decisions – like how many afternoons a week Mia will attend nursery, as she's the one most affected by those decisions. I can feel a bit powerless.*

Mel: *We've had a few emergencies with my health – trips to hospital in ambulances and enough stuff going on to shock my mother-in-law into helping. She even stayed the night and looked after Max [aged eighteen months] as I was on sedatives. I'd never ask her to help us on a regular daytime basis, but at least she's willing to babysit and forces us to go out.*

Yvonne: *My in-laws have been brilliant. They have such a close relationship with their grandsons. Yes, they give the boys chips, which we don't have at home. But it's a sad state of affairs if you can't have a treat at Grandma's.*

Is home working the answer?

Apart from a brief and rather tense return to a real office, I have worked from home since becoming a mum. 'You're so lucky, not having to drive to work,' my neighbour says, lounging on my sofa as she sips her coffee. My back teeth are jammed together. I'm wondering when she's intending to leave so I can get on with some work.

I love having visitors but when anyone pops in on a work day I'm aware of a loud tick-ticking between my ears, reminding me that the precious day is slipping down the plughole. No one thinks you're actually working if you never actually go anywhere and merely twiddle about on the computer. You're not a professional person in your bobbly sweater and slippers. You are the Pop-in Café.

Yet working from home has whopping advantages, like working to your own infinitely flexible schedule. You can spend all day repeatedly opening and closing the fridge door, then stay up slogging away until two am. If your child emerges from his bed as one enormous crusty chicken pox, you can take time off without having to ask for permission and (here's the crux) work all weekend to catch up.

Of course, unless you're prepared to toil away in the wee small hours, childcare is still required. My kids don't understand this. Young children have zero concept of why we work or need some degree of solitude in which to do it. I was gobsmacked at reading that novelist Tony Parsons managed to tackle proper, grown-up tasks when his son was very young; the kid would play at his feet, tinkering with Star Wars models, apparently. I cannot imagine achieving anything worthwhile without tying up my children, or bundling them into the garage. I did attempt to work when my daughter was a (crawling) baby; she'd happily gnaw at a teething ring next to my chair, then I'd look down to see a baby-free void and finally locate her in the kitchen, licking the pedal bin.

Although forbidden, my sons regularly break and enter my office to steal pens, leaving me to make important notes with a snapped wax crayon. J props up his guitars against my PC. Working from home can also be terribly lonely; I've chatted maniacally to the man who came to pluck all the bra underwires from our washing machine, and often require J – on his return home from his busy stimulating office – to be all-singing, all-dancing Entertainment Man.

For the first two years of freelancing I'd be unable to start work until around three-thirty pm, by which time I'd be sufficiently 'revved up'. These days I'm used to being alone for much of the day, and am grateful that I can take my sons to and from school. Being a home worker also means – and here's the real bonus – that I can escape to a tiny horribly disordered room, not to twiddle about on the Internet, or to idly swing on my swivel chair and pick off my nail varnish, but to work (honest).

I'm a workaholic and extremely well-disciplined. It was bliss to come from a hectic office to the peace of home. People dropping in hasn't been a problem – in London I'd ignore the doorbell and when we moved to Somerset, I didn't know a soul. Managing work and a child has meant heaps of evening and weekend working, but the plus side is huge. James is very confident having both his parents around – we've always managed the childcare between us. Although, naturally, he doesn't always understand that Mummy has to work rather than build a cushion mountain.
Jane, health writer and mother to James, six

My kids can't understand why they can't be there when I'm working. They say, 'We'll just play in the garden,' or, 'We'll sit in the corner and be quiet.' They can't get their little minds around the fact that I have my mum head, and my work head, and the two just don't mix.
Eleanor, bookkeeper and mother to Barney, seven, and Michael, five

When I've been really stuck, and had to make more work calls when they've come home from the childminder, I've

shoved them out into the garden with a whole packet of biscuits.
Beth, freelance journalist and mother to Frank, four, and Milo, two

When I asked my daughter what she thinks I do on my work days, she said, 'You write in notebooks.'
Fiona, the author (whose kids are gutted because the books she writes 'don't have any pictures in')

The school holiday/working mum juggling act

'Don't *want* to go to holiday club,' storms a son. He will not be swayed by the fact that the club is actually called Fun Club and offers billions of activities of the arty/sporty type, plus hordes of other children to play with. He believes that he should not have to go anywhere because, as he reminds me, it's the summer holidays, which means BEING AT HOME and DOING WHATEVER HE LIKES.

Can I point out a few facts? My children are in daycare for around nine days of the seven weeks' hols. They can remember the basic layout of our home and still recognise me as their mother. Yet, despite my protests that I enjoy working and should be allowed to get on with it in relative peace, somewhere inside lies a kernel of guilt.

The guilt button doesn't activate during term time. The boys are at school (which is good for them, dammit), my daughter's at part-time nursery and we all function relatively normally. School holidays change everything. Because I do 'steal' the odd work day, I try to make the most of our time together. We have masses of picnics and days out. My kids believe that, if they weren't packed off to the vile institution that is Fun Club, their entire seven weeks would be spent whizzing down flumes into bubbling pools or romping on beaches. J suggests that Fun Club might be rather more enticing if I ditched the day trips and forced them to start cleaning the toilet instead.

Yes, I could work like bonkers before the hols, then take the entire summer holidays off. Hang on – that's seven weeks! I feel quite bilious just thinking about it. Some mothers disapprove of holiday childcare at all, and say, 'Ahhh, shame to send them away when they're only young for such a short time.' Yes, and isn't that great? In just thirteen years' time, my daughter will be driving me to Glasgow, buying me lunch and carrying all my shopping bags.

Disapproving parent uses emotive phrases such as 'shoving your kids into childcare' and 'palming them off'. I am relieved to note that the Fun Club's sign doesn't read: 'Hey, uncaring parents! Dump your kids here. Collect them at five (that is, if you can be arsed).' What's so great about being at home all summer anyway? The club playleaders aren't forever attempting to have grown-up phone conversations or shove washing into the machine. They are paid to play. Kids are their job.

One local mother said to me, 'There was no need for holiday clubs when I was a kid. We just played out all summer.' She forgets that, back in the seventies, rural communities might have seen a car chugging past every forty-five minutes. More importantly, she does not know my children. Their recklessness means that they will, eventually, be allowed to play out, but only with either me or J lurking nearby, disguised as a hedge.

So I stick to my guns and announce that my sons are booked into Fun Club day. 'I hate Fun Club,' one son rages. His brother is in tears, refusing to clean his teeth, and heads for his bedroom to hunt for a toy which he's never given a monkey's about, but must now be located before he'll agree to leave the house.

Later that afternoon, I set off to pick up the boys. I'm wondering if it's worth it – all the angst, the wet cheeks, the pleading to stay home. At Fun Club, however, no one appears to be having a horrible time. A playleader beckons over my children and shouts, 'Boys, your mum's here.'

'Aw, not Mum!' a son retorts. 'I don't *want* to go home.'

Working woman needs . . .

Here's what would make our lives so much easier: having someone around to do all those pesky tasks which are so easily forgotten. Stuff like: paying bills, remembering dental appointments, buying birthday presents, disposing of several thousand polystyrene coffee cups currently polluting the car, peering in the fridge and shouting, 'Good God, these eggs are seven months out of date', calling the drain man, locating matching footwear . . .

In other words, a wife. Failing that, a cleaner might save us from chaos, if we could only get over the embarrassment of having someone scrub out our scummy bath. When I interviewed a well-known TV presenter she was happy to rave on about her full-time nanny, but when she accidentally mentioned her cleaner who comes in three times a week – 'Three times a week!' I blethered, like an idiot – she shuffled in her seat and stressed, rather hotly, 'It's because we have a dog. If the hairs weren't Hoovered up all the time, they'd be strewn all over like snowdrifts.'

We don't have a dog – we will never have a dog – but we do, I feel, need some assistance in the housework department. I'm sick of barging aroun, ranting, 'NO, THAT'S FINE, I'LL CLEAR THE TABLE AND WASH UP AND HOOVER WHILE YOU READ THE PAPER, THAT'S BLOODY BRILLIANT, SLAM-BANG-CRASH, YES, I'M ABSOLUTELY FINE!'

One particularly tense day, after such an outburst, I make a note of a number in the newsagent's window. The card reads: ALL YOUR CLEANING PROBLEMS SORTED. NO JOB TOO BIG OR TOO SMALL. A pert-sounding woman says she'll need to come round to 'assess the job' before she can give me a price. She arrives, and immediately registers the lumps of old sauce on the cooker hob, the hunk of old sausage slowly withering under the table, the smattering of pine needles underfoot (this is February). Her eyes take in the frayed knickers draped over the radiator. I am compelled to babble excuses: blaming children, builders, living in the country (all that soil outside!). She says, 'I'd recommend a deep clean to start with. Two cleaners will come in and stay until the job's done.' I picture them scouring for weeks, wearing those spacey-looking suits designed for asbestos removers.

I am now regarding my house with more critical eyes. How could I have failed to notice a footprint on the living room wall? An abandoned banana jutting from a toy box? You think you function reasonably well, then along comes a stranger who says, 'I can see this is a difficult house to manage,' and, 'You're either good at cleaning. Or you're not.'

She marches from room to room now, assessing whether our wooden floors will need to be washed or just Hoovered. My sons' room is its usual putrid state. 'I assume you'll be picking up all these toys before the cleaners arrive,' she remarks.

Hang on: cleaners?

'I'd recommend two cleaners working three hours a week.'

Two people? It sounds terribly task-force-ish. The cleaning woman gives me a big smile and says, 'I promise we'll make all the difference.'

So they start, and our house no longer stinks of decaying fruit. I'm too ashamed to tell my local friends that we have any help, and just hope that no one drops in while the cleaners are doing their stuff. One day, however, Cheryl stops by for coffee. 'Oh, hello!' she says to the overall-wearing stranger in the kitchen.

'This is Jo,' I explain. I'm about to add, 'Our cleaning lady', but it's pretty obvious as she's mopping the kitchen floor.

Cheryl perches on a chair, all uncomfortable and guilty at sipping coffee while someone Hoovers up dried spaghetti from between the floorboards. So we go out, and by the time I come home the cleaners have gone and everything's shiny. The effect they've had on our home is like a glimmer of sunshine peeping out from behind a storm cloud. Later that evening, J's sister comes to stay the night. 'Wow – it's lovely in here,' she enthuses.

'I do my best,' I tell her.

I never imagined I'd find myself in this wifely role but here I am, with my endless lists and diary and calendar, keeping on top of everyone's activities – being Mum to the whole family. Often, I'm still tidying up and sorting out laundry at ten pm. What I fantasise about is a kind of secretary who knows what needs to be done without having to be asked. Someone who always knows where everything is.

Suzanne, a deputy head teacher and mother to Clem, eight, Ginny, six and Megan, four

Having a cleaner has helped to dispel a lot of the bitterness and knock those tedious domestic rows on the head. The only trouble is, Ryan has taken a dislike to Rosa, our cleaner, and runs out of the room crying whenever he sees her. She's so kind, and tries to cuddle him. He just runs away shouting, 'Don't like that lady!'

Jemima, part-time college lecturer and mother to Ryan, three

Most women have three jobs: house, family, and paid job. Of course we want a wife to take care of us. Certainly, paying for help can take the pressure off. Hiring staff is far more widespread now – salary and social class are no longer obstacles here.
Suzie Hayman of Parentline Plus

My daughter once shouted, in earshot of my playgroup friends, 'At our house we have a servant!'
Jacqui, mother to megamouth Lil, aged three

Why family life goes belly-up at weekends

Whether one or both parents has been at their workplace for most of the week, peculiar things happen to families at weekends. It's something to do with the fact that no one can escape to their jobs and are instead squished together in one building. Here's what happens at our house. Saturday morning: newspapers arrive, to be scattered about and defaced with felt tip. For some reason, we expect the children – who are programmed to wake at six-twenty-five am – to detect a whiff of weekend-ness and emerge from their rooms sometime after ten. At this point, the family should arrange themselves around the table for a leisurely cooked breakfast.

On weekdays, when breakfast consists only of whichever sugar-coated cereal offered the most covetable plastic gizmo, no one expects the kids to sit primly and compliment the food. At the weekend, however, when eggs have been scrambled and bacon slapped into a pan, J expects the children to exhibit some appreciation.

An at-table nipping incident results in a PlayStation ban. PS will be put in the attic. No one will have a friend around to play ever again. The kids are too upset to eat; J is wolfing his food in order to escape to the back yard for a fag.

Jolly breakfast over, we make plans for the rest of the day. Or at least I do. Here's where your traditional set-up – man out at work, woman at home – comes unstuck. Partner With Proper Job (ie, out-of-the-house job) wishes to 'potter' about in the house and garden. Partner At Home, who has spent approximately eighty-seven per cent of the week within the confines of these four walls, has in mind a shopping trip in the city, a jaunt to some child-pleasing attraction, plus acres of time in which to loaf in the hairdresser's and sniff body oils in John Lewis's perfume department.

Relationship experts always urge us to compromise. But how to compromise on the do loads/do nothing issue? Do we go out, but not too far – say, to the ironmonger's at the top of the road? Or pack one weekend with activities and stay at home, cooped up and shouting, the next?

As J produces most of the meals at weekends, hanging around at home should be quite restful. However, his disregard for traditional mealtimes can result in frayed tempers. It's lunchtime, but there's no indication of a gas ring being lit. Our son announces that his 'tummy is like an empty cave'. It's now two pm and the lamb is still in the fridge. Judging by the size of the beast, it will take at least four days to cook. There's a gentle rustle of newspaper as J checks the Motherwell scores. My son repeatedly opens and closes the fridge. 'I'm going up for a bath,' J announces, telling our son off for swinging on the fridge door before disappearing upstairs for a soak.

By three-fifteen, our daughter has constructed an unstable structure of piled-up toy boxes in order to access the biscuit tin. Our sons are pale-faced and ill-humoured. I swear, they're thinner than when they woke up. I make them toast, then let them scoff Party Ring biscuits, and warn them not to tell Dad.

Finally, he emerges from the bathroom, takes half an hour to 'oil' the lamb, snip one sprig of rosemary into tiny pieces, and carefully place the masterpiece in the oven. Our daughter gnaws hopelessly on a four-day-old baguette. By the time the meal is served, the kids are so stuffed with illicit snacks that the rosemary-infused dish is merely poked with forks and left to go cold before being slung in the bin.

'What's *wrong* with you all?' J thunders. 'Can't we enjoy a nice dinner together, like normal families do?'

'I thought it was lunch,' our son whispers.

Some of these parents have weekends figured out better than others

Kat: *I love weekends because work doesn't get in the way – it's all family stuff. You feel less compromised. We go to farmers' markets, museums, National Trust houses, see Granny, veg out in front of videos. It depends on finances, weather and levels of energy. And we make sure we get one lie-in each.*

Mollie: *Saturdays are great. We watch our sons [aged eight and six] playing football, then have lunch out. By Sunday, the kids are missing their school friends and starting to bicker. There are petty rows about stupid stuff like tidying their rooms, and everything starts to disintegrate.*

Lou: *I find myself compensating for the amount of time Eliza's spent away from me during the week, and end up making fairy cakes with her at six am.*

Pam: *Dan and I have more rows at weekends – mainly because I think he should spend time with Ellie, just chatting and playing, as he's been working all week and* *usually gets home after she's gone to bed. But all he wants to do is sit on his arse.*

Mark: *Everyone should be allowed to sit on their arse sometimes. Sophie, my girlfriend, likes weekends to run to a schedule so we're out and about a lot, as she works from home and gets stir crazy. All I want to do is relax at home, wander round the charity shops with the kids, play football, work on the veg garden.*

Miranda: *As a curate I work Sundays and am on call Saturdays, but we try to do something nice – even just going to Pets' Corner and having an ice-cream, or lunch out. And we try to go out on Friday nights to make the weekends seem longer.*

Cecile: *Saturdays are pretty structured with swimming, supermarket and my Pilates class. Sundays can go haywire with my relying on CBeebies and scourging myself mentally over all the jobs I should be doing – stuff I never get done in the week, because of work! If you work full-time, at least half of the weekend is gobbled up with catching up on chores.*

Mark: *When both partners are working, everyone has very high expectations of their weekends. They can be very hard to get right.*

Things that have made our weekends better

Taking turns to lie in.

Accepting our crapness at DIY, and waiting until we can afford to pay someone to do it.

- Roughly speaking, having a mooching-at-home day, and a doing-something day (instead of me barking a schedule at J).

- Taking up running. (My escape route for when my dear, beloved family are getting right on my wick; after all, you have to get out of the house to run properly. Running up and down stairs isn't the idea at all.)

- Learning how to grow things in the garden.

So is it all worth it – the mess and the rushing and chaotic attempts to keep two lives (Mum life and work life) together? Recently my son said, 'Remember that school concert when you couldn't come because of work, and I cried?'

I wanted to snap that his gran went instead – she'd endured a three-hour bus journey so she could go – but just murmured, 'Yes, I remember, and I'm very sorry.' I never told him that the work trip had involved staying in a lovely room at Malmaison, and sipping champagne and raspberry cocktails in the bar until two-thirty am.

If you asked your kids, they'd probably prefer you to never do a day's paid work until they leave home. I know for certain that mine despise my desk and computer, because activities connecting to these things take me away from them. Given the choice, they'd have me attending to their needs eight days a week, and forever making fairy cakes.

Actually, scrub that. My children have encountered my fairy cakes.

7
kids at school

**Wobbly lip at the school gate (and that's just the mother)
• how school changes kids • the impossible lunchbox
challenge • good reasons to walk to school • trauma-
free homework • kids who do too much after school •
school friends . . . and enemies • parents' evening and
the yearning for beer • why teachers don't want your
cheap bubble bath • the school concert (or: the day my
son tried to cut up
his brother)**

The day your child starts school is weird, weird, weird. For years now she's been buffeting around your ankles, demanding to finger-paint and make muffins, then she's gone, catapulted into the education system, her life to be dominated by Miss this or Mrs that (male teachers are still a rarity in primary schools). And who is this woman exactly? Someone you know nothing about, who is extraordinarily pretty, and – the hardest factlet to swallow – born in nineteen bloody eighty-three.

My boys started school two years ago. As the big day approached, I started to experience waves of joy and relief. My sons were no longer thrilled by the eggbox crocodiles I forced

146

them to make. They were sick to the back teeth of my foul face. School was what they needed. Structure and discipline. By God, it was time to knock some sense into them.

So I'm all hard-nosed the first time I march the boys up the high street to the great Centre of Learning. Their immaculate blue and grey uniforms make my guts perform a weird kind of somersault, but it's fine. I'm just not used to them looking so pristine.

J has taken the morning off work, and is behaving in a ridiculously casual manner – as if this is just a normal day! The lollipop lady looks like she's coming over to wish us luck but I hurry on, aware of a bubbling sensation in my throat. Then school's in sight, swarming with massive kids who look about twenty-six, and we're into the classroom, ramming my daughter's buggy between little plastic chairs and primary-coloured tables. There are pots of felt tips, and jigsaws on each table. It's all very welcoming and jazzy-looking.

For some reason, I'm no longer fizzing with delight that two of my children will be out of my hair for six hours every weekday. I can't feel excited at the prospect of living in a house that appears to be reasonably well-functioning, rather than recently burgled. J appears calm and relaxed. (Doesn't he care? Doesn't he feel *anything?*)

Don't cry, I tell myself. Snivelling is pointless and terribly unfetching. A wet, collapsed face does nothing for your image as a competent adult. Your eyes acquire a pink glow. Cruelly, your nose becomes equally fluid, and you're barging into the school loo and mopping your nostrils on a rough paper towel.

Back home, J reads the paper and wolfs a bowl of cereal. The house feels like a morgue. A friend with older children calls to ask how we got on. She says school changes children; they stop needing you so much. She says, 'You won't know what to do with yourself.'

She forgets that, with one child still at home, plus a part-time job, I'm not quite at the lifestage where reading entire glossy magazines and 'sugaring' my legs, whatever that means, are viable options. But she's right. It's eleven-fifteen am. J has fallen asleep on the sofa. Our daughter is quietly colouring in. Yesterday, I was certain that full-time education would be the greatest thing ever. Now, I just want to stomp back to that school, and press my wet face against their classroom window, just to check that they're okay.

J opens one eye and says, 'Look on the bright side. At last, someone's prepared to take care of the boys – for no money.' Yes – someone born in nineteen bloody eighty three!

School makes kids more independent, and attitudey. Your influence ebbs away. They're more critical, as they see you in the context of all the other mums standing at the school gate. Soon after starting school, Isobel said to me, 'Why aren't you like the other mums?' When I asked what she meant, she said, 'Other mums don't wear bright pink.'
Tania, mother to eight-year-old Isobel and Annie, four, who's not sure how to be like 'the other mums'

At first school made Robert quite narky and difficult. He was a young starter – just turned four when he started reception – and he started pooing his pants during the day, even though he hadn't had any accidents in over a year. Gradually he found his feet, made some friends, and 'grew' into school. And the pooing just stopped.
Shelley, full-time mother to Robert, six, and William, two

Bethan won't allow her dad to pick her up from school when he's wearing his plumber's clothes. She's embarrassed because he looks dirty.
Moira, musician and mother to image-conscious Bethan, eight, and Leoni, four

I felt so exposed when Riley started school. Suddenly, I was hyper-aware of the messy hair he refused to have cut, his coat with the scuffed sleeves from being rubbed along the wall . . . There was this whole new world of mothers at the school gate, all checking each other out. And we were usually late, clattering towards school just as everyone was heading away from the building.
Wendy, a town planner and mother to six-year-old Riley, plus baby Lydia, who soon discovered that most other mothers were as frantic as she was (the ones who weren't – who were utterly sorted on school mornings – she didn't bother befriending)

Two lovely books for nervous school-starters

* ✶ *I am Too Small to go to School* by Lauren Child. Beloved by my children, especially when Lola is told that she can't go to school in a crocodile outfit. 'It's not a crocodile, Charlie. It's an alligator.'

* ✶ *Tom's First Day at School* by Beth Robbins. Part of Dorling Kindersley's reassuring It's OK! series (which includes other worrisome events like having a haircut, or a jab at the doctor's).

From free spirit to fusspot

One of the biggest changes I noticed was that my sons, who had previously paid no heed to their appearance, were suddenly concerned that every school-related accessory should be absolutely 'right'. I hadn't realised that something can be right for a certain period – then glaringly *not* right. Velcro-fastening shoes, with discrete dinosaur hologram, were highly desired for the first couple of terms; beyond that, they were deemed 'little-ones-ish' and thereafter shunned, despite costing me a shuddering amount at Clarks.

The boys' first backpack-style school bags were soon a cause of humiliation and even tears ('Too small', apparently, the current style tending towards a massive sack-like structure which causes its owner to stoop and stagger and, on closer inspection, is found to contain just a tangerine and a pencil sharpener). Likewise, lunchboxes. Action Man design for the first year at school? Highly prized. However my sons' relationship with the frozen-faced hero was terminated abruptly – ditto Spiderman, Shrek or any Disney/Pixar movie tie-in – in favour of understated plain black or silver.

As for what goes in the lunchbox: I'll admit it, packing them is not a job I relish, and am usually on autopilot when chucking in edibles (usually a hasty selection from the following: roast chicken drumsticks, tuna/ham sandwiches, cucumber sticks, crisps (tisk!), tangerines, a chocolate coin (*nul points*), sticks of Cheddar, slice of melon, watermelon or pineapple, halved kiwi with teaspoon (the boys eat them boiled egg-style), grapes, Party Ring biscuit (bad, bad mother).

While this list might sound quite fruit-heavy – you're probably thinking, 'smug bag' – can I add that many of the healthier items which I've lovingly placed in my sons' lunchboxes are tipped straight in the canteen bin. I haven't seen this happen; I just feel it in my water. Short of reminding my sons that teeth can go black and fall out, or installing a spy camera in the canteen, there's bugger all I can do about that. (Like most children, my kids surely realise that lunchbox contents are heavily influenced by their mother's mood, and how many parenting articles she's been reading lately.)

I have a weekly lunchbox 'timetable' with a list of items next to each day. That way they're getting a different selection each day and I don't have to think. For instance, Monday's list reads: cheese sandwich, breadsticks, raisins, pear, apple juice, Twix. I keep the list taped to the fridge and couldn't function without it.
Gill, interior designer and mother to Henry, nine, Jack, seven, and Ricky, three

Every morning I put an apple into Phoebe's lunchbox and every afternoon it comes home until, five days later, it's started to wrinkle and gets lobbed in the bin.
Marc, architect and dad to an eight-year-old fruit-dodger

They're allowed a chocolate thing on Mondays and crisps on Fridays. I try to make their boxes reasonably healthy. Like, I'll put in a dinky little Tupperware box of grapes. I'd have loved that when I was a kid. But they just come back untouched and slightly sweaty looking.
Freya, customer services advisor and mother to Sam, seven, and Oliver, five

One day I'd felt too hungover to make up Keiran's lunchbox. When his teacher asked him why he was having a school dinner, he said, 'Mummy drank so much wine she was sick in the toilet. She didn't have time to make my sandwich.'

Alex, full-time mother to Toby, eighteen months, and a five-year-old tell-tale

You'll find kid-approved lunchboxes at:

✱ Good old **Woolies** tend to stock the latest film tie-ins and favourite characters of the moment, but my sons have had plain black and silver boxes from here too. You'll find a better selection anywhere at the start of the new school year.

✱ If you're sick to the eyeballs of movie/TV tie-ins, **John Lewis** have a lovely range of contemporary designs, although not online at the time of writing (visit www.johnlewis.com for store guide).

✱ Most lunchboxes fall to bits by the end of term. What do kids do with them? Kick them around the playground? Jump on them in rage just because you had the audacity to enclose a few dried apricots? Whatever, most boxes are pretty flimsy. Try **www.muji.com** for much sturdier picture-free boxes which your child can customise with his own stickers (and update as often as he likes).

✱ Stuck for what to put in? Grab a copy of *Lunchboxes* (Vermilion) by kiddie food guru Annabel Karmel who, as mother of three children, has packed over 5,000 boxes (a thought which makes me feel quite faint).

✱ At this point I'd like to add that, no matter how lovely the lunchbox, or the care with which you fill it, there is still no escape from the vile task of swilling out a slurry of split juice and remnants of warm tuna sandwich. Truly foul.

The reluctant schoolkid

You can get all the externals right – the shoes, lunchbox, haircut – and yet your child still doesn't want to go to school. With my kids, this happened when they hit a tricky patch with a temporary teacher with whom they just didn't see eye to eye. As their behaviour deteriorated, so the teacher became frustrated, resulting in a steady round of tellings off and negative feelings all round. Happily, we've moved on from that now and yet, occasionally, one of my sons will attempt to pull a fast one. He might develop a mysterious symptom-free 'illness' in the hope of wangling a day off school. The illness often clears up with remarkable speed when I suggest a visit to the doctors.

To my shame, I once bundled my genuinely ill son off to school. He'd staggered downstairs, complaining that his stomach hurt and his mouth tasted so bad that he needed to lie on the sofa and play his new Sonic Heroes PlayStation game. I dragged him out of the house, informing him as we hurried along that 'a morning of sums and writing will take your mind off your stomach'. Less than one hour later the school secretary called to say that he'd been violently sick in the gym hall and must be collected immediately. 'He said he *told* you he felt poorly this morning,' she added.

I think the answer is to ensure that, should your child appear genuinely ill and be allowed to stay home, then his day should be as dreary and unappealing as possible. He'll soon figure out that school is heaps more entertaining than being stuck indoors with a grouchy mother.

Some fun things kids learn at school

A couple of weeks after starting school, Dylan became obsessed with 'wedgies' – a playground craze, apparently. He demonstrated what a wedgie is – your pants pulled tightly up your bottom.
Joanne, part-time occupational therapist and mother to a six-year-old wedgie-demonstrator, plus Hollie, three (who has yet to acquire such skills)

It was only his second week at school when Ciaran came home and asked, 'What's a wanker?' Someone had called him one at school. I chickened out and explained, 'It's what some people call a silly person.' Later I heard him shouting to his brother, 'Harry, you're a wanker.'
Beth, student and mother to twelve-year-old Harry and Ciaran, six

Matthew [then five] had had a nice mix of male and female friends until he started school. He did remain friends with Kirsty, whom he'd known since they were at toddler group. Then one afternoon after school I heard him telling a friend in his bedroom that he'd 'dumped' Kirsty. Later, I asked what he thought it meant to dump someone. He looked sheepish and muttered, 'Er . . . I don't know.'
Debra, cleaning agency owner and mum to 'dumper' Matthew, seven

Teacher, teacher, I declare
I can see your underwear.
Is it black? Is it white?
Oh my God it's dynamite!
My sons plus their mates on the walk home from
school (nice to see poetry featuring on the
curriculum)

Good reasons to walk to school

Raucous poetry renditions aside, we've been lucky in that we've always been able to walk to and from school. For one thing, it means that we don't have to face our disgusting stinky car first thing in the morning. (Maybe that's why eight out of ten kids who are driven to school would prefer to walk, according to research carried out by Brunel University.)

Plus, you can congratulate yourself on the fact that you're not adding to congestion around the school, and that your children are becoming more road conscious *and* getting plenty of exercise. Which mean less guilt when they come home and click on the telly.

You don't even have to do all the walking yourself. 'Walking bus' schemes, where children are picked up en route by designated adults, can be set up with help from your local County Council, who may even provide fluoro jackets and insurance (speak to the road safety officer).

I enjoy the half-mile walk back from school. You just chat
to the kids without thinking about it. It's a good way to
find out if anything's worrying them.
Mil, mother to Bonny, six, and Miriam, four

155

If there's been a screaming fit as you've tried to shove everyone out of the door, at least they'll have calmed down by the time you reach the school gate, and will be ready for a day's work. And on the way home, they can fool about a bit, and expend some energy, after being cooped up for much of the day.
Rosie, mother of three

A short note on homework

I was amazed when, three weeks after starting school, my sons were given homework most evenings. We weren't talking 1,000-word essays, or translating *Pride and Prejudice* into French, but still, it had to be done.

I found it so tricky to fit homework happily into the after-school period. Too soon after coming home, they'd be desperate to chill out, roll on the floor, scratch their bums or watch telly; too late in the evening and they'd be yawning and feigning snoring over small heaps of rumpled paper. Basically, there's a very small window in which a child – at least an infant child – will face his homework. A pretty rigid routine helps, most of the time. For instance, homework just before tea. Or no TV until it's completed. But I'm darned if I'm going to haul my kids home to complete their sums if the sun's splitting the sky and all their friends are heading for the park. At one point I had a quick word with the school head about the fuss my sons were kicking up over such simple tasks. The head explained that, at this early stage, homework merely reinforces what they've done in the day and isn't worth anyone getting out of their pram about.

Some of my sons' homework avoidance tactics:

* ✱ 'Losing' all their pencils (ie, dropping them down the back of the radiator).

* ✱ Having a headache/bellyache/mysterious back-of-knee ache.

* ✱ Failing to bring homework jotter home.

* ✱ Losing school bag (containing homework jotter) at some point during seven-minute walk home from school.

* ✱ Arsing about so much at the table that I've snatched away their pens and jotters, thrust them back into their school bags and not allowed them to do their homework.

What should kids do after school (other than homework)?

I grew up in a West Yorkshire hamlet called Goose Eye. After school, a small gang of us would sneak into the Rag Mill, an enormous, crumbling structure which my parents had bought for something like seventy-five quid. Mum and Dad had no idea that Gill, Jan, Amanda and I spent much of our time creeping around the mill, clambering up its perilous staircases, side-stepping whacking great holes in rotten floors. Everything smelt of old soggy wood.

I don't recall doing much after school apart from playing here. One floor of the Rag Mill was filled with thousands of tiny blue glass jars – we later discovered that these were the liners for silver mustard pots – plus old record books whose pages crumbled as you turned them. It was a truly magical place. Of course, if my own children wished to play in such a dangerous place, I'd go mental. Yet I can't help wondering whether children would

157

benefit more from being able to roam, explore and just diddy around a bit, instead of having their after-school hours scheduled to the hilt.

I remember relentless after-school activities – violin, piano, choir, orchestra – and was never allowed to doss around like my mates. I see kids in the park where I take my daughters; they're totally non-threatening and having a much better time than I did at their age. In fact one of them very sweetly told me where she got her delectable Converse trainers.
Millie, journalist and mum to Laura, eighteen months, and Nina, three

Miranda has her French club, drama group, disco dancing and swimming lessons. It's quite a lot but she spends most weekends at her dad's, where she does nothing, so I'm quite happy for her to fill up her afternoons.
Jo, hotel manager and mum to eight-year-old Miranda

There's nothing wrong with just hanging out at home – even if it means being bored – after school or nursery. A bit of boredom helps to stoke the inner furnaces.
Inner furnaces – I like that (from Millie again)

Classes of thirty kids have to be pretty regimented so they need some free time at home. My boys sleep for around thirteen hours a night, and they're at school – or en route – for seven hours. After eating, and sometimes having a friend around to play, that leaves little time for anything else.
Rosie, full-time mum to boys of five and six

School friends . . .

Pre-primary school, we can pretty much control who our children hang out with. We're their mother, and we're in control. But the school playground is a different matter: largely unpoliced, and populated by enormous kids with unsavoury habits who'll wish to invite our own dear children home for tea.

My sons' latest hero is Danny, a boy of their age, but with arms like hams and a habit of letting his food fall out of his mouth while he's eating. Plus, Danny smells perpetually of rich meaty farts. He's the only seven-year-old I've ever met who suffers from BO.

So my kids are asked round for a play after school, and Danny's mother asks me to collect them at six. 'Really?' I say. 'That late?'

'Two more children won't make any difference,' she insists. However, when I arrive to collect the boys, she has a wild-haired look about her, as if she's been trapped in a wind tunnel and pelted with soil. She says, 'I can't say it's been easy.'

I apologise – for what, I'm unsure – and tell the boys to say, 'Thank you for having me.' I add that we'd love to have Danny for tea, but his mother has already banged the door shut.

The girls come back from friends' houses with their nails painted, clutching pictures they've made. I just can't be bothered with other people's kids. You see them buckling up their shoes and gazing out of the window and you haven't even served tea yet. To be honest, I think they're usually quite relieved when it's time to go home.
Carrie ('hostess with the least-est'), mother to Bella, seven, and Natasha, five

When your kids start school you want to help them make friends by having their mates for tea. Josh now bounds

out of school, saying, 'Can Calum come for tea? Can Jack come to play?' Sometimes we have too many kids over and I miss just being with my boys, just family. Also, Josh will be desperate to have a friend over, then skulk off to a room on his room, and read his Beano *annual.*
Marina, shop manager, and mother to Josh, seven, and Adam, four

. . . and enemies

It's a sad fact that not everyone in your child's life is going to be good to them. At a local summer play scheme, an older kid stole my son's tuck-shop money, then pushed him into the locker room with the light off. I was seething but, as my son chose to share these details weeks after the actual event, there was little I could do, apart from fire off a furious letter to the leisure department of our local council and rant about it to J whenever I'd had more than two glasses of wine. What I'd rather have done was bundle the bully into the locker room, first ensuring that it was infested with cockroaches and rats. Here are more workable measures:

✱ Be aware. Children are often reluctant to admit that they're being bullied. Tell-tale signs might be a reluctance to travel on the school bus, or mystery 'illnesses' meaning days taken off school. He may be moody, unusually quiet, or announce that a favourite possession is 'lost'. A gentle chat – rather than freaking out, and roaring, 'I'll thrash the little swine to bits' – will usually coax your child to talk.

* Your child's class teacher will tell you if they've noticed anything amiss, and may offer suggestions.

* If the bullying doesn't stop, keep a record of events and write to your child's teacher. If the problem persists, write to the head teacher, detailing everything that's happened. Schools are duty bound to act when informed that a child is being persistently bullied (and should have an anti-bullying policy which any parent can see).

* If you need to attend a meeting at school, take your record of events and any correspondence regarding the bullying. If the bully still won't let up, contact the chair of governors.

* Help your child to develop a network by inviting his friends home. Yes, it'll involve feeding the five thousand, all of whom will complain that your fish fingers are burned, but it'll be worth it. Safety in numbers and all that.

Sophia was being bullied by an older girl who would climb up and stare over the cubicle every time she was on the toilet. The girl would take little toys or favourite things that Sophia had brought into school. She told Sophia that if she grassed her up, things would get much worse. I wasn't aware of any of this, although I did wonder why Sophia had become tearful about going to school. When she finally told me I wrote a letter to the head teacher, giving the other girl's name and stating all the events. He called in the older girl for a stern talk and she never hassled Sophia again.
Marina, full-time mother to Sophia, six, and Tilly, eighteen months

How to show yourself up at parents' evening

Bullying aside, contact with your child's teacher is generally limited to snatched chats in the playground, and parents' evening. The whole point of parents' evenings is to have a brief, skim-the-surface discussion, air any concerns, and be kept up to speed with your child's progress. When you're allotted ten to fifteen minutes with each teacher, there's little opportunity to delve into the nitty-gritty. Clearly, slamming your hand on the table is counter-productive and pretty humiliating. As parents' evenings generally take place with the other parents earwigging and checking out each other's facial expressions ('I must say, Stephen Taylor's parents looked pretty pissed off!'), better to keep your cool and arrange a follow-up meeting if there's sensitive stuff to discuss.

I only write this because, after one parents' evening, I was forced to bolt out of the school, red-faced, and into the pub to down three pints of Stella in quick succession. (Which was no way for a mature person to handle a challenging meeting. Although it did make me feel – briefly, at least – a whole lot better.)

If you think you're going to cry or start shouting:

* Try slow, deep breaths, accompanied by rapid blinking (which can sometimes, miraculously, suck tears back in).

* Flick off a piece of jewellery. This allows you a few moments to scrabble about on the floor and get your act together.

* Picture teacher on the toilet.

★ Repeat the following: *You were born in 1983. What do you know? You were born in 1983. What do you know? You were born in . . .*

On the bright side

Your kid's teacher is more likely to be hugely complimentary during parents' evening, and deserves an end-of-term present. Here's the quality of booty that poor long-suffering Teach tends to receive:

I have sensitive skin and am usually deluged with the kind of cheap bubble bath that brings me out in a rash. One of the nicest things I've been given is a set of aromatherapy bath oils which a pupil's mother had made up for me herself.
Jane, a primary teacher currently teaching ages seven to eight

A teacher friend told me that she's besieged by presents every Christmas and at the start of the summer holidays. What I've started to do instead of sending end-of-term presents is bring in a big box of Belgian chocolates for everyone to share in the staff room when everyone feels a bit bleak in January.
Elizabeth, mother to Jessica, seven, Kira, four, and self-confessed teacher's pet

Teachers don't really want anything – especially not orna-ments, as it just amounts to more tat in the house. I don't

163

*want to sound ungrateful, but twenty ornaments a year is
more than I can cope with.*
Ruth, head teacher of a small village primary school

Gifts to get on their good side:

*It's lovely to receive a note from a parent, saying that they
appreciate what you've done. A bunch of flowers is nice –
from the garden or filling station, it really doesn't matter. A
small box of chocs, like five or six in a box, is appreciated.
Basically, edible, drinkable or disposable is best. We don't
have houseroom for stacks of gifts.*
**Miriam, a deputy head and mother to Ginny, fourteen, and
Chris, twelve**

*I once received a mug, a magazine and Time Out bar,
plus a note that read, 'Put you feet up and take some
time out this summer', which was lovely.*
Suzie, primary teacher and mother to Ellen, three

The school concert (or: the day my son wanted to cut up his brother)

It strikes me how fearless children can be when the end-of-term
play or concert looms. At my sons' school the kids can do whatever they fancy: sing, dance, tell jokes, dress in spangly outfits
and form a human pyramid of little Beyonces – or chop up their
brother into lots of teeny pieces, as one of my sons is currently
planning. 'I'm not sure about this,' I tell him as his debut stage
appearance draws horribly closer. 'I just think it might be a bit
. . . complicated.'

He assures me that his 'trick' is failsafe and not at all dangerous. Isa, our friendly local florist, donates the two enormous
boxes he requires. I warn my son that magic – *real* magic – takes
decades of practice and a terrible bouffanty hairdo, like David
Copperfield's, but he ploughs on, ordering his brother to lie in
one of the boxes, then joining the second box to it with loads
of messily-applied sticky tape. He writes things down in a secret
notebook, ignoring his brother's muffled requests to come out
and watch *Dexter's Laboratory*.

'How are you planning to do the actual *cutting*?' I ask
eventually.

'Er, I don't know,' my son replies.

You'd think that a complete lack of technical expertise
would render him rather unsure about his act, and lead him
to the conclusion that – *please, please* – it would be wiser not
to participate in this year's concert. It's not that I wish to deprive
him of his moment of glory; more that I can't bear to witness
him being laughed off stage, or damaging his brother. However,
he is adamant that not only will he appear on the night, but
will be 'brilliant'.

I love this – a child's innate cockiness. Not for them the
ridiculous self-effacing tendencies of adults. When my friend
Nicky sent me a copy of her debut novel, I emailed her immediately to praise its gorgeous jacket. 'Oh, I had a crappy idea,'
she replied, 'which I gave to my sister-in-law, and amazingly,
she made it work.' Another friend, Miriam, confessed that when
her new boyfriend said that he'd loved romping about in bed
with her – that he'd never experienced sex quite like it – she'd
blustered, 'Oh no, you can't mean that. I'm crap in bed.'

So what's made our children so brim-full of confidence?
I don't remember being like this as a kid. I'd stand there,
clutching a miserable gingham apron that had taken me three
terms to construct in needlework class – thirty weeks to stitch

on some rick-rack braid – and the teacher would say, 'Look at this mess! Unpick it immediately!'

I'm sure that teachers these days are so much nicer and smilier – more human, somehow, and eager to boost kids' morale. My sons' teacher gets down on her hands and knees in the school playground to help them chase a centipede into a lunchbox. When I asked my kids if they knew her first name, they laughed and said, 'Of course we do. She's our teacher.' I don't recall being aware that my teachers even had first names, let alone homes and families of their own. I just assumed they sort of melted away at three-thirty pm, or folded themselves up in a cupboard.

Worryingly, my son's teacher has said that she thinks his magic act is 'a fantastic idea' and he comes home announcing that he's figured it out; all he needs now is 'a massive knife'. Occasionally I wish I could be slightly more chilled as a parent, and let my kids just get on with things while I laze around drinking tea and reading *Marie Claire*. But I can't do the gigantic knife, despite my son's assurance that he'll 'be careful'.

The big night comes. My son shuffles on stage and reads a poem about falling down the toilet. People laugh, in a nice way, and there's applause. Later I ask if he felt disappointed at not being allowed to saw up his brother. No, he enjoyed reading the poem – in fact he was 'brilliant'.

And the magic act? 'There's always next year,' says my son.

So your child has survived his first day, or first term, or first year at school. And finally it's the holidays, which should feel wonderful because it's just like the old days – the hazy, pre-school days – when there were no gym kits to find, no school bags to check for rank biscuits/mouldering bananas, and everyone could mill around in their PJs until lunchtime.

However, school hols can feel quite strange. It's common for a kid to exhibit a weird kind of listlessness – sighing, slithering about the house, twanging his nether regions – until he adjusts to being at home again. I think that a child's brain becomes so accustomed to the tightly-structured school routine that a certain amount of de-schooling has to take place before he can fully enjoy the blast of freedom which the holidays represent.

So yes, school is wonderful for keeping them busy, keeping them out of our hair – oh, and learning the odd factlet, of course – and for reminding us, when we find ourselves missing them madly at two-fifteen pm, that the little blighters are rather lovely after all.

8

special occasions

**Birthday party survival • the day my son demanded a
death mask • Can you palm off your kid with carob at
Easter? • scary things about Hallowe'en • Christmas pre-
and post-children (spot the difference) • some prickly
(and nice) things about Christmas • hangover cures for
haggard parents • kids' over-inflated
wish lists**

Kids' birthday parties used to be so simple. Your mum would
stick a few Smarties on chocolate fingers ('traffic lights'),
blow up balloons to be batted around the living room, and everyone would be utterly thrilled to spend several hours ripping the
layers from a parcel.

Things are different now. For their birthday my sons require
a *something* party, which means themed; after weeks of heated
debate, they decide on an Ancient Egyptian event, requiring the
village hall to be transformed into a tomb stuffed with sparkling
artefacts. More worryingly, one son wishes to sport a replica of
Tutankhamun's death mask which, I fear, will require trickery
with cereal boxes and gold spray.

Party bags are to be fashioned from high-camp sparkly fabric
and filled with pharaoh stickers and foil-wrapped treasure. As

the party approaches, my son keeps enquiring how Tutankhamun is progressing. 'It looks like a *girl*,' he retorts. Music is of concern too. A friend unearths a copy of 'Walk Like an Egyptian' (extended dance mix) but I fear that playing the same song over and over may inflict psychological damage on young impressionable guests. My friend tracks down another stonker – 'Tutankhamun Cha Cha Cha' – but things are not looking good on the fancy dress front. The death mask sits too high on my son's head, like a glistening tower block, and he can't see out.

Meanwhile, the guest list is growing. Somehow, thirty-six children have received pyramid-shaped invites, and everyone is able to come. I wonder what to feed all these children. Prepare tons of food and it winds up being stamped on, then shovelled into a bin bag; offer nothing and kids troop home, hollow-cheeked and crying.

Games, too, are a challenge. I favour the rigid itinerary approach – one game after another, with no gaps – and consider purchasing a giant, kid-scaring megaphone. On the music front, things are looking better. Lifesaving friend tracks down Egyptian Reggae and – a gem by a mysterious artist called Kwentin Quisp – 'The Way Out Mummy'.

I'm feeling way-out mummyish myself when my son – who complained about Tutankhamun's aura of femininity – requests several spangly bangles on the accessories front. And I start to wonder if all this is worth the effort. Instead of hauling home forty-eight loo rolls from the Co-op (for 'wrap the mummy' game) we could have enjoyed an educational family excursion to Glasgow Science Centre.

But the end is in sight. The death mask is finished. I imagine the unveiling of this creation will be greeted with excitement on a par with King Tut's real tomb being opened back in 1922. My son examines my creation, wilts a little, and says, 'I want to go as a mummy.'

Things I wish I'd known about kids' parties

That children still like pass the parcel (and cubes of cheddar on cocktail sticks jabbed into a foil-covered orange). We worry that, to be truly spectacular, the event must feature a clown/entertainer and, ideally, some kind of 'workshop' (ie, magic tricks taught by a real magician). Extra points are awarded if a marquee or entire cinema features during some part of the day. Of course this is rot. Yes, my sons are big on elaborate themes but when the day arrives, they're easily pleased. My daughter loved her fourth birthday party which involved little more than running around the garden and screaming. Competitive party syndrome is an adult trait. Clearly, something is amiss if our children are enjoying more spectacular parties than we throw for ourselves.

Kids' entertainers can be very scary. Recently, I attended a three-year-old's party. At the last minute, let down by a highly-recommended magician, the freaked-out parents resorted to a sub-standard clown from the Yellow Pages. This guy had a nasty way about him. As soon as he appeared, the youngest children started crying. That set the others off. The clown made a half-hearted attempt at fashioning animals from sausage balloons before a sea of wet, blubbering faces. He was sent home early and the parents were mortified.

Children think they know what they want. Like, one year, my sons *definitely* wanted a ghost-themed party. 'Are you sure?' I asked, over and over. Oh, yes. They wanted cauldrons, 'blood' drinks, spooky everything. It took me two hours to transform a very ordinary chocolate cake into an authentic spectre.

But they don't. My sons changed their minds. One now wanted a *Hong Kong Phooey* cake. His brother required a precise replica of the Laughing Cow cheese box.

The child who 'needs' the entire house decked out as a fairy grotto is having a laugh. What better entertainment for a child than watching her parents balancing precariously on stepladders and detangling yards of fairy lights?

The more effort you put into planning the games, the least likely are your own children to join in. In fact they'll just want to watch telly.

You don't have to do everything yourself. Some people who can help you:

- **www.partytreasures.co.uk** offers a vast range of party bags, and little goodies to fill them, plus balloons (with disposable helium canister), themed tableware – every celebratory doo-dah you can think of.

- Or try **www.partybox.co.uk** for similar, plus a range of bright, fun 'pinata' – models to fill with sweets or goodies for the kids to smash open at the end of the party.

- Not all kids' entertainers are scary and horrible. A good one can take most of the strain and keep everyone entranced while you sip wine with your friends. Of course, you can scribble a fat cheque and place the entire party in someone else's capable hands.

Children's parties are becoming more extravagant with money being no object. We've organised a jungle party where the whole downstairs of the house was clad with camouflage nets and decorated with life-sized fibreglass zebras. Once children reach six or seven they have a clear idea of what they want. The child wants a party as flamboyant as the ones they've been invited to, and the adults want to get together in another room and drink champagne. It's exciting for everyone.

Kim Einhorn, spokesperson for event-planning company Theme Traders

As my sons have grown older they've started to pooh-pooh the traditional musical bumps-type party. They never joined in anyway, and it was always so embarrassing – I'd be bouncing around, getting everyone into the games, and they'd just skulk in the corner. The boys now have outings instead. Gemma still loves parties and, luckily, it's usually good weather so I haul our massive assortment of kids' tents and collapsible tunnels out on to the lawn and they spend half the party diving in and out of them. Parties for two- to four-year-olds are a joy because they're still very easily pleased.

Miff, full-time mother to Luke, eight, William, seven, and party girl Gemma, four

I'm happy to do kids' parties but one thing I can't stomach is party bags filled with more sweets, and more plastic tat, after they've been guzzling sweets and winning plastic tat for the past two hours. What I did for Jacob's birthday last year was give every child a strawberry plant to take home.

Sophie, play therapist and mother to Jacob, four, and Milo, one

172

I don't like party bags, but still do them, due to intense pressure. I did take Grace to a party where no bags were given out. They'd had a lovely time, but were so crestfallen at not having anything to take away that they all went home sobbing.
Rhiannon, graphic designer and mum to Grace, aged five

Two and a half hours is the maximum length for a kids' party. I usually round off by getting everyone to sit round while I read a story that's linked to the party's theme – like a Funnybones book for a ghostly party, or a fairy story at a princess party. It helps to wind everyone down.
Maggie, part-time painter and mother to Jasmine, six, and Laurel, four

When is everyone going home?
One of my sons, at his fourth birthday party

Choc-ful of chocolate: it must be Easter

First day of the school Easter holidays, and the kids and I have arrived at my dad's. With two weeks to fill, I'd intended to kick-start the hols with a fabulous day out; my dad, as is custom, doles out a vast selection of Easter eggs so everyone's brown-lipped and jittery and it's only ten-thirty am.

The plan is, Dad and I will take the kids to a (since defunct) museum of inventions, a gaudy explosion of kiddie-friendly exhibits and science shows. On the walk here from their grandad's house, we stop to admire snails on a path. I stand there for well over fifteen minutes, tapping my foot, and start to fuzz off into a parallel universe. Well, snails are hardly the most entertaining of creatures. We finally make it to the museum, where we fork out a £24 family admission fee, £15 on chicken nuggets, chips, coffees and sad-looking soup, plus another £7.50 on three 'inventor kits'.

This feels rather excessive. To round off the day perfectly my daughter announces that she 'can't walk' back to Grandad's – probably due to the gallons of molten Easter egg swishing inside her – and one of my sons is chundering on about Jesus, and how he came back to life with bleeding holes in his hands. His brother is too queasy to speak. Later, when I ask Sick Boy what he enjoyed most about our day, he looks up from his pillow and mumbles, 'The snails.'

Instead of pocket money, I've introduced holiday money for the oldest two – a tenner each at the start of the summer, Christmas and Easter holidays. I'll still give them a small Easter egg each but they're more excited about buying a toy of their choice. To Lewis, a super-soaker water gun is far more enticing than chocolate.
Jenny, social worker and mother to Lewis, eight, Ashleigh, six, and Robert, two

Emily is totally over indulged by my sister and both sets of grandparents at Easter. I let her have one egg on Easter Sunday – plus we do an egg hunt with little foil-wrapped eggs hidden all over the garden. The rest is offered in dribs and drabs, sometimes stretching until July when it's started to look a bit speckled.
Niall, furniture-maker and dad to Emily, five, and Joe, nine months

Since Freddie turned four I've relaxed my rules and let him have as much choc as he wants on special days. At Easter he gets two or three eggs and is smeared in

*chocolate all weekend. It's a sort of up-yours to the
disapproving rice cake brigade and makes Freddie
extremely happy.*

Naomi, a teacher on maternity leave with her second child due
any moment. (She says that one day Freddie might come to
the conclusion that there are more exciting things in the
world than chocolate. He just hasn't thought of them yet.)

Confession

I once bought carob bars for Easter. To my sons, then four:
'Would you like to try something that's as yummy as chocolate
but much better for you?'

Son one: 'Yeah!' He nibbles a lump of dark brown stuff.
'Disgusting! It's not fair!'

Son two: 'I'm not your friend.'

Scary things about Hallowe'en

My children love Hallowe'en. In the hierarchy of special
occasions it ranks just below birthdays and Christmas. It's the
spookiness and gore that appeals: Dracula masks, flickering
nightlights in pumpkins, and being allowed out after dark. Plus,
it really is a kid thing. Only children should be allowed to
dress up and go trick or treating. Grown-ups in fancy dress? Not
fetching. J recalls the last Hallowe'en party he was forced to
attend where two latecomers arrived in remarkably authentic
police outfits. 'Great costumes!' the host exclaimed. 'You look
like real police!'

'We are the f-ing police,' came the reply.

Here are more scary things about the witching hour – other than the rather grubby plastic fangs which my son found behind the radiator, nestling by a small pile of ancient Sugar Puffs and an end of fish finger:

◎ **Crazy neighbours.**
Ours once shouted at me for having 'an attitude', and takes great delight in blocking our gate with a row of wheelie bins. However she also dishes out highly desirable Hallowe'en sweets, like those horrible pastel pink 'prawns'.

◎ **Damaging yourself with a serrated knife.**
The more children you have, the more pumpkin lanterns you are expected to construct. Each pumpkin weighs around the same as an Afghan hound. You must haul them home from the shop, then carve them artfully. Your children will then complain that they don't have teeth.

◎ **Putrid sweets.**
My kids look upon apples and monkeynuts (the usual booty when I was a child) as if they were poison. What they don't realise is that many of the zingy sweets they're given are actually older than they are. (Hallowe'en, as anyone knows, is a prime opportunity to offload all your out-of-date goodies. Last year my daughter tore the wrapper from a finger of Fudge which must have been manufactured pre-decimalisation.)

◎ **Songs which go on for a thousand years.**
Kids will blast out these on your doorstep to 'earn' their treats. Like a speeded-up film of a decaying flower, you'll

feel yourself ageing – hair greying, face withering, your lifeblood seeping away. You can, of course, pretend to be out, which will require you to sit in the dark all evening.

◎ Needing a wee.

At the furthest point from our house, my daughter will announce that she needs a toilet. A design fault of Hallowe'en is that it occurs when it's achingly cold, causing everyone to need a wee. (This doesn't affect J as he remains at home, in front of a roaring fire, quietly flicking through *Mojo* magazine.)

Trick or treating is all well and good if you live in a village where everyone's friendly and has bags of sweets ready to give out, but where we live there's a high proportion of National Front supporters and you wouldn't want to go wandering around in the dark with your children. As India's friends live too far away to visit on foot, we have a get-together after school with pumpkin lanterns and a big cauldron full of red jelly and sweets.
Suzie, nanny and mother to India, five

Part of the fun of Hallowe'en is the kids dressing up and having their faces painted. I'm useless at sewing but any idiot can make a cape by gathering one end of an old piece of fabric. I've used horrible dark green velvet curtains – Hallowe'en's a great opportunity to use up your old tat.
Anita, full-time mother to Thomas, six, and Tabitha, five

Christmas through the ages

First Christmas with J. Just me and him, in our Hackney flat, piddled on sherry by ten-thirty am. Run out of ciggies and all shops closed. Locate tragic pub open on Upper Clapton Road. Drink some more and totter home, giddy and stupid.

First pregnant Christmas. Our flat is packed with J's friends, including an old bandmate from his punk days who's come over from Sydney. Sydney mate has brought his new girlfriend; she has gorgeous auburn hair, porcelain skin, looks like a pre-Raphaelite painting. I've gained four stones and can wear only outsized army surplus dungarees. Sydney mate and his girl snog all the time. I have already decided that J and I will never get up to anything intimate ever again.

First Christmas with twins. The only clue that there's some kind of religious festival going on are the heaps of mail that plop through our letterbox. The boys are ten months old: cruising, falling over and clonking their heads several times an hour. We're so sleep-deprived we can hardly speak. I buy J an exciting pair of sheepskin gloves.

Up the duff again. We've moved from London to rural Scotland. A vast array of J's Scottish relatives sit around a long trestle table. Some of these rellies verge on the stern. J's cousin whispers that 'it's like the Nuremberg trials'. To make our crumbling house look a little less squat-like, we've splashed white emulsion over embossed moss-green wallpaper. The swirly pattern still shows through. J is trying to cook dinner for eleven people using a cooker that's so decrepit, its temperature markings have worn off. The oven door won't close. J tries to jam it shut with a folding chair.

J's cousin to the rescue. The boys are three, our daughter eight months. We're at cousin Adam's and it's lovely to be fed and looked after. The boys amuse themselves by turning the TV on and off and snatching at fragile ornaments on the mantelpiece. One of my sons opens his present from J's cousin – it's a Buzz Lightyear outfit – and mutters, 'I don't like Buzz Lightyear.' I could die with shame.

There follow several years of Christmases at home, and it has become easier, simply because I've knocked on the head any notion of the 'perfect' festive season. I used to imagine our house filled with just the right amount of people: close friends, the family members we actually like, with no one poking their head into the mysterious dank space off the kitchen loosely termed as 'the pantry' and gasping, 'What a lot of wine bottles! Don't you ever go to the bottle bank?'

Over the years I have grown used to the fact that Christmas is chaotic and verging on out-of-control. After all, it's designed with the under-tens in mind: free toys, billions of telly, limitless sweet junky food. A design fault of kids is that they find the whole experience 'too much'. This results in tears and stomping over mountains of toys and an older child informing his younger sibling that 'Santa isn't real, you know. It's just Mum and Dad, in the night.'

You'd think that adults would be somewhat more gracious. Last year a family member in her fifties examined the classic – and, hell, painfully expensive – black sweater I'd bought her and said, 'Hmm. It'll be handy for gardening.' As for my gifts, most years I'm presented with a breadboard or curious revolving 'platter' on which hors d'oeuvres can be placed which, although useful and appreciated, reminds me in no uncertain terms that I am no longer twenty-two and can, in fact, list all of Spandau Ballet's top ten hits.

Ways to a relatively snarl-free Christmas

If you didn't start preparing for Christmas months ago, you're already too late. Delia had *her* cake baked months ago. But you're not Delia. And you had better things to do than weigh out dried fruit in September.

Try to avoid a huge pile-up of people. We arrange to see people the weekend before Christmas and right through to the New Year. It spreads it all out, no one's insulted by being left out, and we have a better time this way.
Professor Stephen Palmer, director of the Centre for Stress Management in London

Last year, my mother gave Chloe a pop-up tent. It's the best thing anyone could have done for us. Chloe sat in it over the whole Christmas period. We just posted in the odd drink or snack. It's almost like she wasn't there at all.
Jess, writer and mum to Chloe, six

I'm Jewish and French. There have been years when some family members wanted to celebrate Christmas, while others didn't. Some spoke English, others only French. My solution was to throw myself into cooking and feeding everyone. It helps you steer clear of tension. I'd advise anyone hosting Christmas to be organised, prepare to compromise, and don't let the niggly bits overshadow the day. It's only a day, after all.
Claudine, a counsellor and mother of two

The case for severely editing the present/card list

I am in awe of J's approach to Christmas shopping. Every year, at around 21 December he requests a child-free day in Glasgow during which he visits several old friends and manages a three-hour amble around Borders. Yet he still shows up with acceptable carrier bags (ie, not Everything Under a Pound) and the announcement that his shopping is all done and was, in fact, most enjoyable.

My festive shop is not like this. The fact is, most women's Christmas lists run to twenty or thirty people, partly because we tend to have more dealings with other people's children, and make ourselves sick with guilt if we forget the lollipop lady or that friendly lad who lopped down the sycamore and left branches strewn all over the path for us to trip over. No wonder we start formulating present lists in early November.

It's a terrible affliction, this desire to please. When we moved into our small town five years ago, I spent months smiling hopefully at every resident, even the fierce lady in the grocer's who sucked in her lips whenever I had the nerve to enter her shop. Unwittingly, I launched a 'Like Me' campaign. I'd bound in, compliment her on her fine range of breads and place my purchases ever so neatly on the counter. She still looked like she might haul me into the back room for a good spanking for spending so much on wine and fags.

Recently I've toughened up and have managed to edit my Christmas list. Friends are doing likewise: one has even struck off her own husband, claiming, 'Neither of us needs anything. We're just buying something practical.' Is anything more tragic than buying 'something for the house'? Our home is such a manky, unloved heap that it doesn't deserve a present. It has

181

behaved particularly badly this year: kitchen cupboards emit a murky stench, the toilet repeatedly flushes itself.

So that's one gift I can strike from this list. In the meantime, I am willing to make a generous cash offer to anyone willing to finish my Christmas shopping. If it all gets too much, you can dump the carrier bags with me. I'll be having coffee in Borders.

Some prickly things about Christmas

- In-laws saying: 'Don't feel bad about not coming to us. We'll have a nice time. On our own. Without you . . .'

- Too many people jostling at your sink, all trying to wash up.

- No one trying to wash up.

- Family members in conflict. Your mother: 'See how your father behaves? And I have to put up with this, day in, day out, you wouldn't believe what he . . .' All the adult offspring can do is remind ourselves that we had the good sense to make a speedy getaway years ago.

- Crowing round-robin letters: 'And of course, Tallulah always wins the gold at gymnastics . . . and Jasper has learned to read – and he's only nine months old! Did I tell you that Josie can speak fluent Russian?' Blah-di-bloody-blah.

- Other parents bragging that they've made iced biscuits to hang on the tree, printed their own recycled paper with a star stamper and gold paint, *and* hand-drawn all their cards.

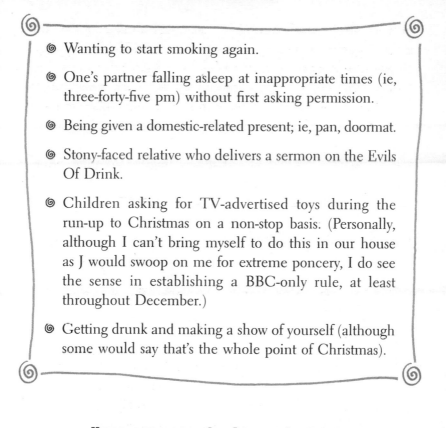

- Wanting to start smoking again.

- One's partner falling asleep at inappropriate times (ie, three-forty-five pm) without first asking permission.

- Being given a domestic-related present; ie, pan, doormat.

- Stony-faced relative who delivers a sermon on the Evils Of Drink.

- Children asking for TV-advertised toys during the run-up to Christmas on a non-stop basis. (Personally, although I can't bring myself to do this in our house as J would swoop on me for extreme poncery, I do see the sense in establishing a BBC-only rule, at least throughout December.)

- Getting drunk and making a show of yourself (although some would say that's the whole point of Christmas).

Hangover cures for haggard parents

For all you festive over-indulgers out there, with your carpet tongues and rank-canal breath, I've been researching hangover cures. Unless your partner is especially benevolent, or your children have been temporarily removed to another county, you simply cannot lie in until midday. It's not allowed.

I'll confess something here: as I write this I'm feeling a little hot around the cheeks, and furry of mouth, probably due to the wild gang of hoodlums who strapped me to a chair and forced a funnel into my mouth, through which they administered alcohol. I think that potent substance, After Shock, may have been involved. No one warns you that, with its vivid colour and sweetie-medicine taste, it is intended for consumption by those slightly younger than ourselves.

The trouble with hangover cures is that they force you to consider what you've done to your insides. Milk thistle is a hot favourite; apart from sounding ever so wholesome, it has a beneficial effect on the outer membrane of the liver. The thought of the liver having a membrane at all – so fragile-sounding – is not what you want to hear after a night during which you were rather free and easy with your affection. After a sesh, I like to think of my liver as virtually indestructible, possibly constructed from breezeblocks, and not a quivering organ kept intact by a mere *membrane*.

Artichoke is another proven cure and is available in capsule form. But let's get real here: you want food – big hefty food – not capsules. Carbs plus lovely, slimy fat, to mop up excess juices. Better still: lots of rest, in a darkened room, with no one shouting or parping a trumpet into your lughole. With luck, the children can actually be worked in as part of the hangover cure. You want to be flat on your back with someone stroking your head? Dig out that toy medical kit. While your offspring busy themselves with plastic stethoscopes and syringes, you can lie down, 'being the patient'.

Of course, by rights, parents shouldn't be in licensed premises at all. But our kids, and their enormous wish lists, are the very reason we drink.

Present overload

I was wrapping up Jenny's presents a couple of Christmases ago. I'd bought more and more as Christmas approached without keeping track. It was obscene. Half of it ended up

stashed away for future birthdays and Christmases. You get carried away, sucked into the whole consumer thing, and they start flinging it all about, then fighting over something insignificant, like a yo-yo.
Fiona, restaurant manager and mum to Jenny, eight, and Amy, five

It's easy to be swept along with the hype, the goodies on offer, in our desire to please and have a quiet life. We can't bear the thought of our kids being disappointed on Christmas day. But it's far better to say how much you can spend and involve your child in making a choice. Rather than being guided by ads, where everything is shinier and bigger and better, let them see real things in shops. Then they can see for themselves if it's still what they really want.
Suzie Hayman

Sophie loved the play kitchen at her friend Rachel's house, but when we bought her one she wasn't remotely interested. It's just this massive eyesore in the living room. This year I'm using the kids' lists as a guide but finding out what grandparents and aunties are buying so, hopefully, there won't be any unwanted or duplicated presents.
Heather, language teacher and mother to five-year-old Sophie and Morvern, three

Medium-priced toys – the £19.99 price range – can be a complete waste of money. You might be better clubbing together with relatives for something bigger which offers far more play value. Don't forget, though, that kids love cheap trash too. It's fun, and no one cares if it's broken by Boxing Day.
Lesley Steyn, couples therapist

My girls usually want clothes, which we choose together. I wouldn't dream of venturing into Gap without them. They also love art stuff and books. Christmas becomes easier as they get to know their own minds and understand money.
Tim, father to Gemma, ten, and Kate, nine (he does admit, however, that 'Gemma cried last Christmas because I'd got her the wrong Nokia phone')

You may have to knock the Santa myth on the head and show your children that real toys come from real shops, and are paid for with real money.
Suzie Hayman again

As for my own kids, each year the wish list becomes longer. Yet too much of everything is, perhaps, the whole point. Christmas is more than the average brain can cope with. There's nothing for it other than to glug your wine and flop out on the sofa, while congratulating yourself that, for another year at least, you've survived.

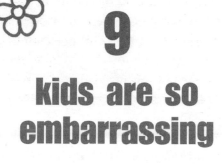

9
kids are so embarrassing

'That man's so fat!' (and other terrible things children say) • why kids are obsessed with our bodily functions • lies, damned lies • foul language • sex education: how long can you blether on about 'special cuddling'? • nit infestation . . . and extermination • kids who won't play by the rules

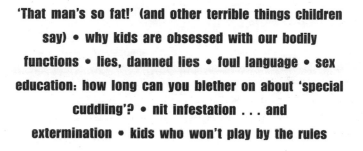

As a habitual blusher, I've always found life pretty embarrassing. Periods, boys, going for a summer job interview as a hospital orderly and being mistaken for a patient – then told to go into a curtained cubicle and pee into a kidney bowl (and being unable to expel a drop, despite thinking desperately of waterfalls and gushing taps) – all guaranteed to trigger simmering neck-rash and intense mortification.

Yet nothing is as embarrassing as children. The other day, harassed after my sons' spectacular behaviour at the hairdresser's (careering around, making chairs go up and down), I bent down to gather up two schoolbags and lunchboxes, four jackets, plus two carrier bags of shopping as we prepared to make our exit from the hair salon. 'Mum!' my son hollered. 'Pull your trousers up. I can see your knickers!' Tempted though I was to growl, 'Actually, sweetest, I don't give a flying f-' I just muttered a terse, 'Oh, really', and shoved the three of them out of the building.

So, yes, children are embarrassing. They may possess many charms – innocence, humour, peachy complexions – but decorum? Not a hint of it.

Cringey things my children have said in public

❀ 'Why were you and Daddy shouting last night?' *My daughter, at the supermarket checkout queue*

❀ 'Imagine if Adam and Eve made everyone in the world. All that sex!' *Seven-year-old son during creation-versus-evolution discussion at an elderly relative's house*

❀ 'The doctor put something in you so you don't have any more babies.' *Same son, at dinner table, in the presence of both of his grannies*

❀ 'You have fat bosoms.' *Daughter, on spying me getting dressed*

❀ 'I hate it here! It's too small!' *The day daughter and I visited a friend's picturesque cottage*

❀ 'Peter's got a fat belly!' *My son, a mere three feet away from our dear friend Peter who had driven 400 miles to visit us*

Awful things other adults have said to us

❀ 'Is there a helpline you can call for that kind of behaviour?' *Our neighbour, watching our sons whirl around the garden, knocking merry hell out of each other*

❀ 'Do you have a cloth?' *My mother in-law, on entering our kitchen*

❀ 'Sam said that, at home, he's only allowed to use the dirty downstairs toilet.' *My darling son's teacher*

Kids and our bodily functions

I fail to comprehend why children are so fascinated by their parents' intimate activities. Surely, this a modern phenomenon. I was born in the mid-sixties, and never once saw my own parents naked, or even half-naked; yet my children have followed me into the bathroom on numerous occasions, and watched all kinds of personal stuff that I'm reluctant for even J to witness. To give a hint, I recently extracted a tampon from my shoulder bag instead of a pen, and tried to use it to sign a Switch receipt at the grocer's. 'That's not a pen,' my son snorted. 'That's one of them things ladies stick up their butts!'

An even more harrowing event occurred during our family holiday in Brittany. My French is pretty rusty, and I was already stressing over how to explain to the holiday house owner that our daughter had climbed on to the fragile wall heater in the bathroom, sending the appliance crashing to the floor and leaving a raggedy hole and small heap of dust balls and antique wiring. I looked up 'I'm sorry' in the shrink-wrapped fifteen-Euro book which we thought was a French-English dictionary but turned out to be a phrase book with none of the words you really need. I cobbled words together (sticking to the incorrect but safer present tense) but it sounded too dramatic: 'Nous avons un accident dans la salle de bain. Je suis desolé!' It's amazing how your brain can be stuffed with irregular French verbs in your youth and yet, two decades later, has somehow been

Hoovered of all useful vocabulary. In times of stress, all I can recall is, 'Où est ma valise?'

Things became more desperate when, later in the holiday, one of our party required an urgent application of pile cream. How to request such an item in a French pharmacy? They're so different to ours: so posh and gleaming, with shelves of unfamiliar white boxes, staffed by immaculate ladies in their forties and fifties. I took my daughter in for a recce, but couldn't spy any product remotely resembling Les Germaloids and just kept scanning the shelves with wild, staring eyes. 'Oui?' said a matronly lady behind the counter. She looked like a friend of my mother's from her quilting club.

'Bon-joowa!' my daughter shouted. 'What do we want?'

'Cream,' I whispered.

'Bottom cream,' she added, loudly. My mouth opened and shut. Obviously, miming the condition to this elegant lady was utterly out of the question. What was French for piles? Les piles? No, no, that's batteries. I didn't want this stranger assuming that I was intending to conduct a risky experiment involving my bottom and batteries. 'Tell the lady!' my daughter thundered.

We hurried out, clutching our purchase of hair conditioner and blue nail polish.

Lies, damned lies

To embarrass us further, kids lie. Why do they do this? To embellish, to make life more exciting, to cover their backs: 'The vase just fell off the shelf.' 'The remote dropped into the toilet.' One day, when I asked my three children why a gigantic hole had been picked in a chair's upholstery, my daughter just shrugged and said, 'It made the hole all by itself.'

Well, of course it was possible. Fabric can just . . . disintegrate. A prized 1930s opaque glass vase can, over a period of several weeks, gradually shuffle itself to the edge of the shelf – and fall off. It's more likely, though, that your kid is fibbing wildly. He may be utterly crap at it – when any of my children fib, they adopt this really shifty, staring-into-dazzling-lights expression, or try to pull their jumper up over their head. Face concealed by knitwear? That means he broke it, then.

For the past eighteen months Harvey's been fibbing constantly. There's the wild embellishing like, 'Mum, I scored three goals at football . . .' When I say, 'Did you really score?' he'll look shifty and say, 'Well, nearly.' He's more likely to admit to more serious lies if I'm gentle and patient, rather than flying into a rage. You have to make it easy for them to confess.
Fran, acupuncturist and mother to five-year-old Harvey

It might be hard for your child to distinguish between accidentally damaging something, and deliberately damaging it. To him, both simply mean 'naughty'. You could give him the benefit of the doubt, suggest that he probably didn't do it on purpose. Then explain that it's only bad if he actually meant it.
Psychologist Dr Dorothy Einon

Elise [aged four] kept complaining that her eyes were hurting and she couldn't see properly. I ignored her until she started saying, 'Mum, I'm going blind!' I was terrified and took her to her GP. She was fine. It turned out that her best friend had just been given glasses, and Elise wanted some too.
Lizzie, psychology student

We kept finding piles of poo in our outhouse. Felix [then three] said he'd seen a large dog sneaking into our garden so we started chaining our gate shut. It's five foot high, so we figured a dog wouldn't be able to get over it. But the poos kept appearing. Felix said he'd seen the dog flying over the gate. I had to have a stern word with him about never, ever doing the toilet in our outhouse and, oddly enough, the poos stopped after that.

Mo, full-time mother to Felix and three-month-old Ella (who hasn't figured out the fine art of fibbing . . . yet)

Lies can do good, by encouraging imagination. You can play along, by saying, 'Did you really go to the zoo? What did you see there?' or acknowledge that it's not strictly true by saying, 'That's a nice pretend game . . . so which animals did you meet today?' Without this kind of exaggeration – these wonderful, puffed-up tales – life would be terribly dull.

Dorothy Einon again

Embarrassing foul language incident #1

We're cutting it fine to make it to Newcastle Airport to catch our holiday flight. J is stamping on the accelerator, his brow dowsed with sweat, and cursing in a most un-child-friendly manner. 'Ucking-ell! Ucking-ell!' chirps one son, then four years old, as we swing into the long-stay car park.

J's foul-mouthed outburst thrills our children. As we tear through the airport, and I bark at the boys to 'Stop using bad words – I never want to hear you say that again, do you hear?' it strikes me that neither I nor J have any business coming over all puritanical. We're mortified when our children swear in public, and practically *faint* when one of our infants mutters, 'I can't get my bloody shoes on', yet spurt a stream of obscenities the minute they're out of earshot. Who are we kidding? That it's normal behaviour to murmur, 'Dearie me!' when the rear of our car crunches into a gatepost?

We reach the departure gate with two minutes to spare and are, miraculously, allowed on the plane. Fellow passengers beam hatred. Announcement over the Tannoy: could my family please make itself known to the cabin crew as we have left all our traveller's cheques, plus two pairs of sunglasses, on the check-in desk.

'Bugger!' bellows my son.

Embarrassing foul language incident #2

It's the last day of term. Lovely teacher has asked the kids to bring in CDs for their classroom party. J gives one son The Thrills (completely acceptable, and highly approved by Teach). His brother takes Fatboy Slim which is swiftly removed from the classroom CD player, the teacher blustering, 'There are bad words on it. Words that no one should ever say.'

I was horrified when Alistair's teacher called me aside after school and whispered that he'd rearranged the magnetic letters on the whiteboard to spell the F-word.
Sam, business studies lecturer and mother to seven-year-old twins, Alistair and Mark

The kids and I were invited to tea by our neighbours, who are quite churchy and also veggie. Lily, who's three,

*gamely tucked into her red pepper soup, but James just
stared at it, looking disgusted, and cried, 'Jesus wept.'*
**Moira, mother to five-year-old James and his more
adventurous little sister, who have yet to be asked out to tea
again**

*I'd been breastfeeding on a park bench. It was a freezing
day, and someone I knew from the school gates invited me
back to her house, where I'd be more comfortable. She
was so kind, bringing puzzles for Isabelle to play with,
while I fed the baby. Then Isabelle needed the loo, and
came running straight out, shouting, 'I can't do it in
there. It stinks of shit.'*
**Pip, an auxiliary nurse currently on maternity leave, and
mother to Isabelle, five, and baby Jemima**

This was told to me by Pam and Jock, who have six grown-
up children and 'hordes' of grandchildren:
*Our grandson [aged seven] is playing with his friend
in the playroom. Our daughter – his mum – hears the
friend say, 'You're stupid.' Grandson says, 'You're not
allowed to say stupid. It's swearing.' Friend says, 'It
isn't!' Then five-year-old granddaughter announces,
'No, that's not swearing. Fucking hell is swearing.'*

'How are babies made?'

Thankfully, our children have not yet reached the stage where
detailed explanations about sex are necessary. I've told them bits
and bobs about sperm, eggs, and special kisses between mums
and dads. J has said, 'Ask your mother.' However I suspect that
my sons and their friend Ed are enjoying a right old tee-hee

about sex in their bedroom. Without wishing to eavesdrop, I jam my gigantic, flapping ear against their door. 'And this,' Ed announces, 'is yer balls.'

The room trembles with hysterical laughter, threatening the very fabric of our home. I hurry downstairs, clutching my simmering lug, appalled at the swift disintegration of my sons' innocence. Foolishly, I'd imagined we could get away with wiffling on about babies being created by seed and egg, via 'a special kiss' for some decades to come. So what's happened? One minute, your offspring delight in being presented with Fuzzy Felt Cowboys and Indians. Then, in what feels like a blink, they've shunned the little felt people and 'magic' green board in favour of shouting, 'Sex is when two grown-ups roll around on a bed, ha ha!'

It's all too sudden. Why can't children come equipped with some kind of warning system – like the bleeping noise your car makes when it's on the verge of running out of oil or water – at which point your kid might suggest, 'Just to let you know, I'm going to be asking those questions that make you go all sweaty over the next few weeks, okay?'

In a panic, I consult Miriam Stoppard's book, *Questions Children Ask & How to Answer Them.* It would appear that, as parents, we are lagging way behind in matters of sex education. For children aged two to four, Miriam suggests an explanation along the 'special cuddling' lines which is virtually identical to our preferred bland (and clearly inadequate) answer – and our sons are seven! We'll probably be chundering away about special cuddling when they're massive hairy near-adults, who'll return from the cinema to explain, 'I liked the film, but it had too much of that special cuddling that mummies and daddies do.'

I don't recall asking my parents one single sex-related question. By the age of nine or ten, I still assumed that, in order to make a baby, a boy and a girl just had to sit together in the playground with a coat spread over their knees. J's sex education was similarly patchy. On spying hormone rooting powder in the shed, his adolescent brain made the following connection: hormone = sex, rooting = sex, powder = drugs. So that's why his dad spent so much time in the hut.

How much nitty-gritty do they really need?

Tell them too much too soon and you'll horrify them. You hear three-year-olds talking about penises and 'ginas' and it's just ridiculous.
Terri, sports coach and mother to Aaron, seven, and Alfie, four

I'm desperate to tell Lily [aged ten] the facts of life. I know I'll be really good at explaining stuff. But whenever I broach the subject she clamps her hands over her ears and sings 'La-la-la-la-la' very loudly, drowning me out. The only sex question she's ever asked is, 'Do you and Daddy do it while I'm asleep in bed?'
Lorna, a freelance copy editor who's still waiting for her big moment

Sex education should start very young and very gently. Begin with the physical identification of parts of the body. With older kids it depends on the sort of relationship you have. Don't expect to suddenly come over all detailed about sex if you haven't talked about anything other than the weather or schoolwork for the past ten years.
Nick Fisher, dad to three sons and agony uncle for a teenage magazine for eighteen years

I believe in being quite frank and answering questions as

*honestly as I can. But I just wanted to run away when, in
the park, Nathan yelled at the top of his voice, 'So,
Mum, the man's hard penis goes into the soft vagina . . .'*
Sue, researcher and mother to Nathan, eight, and Charlie, five

Embarrassing little visitors

At least sex conversations do, for the most part, take place in the
home. No one else is involved. Not your child's playmates or
school friends or those friends' parents. When nits sneak on to
your kid's head and stealthily invade the hairdos of each family
member, there is no chance of such discretion. They are – let's
not put too fine a point on it – a complete pain in the butt.

Primary schools are experiencing nit invasion on a major
scale. Something to do with overly-heated houses – all those
toasty regions at the backs of necks and behind the ears – and
non-existence of nit nurses. Apparently someone decided it wasn't
PC to have fearsome ladies raking children's scalps. You always
knew who had them, of course. At my tiny West Yorkshire primary
school, you were given a vivid blue card to take home to your
mum, thus giving classmates licence to tease you mercilessly for
months on end and conclude that, as a host to an extended
family of wriggling insects, you lived in a dirty house and no
one wanted to sit next to you for fear of contamination.

At least my sons aren't subjected to such humiliation. I simply
slather all of our heads with pongy lotion. Quellada, the nit-
zapping stuff, sounds pretty sexy – a pheromone-stirring love
potion, perhaps. Before today I might have even agreed to a
spontaneous Quellada session as long as it wasn't too tiring and
didn't mess up the house.

On the plus side, at least nits aren't as troublesome as some
uninvited guests – mice, for instance. They don't freak you out

by darting across the living room, or eyeballing you from behind a speaker. And so many of our children's friends share the problem that I feel certain there's no longer a stigma. I do notice, however, that for several days our house is eerily free of visitors.

Nit-busting tips from infested parents:

Dee: *You have to nit-comb every day if they're going around school. Cover the hair in conditioner to make the comb glide through more easily.*

Louisa: *We had Amy's long, thick hair cut to a shoulder-length bob to make combing and checking so much quicker and easier.*

Fiona: *When the kids are bored it's fun – educational, in fact – to tap them from the comb on to white paper and examine them under a magnifying glass.*

Claire: *Tea tree oil doesn't kill them but it is an effective deterrent. Use a tea tree shampoo regularly. Also, don't freak out and start washing pillows and bedding because the little buggers can't live anywhere apart from on human heads.*

Liam: *Remember to follow up with a second application of lotion a week after the first – that way you'll zap any eggs which escaped extermination first time.*

Our embarrassing football incident

My sons have so far shown little interest in football, rugby, karate or any other sporting activities which go on in our town. Yet I do feel that they should do something, and take them along to a footie session at a local sports hall. 'Well!' the coach says on my return. I'm thinking: he's amazed by their brilliance. Football is, perhaps, not just a tedious green rectangle perpetually shimmering in our living room, but the solution for reckless behaviour, tiny attention spans – everything. 'I don't know how to put this,' says coach. He's sweating a little, and shuffling uncomfortably as if trying to chuck a girlfriend, but in a nice way ('It's not you, it's me . . .' etc etc). 'Your boys are quite a pair,' he says tentatively.

'Really?' I manage.

'They won't take direction.'

Ridiculously, my eyes fill up, not because of football, a dumb game anyway, but due to the fact that mothers are incapable of hearing even the mildest criticism of their offspring without blubbing pathetically, requiring rapid blinking and talking in an extremely awkward, head-down manner. 'They're distracting the others,' coach says in a gentler voice. 'Of course, you're welcome to bring them back . . .' *But I'd rather you didn't,* he adds, silently.

By now my eyes are wobbling with saline solution. How awful, to cry in front of coach in his shimmery tracksuit, with the surly sports centre staff lurking nearby. I want to run out of the building, and drink wine. 'That's fine!' I blurt out, grinning wildly. 'They're probably too young anyway! And we're terribly busy!'

Other people's kids burst out of the changing room, having channelled all that surplus energy in a constructive manner. My pair straggle out last, babbling that they've made new friends and loved skidding on the shiny wooden floor. 'Can't wait till next week,' one son announces.

'I thought we might try gymnastics,' I tell him.

At times like this, I try to remind myself that all children are embarrassing sometimes, if not pretty much *all* the time. Let's face it: no adult would bellow, 'What's gay sex?' at top volume in a busy Tesco Metro store. Only a kid would yell, on hearing his mother being asked if she'd like another drink at a barbecue, 'Yes she would. She's an alcoholic!'

Both of the above happened to friends of mine. These women – in fact most parents I know – have grown accustomed to being shown up in public, and have perfected a quick raise of the eyebrows, coupled with a shrug of the shoulders (their 'Kids, eh?' expression). If you're tempted to crow that your child behaves impeccably, and never causes you embarrassment, please be warned that bragging about one's child is his cue to pull out his thing in a public place – like in front of the school, with head teacher peering out of a window – and start peeing.

10
kids will be kids

They're scared of non-scary stuff • and make us throw
adult tantrums • they won't go to bed • have nightmares
• won't eat • or let us use the telephone • they're
obsessed with Portaloos • and the little light inside the
fridge • boys are so boysy • why kids worship men •
some children are truly hideous

All is calm in our house. My sons are playing in their bedroom, my daughter is quietly colouring in at the dining table. On such occasions, J and I are able to pore over the newspaper, uninterrupted by hair-pulling incidents or having to drive swiftly to A&E, and no longer find ourselves reading the same paragraph over-again-same-paragraph-over-again.

I start thinking: is this really my family? It's actually quite pleasant, living here. Finally it may be worth investing in proper attractive furniture, like normal people do. Until now, J has insisted that it's 'not worth' buying anything decent for the house, pointing out that our £9 B&Q folding chairs will 'do just fine' until the children leave home; when nagged mercilessly, he grudgingly agrees that we might possibly invest in a new rug once our daughter starts secondary school. But it will have to be rolled up and put away during the daytime.

201

So the boys have reached seven, our daughter four, and I find myself bragging to my mother on the phone that 'the children are no trouble these days'. At that precise moment, I hear something breaking. My daughter has smashed the toy china tea set I've treasured since I was three years old. 'MY TEASET!' I roar. 'Heh-heh,' says my daughter. I'm shocked, dismayed. The trouble with surprise bad behaviour is that it's so deeply disappointing. You think you can read your paper, nibble your croissant, be a glossy-magazine family with your fresh coffee and Bonne Maman Wild Blueberry Conserve – but no. You've been conned. Let's not forget that, while our offspring may put on an occasional show of extreme grown-up-ness they are, beneath their spooky good manners, still kids. And, despite the fact that we've incubated and reared them, we will never have their funny little brains completely figured out.

This chapter is all about the weird things that kids do.

They don't like the places they're supposed to like

J would have it that I disapprove of soft play centres because, like Fruit Winders and PlayStation, they didn't exist when I was a child. Actually, as he has visited a soft play centre only once in his life – during the winter of 1999, if I recall – he has no business commenting on these places at all.

Admittedly, I do try to reserve such excursions as rainy-day last resorts. Who'd wish to spend more time than necessary in a vast warehouse with no natural daylight, dish-watery coffee and hordes of purple-faced, sobbing children? However, my children adore these places, so here we are. At least, I thought they adored them. Today they keep bounding back to the adults' table, demanding sweets and Slush Puppies. Irritatingly, they're hardly bothered with the play equipment at all. My daughter is more interested in the machine which pops out about three jellybeans straight on to the sticky carpet for 20p. My sons just want to crawl underneath the toilet cubicles and spy on me while I'm peeing. Perhaps this is a sign that they're outgrowing these places, and will soon prefer to loiter in the Gap changing rooms, murmuring their approval as I try on lots of different tops.

One of my sons announces – yesss! – that he wants to go home. I'm shoving trainers on to feet when there's a terrible howling. A kid is carried from the 'fun zone' to the reception area. He's around three years old. The back of his head is being dabbed by a gaggle of frantic adults. There's blood oozing out and dripping on to the floor, then the ambulance men arrive and whisk the child away.

My son gawps at the little splatters of blood on the floor. 'Cool!' he whispers.

They're scared of un-scary stuff

It's surprising, when you consider how eager most children are to scale precarious walls and perform on stage in front of hundreds of staring grown-ups, that they're actually scared of lots of things. I quite like this quality. It reminds me that they are, well, *children*, and not scaled-down versions of cynical world-weary adults.

Sometimes their fears develop in response to a horrible incident. Since the day my son disturbed a wasps' nest and ran screaming, with at least fifteen of the buggers trapped in his hair (which I was forced to pluck out with my bare hands – that's devotion for you), he's not been a friend of the vicious little creatures. Other fears just seem to be part of a child's make-up, and individual to that kid: between eighteen months and three, both of my sons would be terror-struck, and start screaming, if they glimpsed anyone wearing a baseball cap or indeed any peaked headgear. They refused to be seen by a dentist until they were almost four years old, yet my daughter has happily opened wide since she's been in possession of teeth, and enjoys the whole whizzy-chair experience.

Here are some common (and pretty weird) kiddie fears, and how you might try to allay them.

Haircuts. You'd think they'd enjoy it – having someone fiddle with their hair, chatting idly about holidays and whoever's on the latest cover of *OK!* – but no. There's crying, screaming, an unwillingness to sit on the chair in the big black cape – and no hairdresser on earth can tend to the locks of a thrashing wilde-beest. Our local hair salon has a racing car seat, which can tempt some kids to cooperate, although my brood is more impressed by the jar of sherbet lollies (vehicles just don't cut it for them).

If your kid kicks up a stink you can leave his hair to grow wild and try again in a couple of months, or hack at it yourself while he watches a video. You can also let him watch you having your hair cut. ('See – it doesn't hurt!') However, I suspect that none of these tactics is half as effective as good, old-fashioned bribery (ie, sweets or hard cash).

Eye tests and glasses. When one of my sons needed to wear glasses for year or so, it helped that he'd witnessed me having an eye test. (In fact all three kids had been there; as a result, I'd taken about 1.2 seconds to choose truly vile shimmery rainbow-coloured frames, like those belonging to a slightly more subtle Su Pollard, which were never worn and finally flung out in disgust.)

It helped that Matthew had worn sunglasses for virtually our whole summer holiday, so he was used to the feeling

*of something on his face. Plus, the place where he got his
glasses had a computer screen so he could see his own face
with all different frames. Just a gimmick, but it worked.*
Julia, pool attendant and mother to six-year-old Matthew

Lifts. Terrifying for some, thrilling for others. My own children
could amuse themselves going up and down the lift at our local
swimming pool for an entire afternoon.

*Marsha [then aged four] skipped ahead of us and into a
lift, which whisked her upwards, and was terrified of lifts
for months afterwards. A good way to distinguish a real
phobia from an attention-seeking tizz is to offer chocolate.
If they cooperate, you know they're just trying it on, and
can get tough next time.*
Annie, chef and mother to a five-year-old lift-phobic

The doctor. A sensitive matter if your child vividly recalls that, on
his last visit, he was jabbed in the arm with a scary needle. I've
found that it helps to have something fun to do afterwards, like
going to a café for cakes, or renting a new vid, or choosing a
small treat like stickers, a comic or tiddly toy from the newsagent's.

*I lied when I took Marco for his pre-school check-up. I
knew he'd be having a jab, but said that I didn't think
anything nasty would happen. I wish I'd been straight.
Now, whenever he's ill, he thinks I've conspired with the
horrible doctor and that he'll be jabbed again.*
Paul, dad to six-year-old Marco and Lucas, two

The dentist. You get kindly, child-friendly dentists, and the other
kind of dentist – the sort who once snapped at me, 'You should
brush your teeth for four minutes, twice a day, and floss them',

and when I balked at the time this would take, snorted, 'So what do you do all day?' Anyway, dentists are changeable. During my sons' scaredy-cat phase, a friendly (lady) dentist gave me a pile of disposable gauzy masks so we could play dentists at home.

Pigeons and assorted wildlife. Between the ages of eighteen months and three, my sons were terrified of clucky farmyard birds all because a turkey had made a terrible gobbling noise as we walked past its cage at a city farm. This incident meant, for a while at least, no more visits to stinking city farms. Hallelujah.

They refuse to go to bed

New rules are being laid down. Thou shalt ensure that bath water remains in bath and is not sloshed on to mirror, floor or the faces of craggy musicians on Dad's teetering pile of *Mojo* magazines. Thou shalt go to bed at a reasonable hour (ie, seven-thirty pm) in order to be bursting with brainpower and festooned with house points at school next day. Should thou be unable to fall into deep slumber immediately, thou shalt indulge in a noiseless activity – ie, reading, drawing, or picking up glitter, particle by particle, from thy bedroom carpet – until a state of restfulness is achieved. Thou shalt not, under any circumstances, upend toy boxes, use bed as bouncy castle or plunge a pyjama-clad arm, up to the shoulder, into thy festering fish tank.

Rules agreed, I look forward to an evening of reading a juicy new novel, without the niggling fear that the upper half of the house is being dismantled and put back together in the wrong order.

6.45 pm. With one son in the bath, and another happily swinging on his bedroom door, I read my daughter's bed-time story and notice, with pleasure, that her eyelids appear heavily weighted. On investigating the bathroom, I discover that my son has had a foam fight with himself, dolloping froth on to every available surface, including the inside of my make-up bag. Decide it's not worth getting out of my pram about.

7.30 pm. Read sons story, ensure that refined sugar is scoured from teeth, and usher my offspring bedwards.

7.45 pm. Scamper downstairs, open wine and novel.

7.47 pm. Back upstairs to investigate awful screeching noise. Quietly reprimand my son for leaping gracefully from one bed to the other, and congratulate myself for remarkable self-control. I am feeling calm and powerful. J is away on a course, and I am coping well. I am mistress of this house.

8 pm. Read first paragraph of novel. Hear crazed laughter from bathroom. Thunder upstairs where my sons have secured balloons to the bath taps. The balloons bulge dangerously, then ping off with a dramatic explosion of water and cheering. Feel the F-word bubbling in my throat and make the kind of noise that comes from the nearby abbatoir. Thunder downstairs in foul temper.

8.20 pm. Career upstairs at sound of high-pitched screaming, the kind that makes dogs go crazy and run round in circles. My son has slammed a door in his brother's face, which is now bleeding. Attend to bloody son with cold compress while roaring at non-bleeding son. Once I've started yelling, I can't stop. I'm an out of control stereo, jammed at full volume with no off button. Tears spill down non-bleeding son's face.

8.45 pm. Back downstairs. Try to re-read first paragraph of novel but my vision is blurry and some kind of saline solution is dripping on to the book. Can hear my sons whimpering upstairs: bleeding son because it still hurts, non-bleeding son because his Yu-gi-yo cards have been confiscated and will be offered to a child who deserves them. Non-bleeding son pokes his head round the living room door, says, 'Can we be friends?'

8.55 pm. Run upstairs in response to demands for water. At least I'm getting plenty of exercise. Women's mags are always urging us to use the stairs whenever possible.

9.15 pm. My sons are asleep. No they're not. My daughter wakes with a shrill cry as the boys – now fully recovered – pile the 276 soft toys which reside in this house on to her bed 'to keep her company'. Stamp my foot so hard, my heel throbs. One son laughs in my face. The other salutes me. Unconnected to my brain, my hand flaps through the air, landing pathetically on non-bleeding son's rump. He howls. Why did I do that? Modern parent knows that Smacking is Bad. We're giving the message that it's okay to hit. The guilt which follows makes it difficult to breathe.

10 pm. Mull over the evening's events, make a mental note to try harder for the rest of my life. Non-bleeding son appears in the living room with a Lego model he made for me. I feel the size of a chickpea. 'Can I stay up for a bit?' he asks meekly. Wearily, I agree. He snuggles into me on the sofa, smelling warm and lovely. Cheer him up further with a bowl of microwave popcorn and give the Yu-gi-yo cards back.

10.25 pm. I creep into my sons' room and stare at two sleeping faces on pillows. They look very small, very butter-wouldn't-melt.

On nights like this, I really feel like I don't deserve them. And my ankle is throbbing.

On days when I've really had enough, I fiddle the clock in their room and tell them it's eight o'clock – their bed time – when it's only seven. You love their little faces but there comes a point when you need to have those faces out of yours.
Beth, full-time mother to Lara, five, and Olivia, four

The boys learning to read has been a big turning point for us. They go to bed at eight-thirty and may not be ready for sleep, but are happy to snuggle in bed with their Dennis the Menace *annuals and their reading lights on.*
Maggie, carer and mother to seven-year-old twins Josh and Paddy

You have to be firm, and enforce a bed time. There's no point in asking, 'Are you tired yet, sweetie?' because they'll always say no. Our kids' bed time crept later and later – now they only get pocket money if they've settled to sleep or are at least quiet by nine pm, all week. We use a star chart. My boyfriend and I need time to talk to each other without the kids around, earwigging and firing questions.
Paula, full-time mother to Georgie, seven, and James, six

They make us throw adult tantrums

The day after my angry outburst over my son's bleeding head, J returns from his course and examines my foot and ankle. I have an anger injury. This is far worse than a drinking injury in that no boozy night out – in fact, nothing remotely pleasurable – was involved. In an act of great benevolence, J goes out for Nurofen, Ralgex and an ankle support. It's made from cotton, nylon, rubber and Spandex, is the colour of waterproof plaster and hardly the kind of saucy attire I had in mind for our looming Cornish holiday. While I tried on a new swimsuit in Oasis, the girl in the adjoining changing room yelped: 'God, this bikini makes me look really thin!' I, on the other hand, will be sporting a super-sexy rubber ankle support, and stinking of Ralgex.

I'm never proud of throwing what can only be termed an Adult Tantrum. This tends to happen as I try to chivvy my two sons into their school uniforms, and my daughter into anything which isn't blatantly pyjama-ish. The clock's ticking, and I keep glimpsing school-bound kids trooping past our gate. One son is upstairs, hunting for his monkey-with-Velcro-paws. His brother is idly stirring a glass of water with his toothbrush.

Usually, I'll keep it together – just do some Mutley-style teeth-gnashing – and we'll just be late for school, and so what? My kids won't be expelled. But on one particular morning, my lid truly flips: one minute, all you can hear is the gentle tinkle of toothbrush in glass. The next, I'm flinging school shoes (they hit the wall) and raging in a most unphotogenic manner. I'm only like this with the kids – never with J. There's no point: we have such different arguing styles that to lose it with my beloved would be totally unsatisfying. The most dramatic thing I ever did was throw a baby vest at him. When I'm mad at J, I want some shouting back – not for him to calmly start making a sandwich.

With my kids, I can't help going loopy occasionally. I'm horrible: a frothy-mouthed monster who throws size thirteen Clark's shoes at a person who only comes up to my chest. When they're teenagers my kids will probably divorce me, like feisty Hollywood actresses do. I prefer to forget that it has happened so, hopefully, my children will forget about it too. But my daughter remembers. 'Mum had a tantrum,' she announces loudly in her nursery's reception area. 'She threw Sam's shoe and started crying!'

'Hahaha,' I manage, before fleeing for home to splash water on to my smouldering face.

* On a real arse of a day when, as my friend Fliss puts it, 'You feel yourself unravelling, like a piece of old knitting', you can do worse than log on to one of these parenting sites:

* **www.babycentre.co.uk** A wealth of into for the very early years.

* **www.ivillage.co.uk** The fattest women's magazine you can imagine – online. All the usual mag stuff: relationships, celebs, health, sex, a vast parenting section, plus lots of fellow parents to have a natter with.

* **www.mumsnet.com** My absolute favourite. Start a 'thread' (conversation) and you'll be inundated with advice and feedback. Everything is discussed here – from philandering partners to what to cook for tea and why someone's child might have developed a cheesy head. Like most highly pleasurable things, it's horribly, horribly addictive.

I threw a wobbler after swimming when Freddie refused to get dressed until he'd checked every locker for abandoned 20p pieces. I was roaring at him in our cubicle when

*another child piped up, 'Why is that lady being horrible
to that boy?' I was so ashamed.*
Adele, a painter and mum to Freddie, six, and Raffy, four

*It's unrealistic to say that children should never be exposed
to anger. Jill and I row in front of them occasionally – it's
not ideal, but it's okay as long as they see us making up.
And yes, we do shout at the kids. Adults get angry and they
should experience that. I don't want them falling to pieces
at school the first time someone raises their voice at them.*
Billy, photographer and dad to Petra, four, and Harry, three

*I always try to compensate for being horrible by being
extra-nice. So I'll shout at the kids on the way home from
school, then make them pancakes with Nutella and let
them stay up late. It's confusing for them, exhausting
for me.*
Jenny, midwife and mum to Kirsty, six, and Samuel, three

When they're finally in bed, they wake up

Our kids are suffering a flurry of nightmares. I suspect that
this disturbing phase is loosely connected to a recent incident
at Glasgow's UGC cinema. Despite the fact that J had taken
our three to see the mildly scary (ie, Disney-scary) *Haunted
Mansion*, what they witnessed instead was a slew of trailers for
non-nipper-friendly movies, ranging from *Shaun of the Dead*
(faintly disturbing to a seven-year-old) to *Gothika*. (Driving
through country roads on a wild stormy night, driver sees small
child in the road with her head turned away and you just know,
when she looks up, that her face will be NOT AT ALL NICE . . .
and you're right! She's not a sweet little child but some vengeful

spirit with horrible opaque eyes and pointy teeth . . . *mammeee!*)

Then the main feature starts. It's not *Haunted Mansion*. It's *Dawn of the Dead*. Opening scene: a hospital, with someone's leg dangling out of an ambulance. So far, so bearable. However, as it's been preceded by the *Gothika* trailer, our kids are truly freaked. One of our sons is trying to climb inside J's jumper. Parents are leaving the cinema, demanding to know what's going on. Young kids accompanied by older siblings are wandering about in confusion.

To be fair, it's an unfortunate mistake (*Haunted Mansion* is the only kids' movie showing that day) and the cinema's manageress does her best to appease angry parents. *Dawn of the Dead* is stopped, and *Haunted Mansion* begins – but the *Gothika* trailer is still showing in our kids' heads and so J has to usher them out, and cheer them up with sweets and comics.

And so the bad dreams kick in. I don't know if children's nightmares are nastier than ours, but they certainly have a different effect. An adult wakes up, thinks, 'Ugh! I was doing something unspeakable with Paul Daniels, thank God it was only a dream', and slips back into slumber. The child wakes up shouting and pelts towards the parental bed, ranting about some terrible beast or not being allowed to go to Disneyland Paris. You can't shoo him away, not when he's wet-eyed and trembling. So you budge up to make room for him.

By now, he should be snuggling in, and falling asleep instantly. But he wants warm milk, toast, a spit-roasted boar with an apple in its mouth and – despite the fact that he's barely four feet tall – ninety per cent of the bedspace. He complains, 'I don't have any covers.' (Yes you do – in your own room, approximately twelve feet from here.) He's too hot, too cold, and unimpressed by your thin pillow. Dad's too snorey. 'You breath smells bad,' he retorts. 'Clean your teeth.'

Small children have the gall to charge into your private

boudoir, uninvited, then complain about the standard of accommodation. It's on a par with a burglar leaving a rude note, complaining that he didn't think much of your CD collection. And when you wake up, foul of temper and unable to twist your neck, the nightmare sufferer is sleeping blissfully and will lie in for a further two hours.

Some parents welcome this cosy co-sleeping arrangement. They buy or construct a massive bed – the Family Bed – which appeals to earth-mommyish tendencies until everyone's sleep-deprived and one of the adults starts kipping in a single spare bed, or on the sofa. I do have doubts about the Family Bed's appeal when adults seem so eager to sneak out of it.

Since *Dawn of the Dead*, I've been fantasising about another sort of bed: not a Family Bed, but one which is simply child-free. On the rare occasions when no infants gatecrash our bed, J and I wake up feeling ridiculously well-rested, like we've enjoyed a fortnight's holiday without the hassle of packing or encountering biting insects.

And I do feel sorry for my freaked-out kids. Thirty-two years after the actual event, I can still recall my own vivid nightmare in which a wet hairy paw repeatedly slapped my bedroom window. I fear that, in our house at least, the *Gothika* trailer will run and run.

Here's what other parents have suggested to keep the kids out of the adults' bed:

We bought a little plug-in nightlight and made sure Evie's feet were uncovered by bedclothes to stop her night terrors. A friend recommended this, and it worked.
Jacqueline, gift shop owner and mother to Evie, three, and Benjamin, eighteen months

Luke went through a nightmare phase a year ago. We .

bought him a cuddly Sully from Monsters Inc to 'guard'
him at night time. Now, if he has a bad dream, I calm
him down, we talk about it, then I magic it away by
rubbing his forehead. It's nice to know that your kid still
thinks you have super-mummy powers.
Jana, OU tutor and mother to Luke, five

They hate us doing things which don't involve them

One of my sons, who attends at least two parties a month
(compared to our average of three per decade), is feeling dread-
fully hard done by. Mickey is his friend too, so why can't he come
to Mickey's fiftieth birthday party? 'It's a grown-up party,' I explain.

'But why?' he asks.

'Because . . . it'll go on really late.' *Because there'll be lots*
of red wine, and you really don't want to witness your parents'
behaviour after lots of red wine. And . . . we want to go by ourselves.

Sometimes, you just don't want to be around your kids. Surely
this is a perfectly normal and healthy state of affairs. However,
like most parents, I'm plagued by persistent low-level guilt. It
revs up a notch every time my daughter spies the chunky white
straps of my unfetching sports bra and asks: 'Are you going for
a run?' Then she pulls her gloomy guilt-making face, and says
in a very small, eerily polite voice, 'I hope you enjoy it.'

And here's another injury story: J and I leave the kids
with my dad, and stay at Mickey's party till five am. Later, on
post-party day, I realise that my toe has turned a rather startling
hue – ranging from purple to palest green – and puffed up to
twice its normal size. It's horrible, like something you might find
pickled in a jar in a cobweb-strewn laboratory. My children
clamour around it, saying, 'Ew.'

'No more running for you,' my daughter announces.

'Or dancing,' smirks J. My mother, an ex-nurse, shows up and pronounces it 'septic'. She returns from the chemist with magnesium sulphate paste which comes in a little white pot with a label which reads: DRAWING OINTMENT FOR BOILS AND CARBUNCLES.

If I'd stayed home, caring for my infants instead of drinking and dancing, this would never have happened.

They can't sit on their backsides and eat their dinner

We are frequently bombarded with research findings reporting that family mealtimes are good for us. If only we could force everyone to occupy the same table, and consume nutritionally-balanced meals, we'd all get along famously. Let's look at the reasons why family mealtimes are, supposedly, a cure for all ills, and see what actually happens.

Research finding: family dinners encourage children to eat more healthily.

Reality: Occasionally, J and I have forced everyone to sit down and enjoy a Sunday meal together, expecting that our sons will compliment the chef on perfectly cooked carrots. There will be no pained expressions, as if the meal consists of dead rodents with horse manure dressing.

However, there are very good reasons why most sensible adults avoid family mealtimes and would, if it were possible, wolf down their dinners in separate time zones from their offspring. For one thing, there's the actual eating bit. You'd think that children – who regularly pollute their insides by licking climbing frames, and eating sweets they've found in the road –

216

would enjoy shovelling good things into their mouths. Recently, one of my sons reported that he was on a diet. Where had this drivel come from? He is seven years old, and weighs less than one of my thighs. Rather worrying, at least five times during our jolly family meal, he employs the effective avoidance tactic of going to the loo. Clearly, 'needing the toilet' is a contagious condition, as three-fifths of my family members are now jammed into the bathroom.

Research finding: children learn better table manners when they eat with adults.
Reality: Once everyone has been dragged back from the loo, a curious swapping session takes place. Desirable morsels are swiped from adults' plates, and horrible stuff – ie, anything which requires mild chewing before it can be consumed – is deposited on top of my dinner. Amazingly, and although I've almost finished my meal, there appears to be more food on my plate than I started with.

One of my sons says, 'Please may I leave the table?' (good), after consuming a fragment of chicken the size of an eyelash (bad). His brother is bounding back and forth from the fridge to hack chunks from a block of Cheddar, despite the fact that several hours have been put into this meal's production. No one is using cutlery, apart from to rap on the table to attract attention over the relentless din.

Research finding: in households where families eat together, children achieve greater academic success.
Reality: No one wishes to sit next to the youngest member of our family. There is much swapping of seats, and a chair is knocked over. I cannot figure out how any of this will encourage our sons to try harder at maths.

Research finding: family mealtimes encourage more effective communication.

Reality: J tells one son off for yacking too much at the table. But isn't that the whole point – to talk, and have discussions? I figure that now is a good time to address a sensitive school-related issue. The conversation goes like this.

Me: How was school last week?

Son one: She took my drink! I don't want to sit next to her. Take her away.

Daughter: I didn't.

Me: Where am I supposed to take her? She *lives* here.

Son one: Get rid of her.

Son two: Yeah, it was great before she was born. We had peace then.

Me: You don't mean that. She's your sister and you love –

Son two: What *is* this?

Me: Broccoli. You've had it millions of times before and loved it.

Son two: It's disgusting.

Daughter: It's bum.

Partner: Stop talking! Just eat!

At this point I snatch my plate – by now the meal's cold, as appetising as a slab of batter dropped on the pavement outside the chippie – and finish my meal in my workroom. It's a little cave of a room, whiffing faintly of sewage, in which every surface teeters with unattended-to paperwork. I feel rather stupid in here: like the child who's thrown a tantrum, then wishes she hadn't, and isn't sure how to make everything happy and lovely again. Back in the kitchen, J tips everyone's dinners into the bin.

Daughter is hungry. Wants biscuit.

Sometimes, they won't eat anything . . .

. . . according to my friend Marla who, during house renovations, came across an old notebook in which she'd written her hopes and thoughts about motherhood. Her daughter Lottie is now ten. I should point out that, as a toddler, Lottie was a terribly picky eater, which drove Marla to distraction.

I must have started the notebook – a big, red, shiny affair – when Lottie was about two and I was really depressed. I was struggling with the reality of being at home with her all the time. Having worked as a freelance writer for years, I was used to my days being entirely my own. I envied the friends who had to go back to work after having their kids – while feeling doubly bad, because I knew they envied me.

The stress of it all manifested itself in Lottie's refusal to eat. Certain friends, and our health visitor, told me it was her trying to exert her control. I refused to believe a child so young could be that devious – if she wanted love, wouldn't it have been easier to comply than make me so mad that I once threw her highchair tray across the room?

Although Lottie was a decent size, our GP referred us to a children's dietician who suggested keeping the notebook so we could be sure about what Lottie was actually eating. The book breaks my heart now. There's no doubt that Lottie survived on very little food, but it's my own attitude that makes me weep. Every morsel is written down neatly: 'Breakfast – Cornflakes with milk in rabbit bowl. Ate two spoonfuls before crying and pushing bowl away. Mid-morning – half banana while being read a story. Lunch – home-made fish pie with steamed vegetables. Wouldn't try it, cried. Had two cherry tomatoes.'

Some days were marked 'good day' when she'd perhaps had a banana and a piece of cheese. On others, you could practically see my tears staining the page. I was convinced that I must be doing something wrong, and if I could just find the right 'key' – novelty cutlery, a new bowl, eating with friends, eating in the garden – the problem would be sorted. But nothing worked. I remember being crushed when I heard that the health visitor had told my friend, 'She just wants the perfect baby.'

Gradually, Lottie started to eat and the pressure eased. In the back of the book are lists, written at the suggestion of the dietician, doctor, health visitor, whoever: lists of why I wanted to be a mum, what I enjoyed about it, what I found difficult. It's painful reading. Also, more sweetly, are long lists of things we could do together – everything from sponge painting to building an obstacle course or den in the garden and making a pretend shop in the kitchen. I so wanted everything to be 'right'.

When I look back now, although I'm not proud of my feelings from that time, I realise that I did manage to hold it together, and ease off Lottie (and myself) eventually. And I did become a good mum. At least, good enough for me, and for Lottie, and that's what counts.

. . . or let us use the telephone

Children under ten cannot abide the horrific sight of a Parent on the Telephone. It causes them to grope for the wire, with the intention of yanking it out of the wall, while shouting, 'I want juice! Where's my dinosaur book?' over and over. Children will even harm themselves to nab adult attention. One time, when I was yacking happily to my friend Fliss, my son speared his forehead with the metal sticky-out bit of his bedroom lock and had to be driven to hospital for stick-on stitches.

A cordless phone enables a parent to stride away from a barrage of questions and wants; I have been known to run through the house, still yabbering on the phone, with a bunch of children in hot pursuit. Late night emailing is, perhaps, more relaxed, if rather risky. (I have had to ban myself from emailing *anyone* when I'm drunk, as the tendency is to become hideously sentimental: 'I just love you *so much* . . . most wonderful person alive . . . without you I'd be nothing . . .' etc etc.)

You might think that mobiles are the answer. Here's the scam: install yourself on a park bench while your children lash each other with sticks. Yet there's even more potential for injury away from the sanctuary of home. Parks have water features, spiky railings, discarded bottles still half full of cider. And it doesn't do much for your image as a fabulous parent, does it? You should be chasing your kids round the park, being a big bear, or at least helping them to identify different species of fern. Instead, you're resting your delicate rump on a chipped round-about and yawning, 'So did you go for the square or pointy toed boot in the end?'

Maybe this is a female issue. Men do not seem to mind a lack of contact with distant friends. They leave emails unanswered, answerphone messages unplayed. Virtually every woman I know spends at least one fifth of her life huddled over the PC or scrawling thank you notes for her child's birthday presents, just to make sure she doesn't offend anyone. Child-rearing creates enough paperwork for a full-time secretary.

It's so much simpler for J. He sends one Christmas card per year (to his mother – actually, no, *I* send a card to his mother!) and, on the rare occasion that he wishes to communicate with a friend, stalks swiftly to my workroom and bangs the door shut. The phone conversation is conducted with no infants twanging the wire or smearing Marmite on his trousers. I hear laughter from in there, plus a lengthy debate about some obscure album mentioned in *Mojo*. J emerges fifty-five minutes later, during which time I have resorted to some hideous potion-making enterprise with the children, requiring perfectly decent foodstuffs to be blended together to make vomit. 'So what did Craig have to say?' I enquire.

'Nothing,' he says.

They're obsessed with Portaloos

I just had to squeeze this in somewhere. My kids *love* Portaloos. They pile in together, flush the loo umpteen times, bang the door open and shut. Portaloos are their gods.

They're so boysy . . . and girlie

It's a chilly autumn afternoon. A friend and I are watching our kids fling bits of stick into the river that runs through our local park. Her two girls are happy to watch things float, and have 'boat races'. Soon, a small cluster of other children and parents have joined in. My boys soon tire of this game, and jump *into* the river – fully-clothed – and fling slimy green weed at each other. 'God,' my friend mutters, 'aren't boys hard work?'

Boys certainly have a bad rep these days, but are they actually harder to bring up? Another friend, who is pregnant and has two boys, has just paid £85 for an extra scan to find out the sex of her baby. She says that, if it's a boy, she needs 'time to get my head around it'. On scan day she eyes the monitor and later says, 'It's okay. The boys will play together and have similar interests and we won't need to buy any new clothes for this one for years and it's fine, really.' Then she donates her collection of 1970s Barbies to the Bethnal Green Museum of Childhood.

Things (some) boys like to do, by the Editor-in-Chief of Sweeping Generalisations:

* Pee into rivers, marvelling at the sparkling arc they make.

* Wallop each other with sticks.

* Twang their bits.

* Push their willies between their legs and shout, 'Look, I'm a girl!'

* Widdle on the bathroom floor.

* Demand copious cuddles in private, but run away before you can plant a kiss at the school gate.

* Be driven at great speed to A&E.

Young boys tend to move around more and make noise. Girls seem to find it easier to exhibit the kind of behaviour which helps them to get on at school, and make life easier for teachers.
Tim Kahn, primary teacher and author of *Bringing Up Boys*

I grew up with a sister and had no experience of boys. They can be bloody stressful. Josh constantly has bumps on the forehead and bleeding knees. But their energy and

good humour rub off on you. They're not as moody as girls. You're forced to immerse yourself in their world.
Donna, part-time art teacher and mother to Johnny, eight, and Jack, four

Paul and the boys love heading out on bikes and playing football or getting up to stuff with penknives. I can feel shut out from that world. But if there are problems with school or friends, or if they're embarrassed because they've wet the bed, it's me they come to.
Sally, clerical worker and mother to Ben, six, and Daniel, four

If we expect boys to be rowdy and difficult, they will be. We tend to pass on our assumptions that boys should only play 'manly' games rather than talking and empathising with others – as girls are allowed and encouraged to do.
Tim Kahn again

It's a big help if you adopt a curious attitude – of wanting to learn and understand about a boy's world. Little boys learn to love from their mothers. Be kind and warm, and enjoy him.
The fine art of boy-raising according to psychologist and author Steve Biddulph (my hero)

Whatever their sex, they worship men

Certain high-profile dads have been talking about how fathering is deemed less important than mothering. While they may have a point, children at least recognise that men are vitally important. Children love men *so much*. In their small world, populated by predominantly female nursery and primary

224

teaching staff, women are all over the bloody place. (If one parent is at home part or full-time, it is still far more likely to be the mother, and if that woman is to stay halfway sane, she will meet up with other women in similar set-ups.)

No wonder kids go gaga for men. My friend Ella's partner is so popular with their kids that a rota has been set up to determine whose turn it is to sit next to Paul (the problem being that he has three children and only two sides). When he is due to come home, his two sons and daughter sit on the fence, gazing at the road, *willing* his car to turn the corner.

Even foul-tempered, scary-looking (male) bastards are revered. My children still talk fondly about Mr Rose, the sinister owner of our holiday cottage near Padstow in Cornwall. With his blood-stained head bandage, and enormous bulging stomach encased in filthy shirt, he was the stuff of nightmares, the storybook baddie – whom our children adored, and tried to clamber all over in order to stuff sweetie wrappers into his shirt pockets.

Men wear their grumpiness more openly and dramatically than women do. J roars: 'I will rattle your arse!' My mutterings of 'being disappointed', and suggestions that 'you could set a better example for your sister' lack drama and go virtually unnoticed. Meanwhile, J can delight our offspring with threats of 'a good beating with the spikey stick' – just a joke, of course, which makes them laugh their pants off. Sometimes I think, for twenty-four hours or so, I'd love to have dangling genitalia.

They don't give a stuff if we're ill

Children are terribly unsympathetic to adult illness. You can ooze flu symptoms, barely able to remain upright. Do your kids insist you lie down and create a suitably tranquil atmosphere by quietly colouring in? No, they do not. Your fuddled brain must engage in the construction of a Hot Wheels drive-thru McDonald's, swiftly followed by an excursion to the aforementioned soft play centre which they don't even enjoy.

They love opening and shutting the fridge door so they can watch the little light go on and off

Other things kids do when they're doing nothing:

* Swing on curtains

* Bang doors

* Lie on the sofa, kicking idly

* Whine

* Poke each other

* Turn taps on too hard and spray themselves

* Nibble their bogies

They love gardens . . .

. . . but are seized by an urge to destroy them. On the final weekend of the summer holidays, as a sort of finale if you like, my kids charge through my mother's borders, wrecking the plants which she has nurtured from seed. Her garden, once a fine example of what can be achieved when one's children have flown the nest, now looks severely ravaged and results in a prolonged telling-off as we drive home, plus a PlayStation/

Gameboy/pretty much everything ban until 2015, when my sons will be old enough to leave home and trash their own nasturtiums.

They are determined to take the house out into the garden . . .

Children often refuse to play outside without hauling a vast assortment of blankets, cushions and even duvets on to the lawn.

. . . and bring the garden into the house

Here they come with their handfuls of soil and worms and curious-looking beetles to scatter all over our living room. Why can't they just leave things where they're supposed to be?

Some kids are even more out of control than our own

Rude Kid and his parents come to stay for a weekend. Rude Kid looks like a Quentin Blake drawing with his wizened little face – all of Roald Dahl's naughty characters rolled into one peevish Coke-demanding five-year-old boy. 'Ah want COKE!' he roars at seven-forty-five am, on spying Rebel Dad's secret stash in the fridge. 'No,' his mother says firmly. Rude Kid cries some more, and is given Coke, plus about eight teaspoons of sugar on his cereal. My kids stare at the crystalline mountain, licking their lips.

When his scrambled egg turns out to be 'the wrong colour' (what colour should it be? Purple? White with a hint of pistachio?), Rude Kid screams and throws himself to the floor. Even when the offending food has been scraped into the bin, he continues to holler because he can still *smell* 'the wrong colour egg' on his plate.

I feel bad even mentioning this child because his parents are great friends of ours. I hate seeing them so down-trodden, fretting that scrambled egg might turn out to be the wrong shade, their lives ruled by a tyrannical horror who can't weigh more than four stones. I even say I'd love them to come again. To avoid upsetting our friends I have, of course, concealed the child's identity. But really there's no need, because Rude Kid doesn't allow his parents to read books (apart from his books).

At some point they learn to look after themselves

Our friends are having a major night out and ask if their son can stay over. Josh is fifteen and appears to be permanently attached to a lozenge-shaped lump of board. Occasionally he murmurs mysterious terms such as 'ollie 360'. He is adult-sized, yet not quite properly grown-up. He is a very mysterious creature.

To tell the truth, I am worried about being held responsible for Josh. Who knows what this near-adult might be capable of? Our friends tell us he'll be out skateboarding with his mates and will show up at bed time. But who *are* these mates? When *is* his bed time? 'Don't worry,' our friends reassure us. 'Josh can look after himself.' This I cannot get my head around. This notion that, at some magical point, children will look after themselves and no longer need us to check that they've wiped their bums properly. When will this happen in our family, and how old will I be? A hundred and six?

Josh shows up at our house at nine-fifteen pm without the need for frantic torchlit searches or any involvement from the police. I've stocked up on various savoury snacks in Day-Glo packets but he doesn't want them. He doesn't need a drink. He's not keen on reading a Sunday supplement, and he certainly doesn't want a magic painting book.

It's hard to know how to handle a person who doesn't need anything. Small people's demands – 'More juice! Wrong cup!' – keep you so busy that before you know it, the day's over and you're trying to ram the cork into a bottle of wine with a knife. Josh just wants to watch TV. His mastery of the remote enables him to flip constantly while accessing all manner of interactive wizardry – stuff I didn't even know it could do. Heaven knows what he'd get up to if allowed near my computer. There it sits: a whopping heap of shimmering technology, capable of doing my shopping, accounts and access any music I might wish to hear, and it's treated like a gigantic beige typewriter.

Right now, however, I'm wondering if Josh's impeccable behaviour is a devious cover-up for the wildness underneath. He does look pretty eager when Slipknot appear on telly in their rubber fetish wear. 'Oh, I love them,' I enthuse.

Josh just yawns in my face and says, 'I'm off to bed. School tomorrow.'

'But it's only half-ten!' I protest.

'Night-night,' says our guest. I feel utterly cheated. Having Josh to stay brings it home to me that, at some point, our own children will stop fearing the doctor, and no longer slither under the cubicles at the swimming pool, and will virtually look after themselves.

Why doesn't this fill me with joy?

11

you're still a couple, honest

Why adults need to go out after dark • wanted: obliging, trustworthy babysitter • who'll invite boys round and drink all your drink • who says romance is dead? • the adult birthday: what a mother really wants (clue: not a dustbin) • sex: should you make the effort, or just not bother? • what happens to long-term couples • how I tried to rev up our sex life • why parents can't help scoring points (and I'm owed 378 lie-ins)

When the children were younger and we went out for the evening, it was a relief to get back and discover that nothing terrible had happened. We're far less anxious these days. Going out makes us feel human again. My heart sinks if there's a baby at the next table in the restaurant.
Robin, father to Jo, seven, Emma, five, and Toby, four

Being out can feel odd at first, especially when you haven't done it for ages. You lose the habit. You need to switch off and realise it's just the two of you again. The

*more often you do it, the more natural and enjoyable
it feels.*
Robin's partner Lucy

*David and I go out so rarely that it can feel like an
anti-climax. It's bound to when you've looked forward to
it so much.*
**Annette, aromatherapist and mother to Tilly, four and Rowan,
eighteen months**

*Going out in the evening is a bit like sex. Once you've
done it, you feel really pleased with yourself, and remember
that it can be quite fun.*
My anonymous friend (and a full-time mother of three)

J and I were out together, after dark. Our sons, then two, were
in the care of our sixteen-year-old babysitter and her best friend.
We had left our mobile and J's pager numbers, the number
of the restaurant, and detailed instructions on the care of
our offspring.

And it was lovely being out together. We sat opposite each
other, our telephonic equipment winking at us like a heap of
giant eyeballs. 'We should do this more often,' I said. In fact, I'd
been worrying that we were in danger of becoming consumed
by our children and, as a counsellor might put it, 'neglecting
the adult relationship'. ('What adult relationship?' J asked. 'You
know – me and you.' 'Oh, that.')

So there we were – having *couple time*. This is a relatively
modern concept. As a child, I recall only one incident of
being looked after by a babysitter, and being flung into a state
of high excitement by her stack of *Jackie* magazines and habit
of wearing eyeliner inside her eyelids. In contrast, modern
parents are panting to get out of the house. Yet it's not quite as

simple as calling the charming and trustworthy sitter who loves your children so much she'll have them pinging their Duplo at her until midnight, all for £3.50. For one thing, if it's been quite a stretch since you last went out, it can feel rather . . . weird.

After our meal, J and I had wound up in the back room of a shabby pub stuffed with fourteen-year-olds, all snogging each other enthusiastically.

'Isn't this great?' I roared over the music.

'What?' J yelled back.

'I said, isn't it fantastic, being out?'

'*What?*'

We checked our mobiles for missed calls and grinned at each other. We wanted to go home, but would have felt foolish, showing up at nine-thirty. I suggested that J called home, just to check that everything was okay. 'Take your mobile outside,' I ordered. 'You might not be able to get a signal in here.' J stood outside the pub just long enough for the drizzle to seep through his jacket.

He sloped back in. 'So where shall we go on holiday this year?' I shouted. He fancied Scotland; ie, where we live. I favoured Majorca. We started squabbling about it. One of the juvenile snoggers started sniggering, then glimpsed my teary face and pregnant belly and looked quite disgusted. It's much better, I think, to go out as often as you can manage, so it feels normal, and not some once-a-season opportunity to spurt out weeks' worth of gripes and hurtle out of the pub with a wet blotchy face.

It's very common to row in this kind of situation. When you're out together and drinking, you're seduced into feeling comfortable. Defences diminish. Finally, you have uninterrupted time together and no longer have to keep up a pretence that everything's okay.
Sue Maxwell, spokesperson for Couples Counselling Scotland

Wanted: lovely, obliging, trustworthy babysitter

Babysitting is a pretty thankless and sometimes horrific job. As a teen babysitter myself, I was prone to snooping in cupboards and drawers. (Ha! Just as I thought! Cutlery.) Unfortunately, any pleasure I may have derived from prying was sabotaged by Devil Spawn, my four-year-old charge. The minute his parents had hared down the path, whooping and cheering and stuffing fags into their mouths, he'd bound out of bed, rip up his colouring book into a thousand pieces, and bellow: 'AM GONNA SHOOT YOU DEAD.'

'Now, now,' I'd say, meekly.

'Fuck off!' trilled Devil Spawn, before threatening to fling himself over their fancy gallery.

No wonder his parents looked so pleased to be going out. I started to worry that they might never come back, and weren't really heading for an Italian restaurant, but the airport. When they did show up, I reassured them that Devil Spawn and I had had a lovely time; yes, I'd be happy to babysit again. Then I snatched my fiver, pelted home, and had a big swig of Gordon's from my parents' drinks cabinet.

Is it any wonder that willing, reliable babysitters can be so hard to come by? Even parents with impeccably behaved kids can hit sitter problems.

We returned home to find our daughter's buggy overturned in the herbaceous border. Our sixteen-year-old sitter confessed that her friends had popped by and given each other rides in it.
Muriel, social worker and mother to Kit, five, and Molly, one

We'd just moved into our small town. A babysitter whom we hardly knew was in sole charge of our three children.

233

She was nineteen, came highly recommended, and had brought a whopping pile of college work to keep her occupied.

We came home half an hour early. An unfamiliar male – who was clearly unhappy to see us – levitated from our sofa, almost dropping his bottle of Grolsch. On TV was one of those movies in the Porkies genre. In a case of terrible timing, two characters started to engage in extremely noisy sex. Later, my husband muttered: 'We'll never go out again.'
Helen, full-time mother to Felix, eight, Daphne, four, and Imogen, two

Our babysitter sprang out of our bedroom, babbling, 'Hi! I was just. I was, er, just-just-just . . .' Obviously she'd been having a rummage about. I was pretty flattered by this – that this gorgeous young girl thought that a couple of clapped-out, sleep-deprived parents might have anything remotely interesting in their bedroom.
Simone, full-time mother to Luca, three, and Evie, twenty months

Don't let these experiences put you off. While your parents or in-laws may not reside in the next street (for that, you may be truly thankful), there are ways to sniff out a willing and able sitter. In other words, no excuse for not going out.

Local friendly teenager.
They're not all intent on romping about with their boyfriends or stealing your drink. Some may be keen to rake in some cash while watching your telly, which means they're probably available at short notice. Disadvantages? The teen sitter is invariably slender, with the complexion of a baby, and wears clothes designed to

flash her taut tummy. Plus, even the sweetest, most wholesome babysitter will snigger over your antique Van Morrison records and the big damp bra draped over the radiator.

When our sitter arrives, my own clothes deteriorate instantly, as if they've been gleaned from the bottom of a skip. Her dinky bag reveals a lot about her lifestyle: tiny, with room for just lipstick, purse and phone. Even when I'm off out for the evening, I tend to haul along a sack-like bag stuffed with dribbling juice cups, spare age 4–5 trousers and some sinister brown speckled disc which might once have been salami.

Babysitting circle.

These usually work on an 'exchange' system, either informally, or with the earning and spending of tokens; ie, you help out others in the circle, and they'll babysit your kids. On the plus side, this method is free, and the other adults (being local parents) are likely to be familiar to your children. Some highly organised circles operate online, putting like-minded parents in touch and emailing all member families to see who's available. Others are no more formal than one gagging-to-get-out mother issuing sheets of participants' phone numbers.

The disadvantage is that you're required to return the favour – although some parents (myself included) are happy to scamper out to someone's house on the occasional week night, particularly if their children obligingly fall asleep by seven pm.

Babysitting agency.

Pricey, but guilt-free. Some agencies charge quarterly membership fees, and the sitter is paid by the hour. A real bonus is that she'll want to zoom off as quickly as possible – not hang about, sipping tea – which is just what you want when you're pulling your I'm-not-drunk face.

We use a mish-mash of other parents who live nearby,
and an agency babysitter. Yes, it costs, but you're not
obliged to spend your valuable Friday or Saturday nights
at someone else's house, returning the favour, or dealing
with friends who never offer to sit for you.
Johanna, health visitor and mother to Keir, five, and Morgan,
two

Who says romance is dead?

I forced Lola to tell me this, as she thinks it's 'highly embarrassing'. During a babysitter drought, she and her boyfriend
Jed decided to make Fridays sacred. No taking phonecalls, no
blobbing out on sofa, picking at each other's spots. He'd bring
home special food and cook her a meal – that particular kind
of man-cooking which involves everything being sizzled on the
hob. She'd assist by, er, watching him from her stool in the kitchen,
and drinking wine. Being a kind of Creative Director of Dinner.
She says: 'It's become our way of catching up with each other
at the end of the week, and chilling out, knowing we don't have
to get up for work in the morning.' J and I tried this. I even
dressed up, but felt rather foolish, clomping about our scabby
kitchen in my strappy heels and a clingy Karen Millen dress.

I don't think there's any point in lamenting the fact that
'things aren't like they used to be'. If they were, J and I would
be heading for bankruptcy via the Priory Clinic. Yes, we used
to book airline tickets on the sly, fishing out each other's
passports, wear chafing underwear (the things he did for me
then). We wrote love letters even after we'd moved in together.
Now, if he spotted my handwriting on an envelope, he'd assume
I was communicating via the Royal Mail because we're supposed
to be Not Speaking.

In some ways, I'm relieved that those heady days are over. Take the sharing of baths. If it's so romantic, why are couples so keen to stop doing it? In most households, the bath is conveniently one-person sized. Surely, having a bath is an excuse to be on your own for a bit. You want to stretch out, read the paper, glug wine. The last thing you require is a six-foot male sloshing water about, forcing you to sit at the tap end.

I can't help feeling suspicious of the overtly I'm-*such*-a-romantic male – the kind who wants to feed you strawberries, and keeps pushing succulent morsels into your mouth (if you get my drift). It's one of those little rituals which should be quite alluring – all that licking and nibbling – but in practice just isn't. If J tried to feed me, I'd assume he'd confused me with one of our kids and was concerned that I hadn't eaten enough. I'd then expect him to start growling, 'Think you're leaving the table? I want to see you finish *all* those peas.'

Likewise, the touchy-feely man. Years back, I'd occasionally go out to dinner with a friend called Daniel. Although he'd made it clear that I was the only woman on earth whom he did not wish to shag – bloody charming! – he'd spend much of these evenings tweaking my earlobe, forcing me to jam my back teeth together and a voice to scream in my head: 'PLEASE STOP DOING THAT TO MY EAR.' (The fondled ear would be scarlet. The other one would remain its normal hue. It made me feel terribly lop-sided.) Men like Daniel can make a woman feel pretty relieved that she's shacked up with a sometimes crabby but rather less cheesy individual.

Admittedly, I make zero effort on the romantic front. For a laugh, I did once present J with a Dr Gillian McKeith's Living Food Love Bar, whose ingredients include sarsaparilla root ('regulates the synthesis of sex hormones') and potencywood root (found to 'lessen inhibitions'). The 'wildly grown' foods are blended together with 'unconditional love and light', which gives the impression that the Love Bar is not factory-made, but lovingly created in a remote cottage at the rate of two bars a day.

J assumed a flat voice as he read the wrapper: 'Made with twelve raw superfoods to feed male and female organs.' Oh dear. My silly joke suggested that someone's 'organ' – either his or mine – needed feeding and, by implication, that some vital spark was sorely lacking. We both stared at the rather scary photo on the wrapper of Dr Gillian McKeith, baring her teeth. 'Thanks,' J said. Last time I looked, the Love Bar was jammed in the kitchen drawer along with our mangled takeaway menus and tubes of dried-up Superglue.

The grown-up birthday

My birthday is approaching, and I hope that something exciting might happen, though as yet I'm not sure what that might be. And it's no big deal, is it? At my advanced age you're beyond getting all revved up and excited. You certainly don't rummage in the backs of wardrobes, hoping to glimpse something beautifully wrapped with your name on it.

Even so, it's nice to do *something*. But what? Years back, I might have had a party. Birthdays were such useful occasions: the perfect excuse to prove your popularity and amass loads of presents. You might even have thrown parties on non-birthday occasions, just to cop a snog off someone. You couldn't do something as simple as phone up and ask them out. You had to round up everyone you knew, plus any extras you'd met during the short journey from work to your flat, and watch them stampeding about, grinding fag ends into your rug. It seems a terribly labour-intensive way of getting off with someone.

After house parties came dinner parties. Somehow, these were never as enjoyable as I'd expect them to be. However casually

I behaved, sloshing my cold-pressed extra virgin olive oil about, the whole thing stopped being fun the minute we sat down to eat. We'd all stare at some enormous dollop which had been sizzling in the oven for so long, I couldn't remember what it was supposed to be. I'd want to drink loads, but was aware that six individual crème brûlées were blistering under the grill. I'd want to run away, to escape to the fag machine. But this being my flat, there wasn't one.

Back in the nineties, dinner parties became so competitive. (Think you're flash with your tart tatin? We're doing individual fish tartlets with each person's name stuck on top, in pastry.) Where do you go from here? Flaming desserts? Ice sculptures? Not practical with children in the house. Childbirth wrecks any cooking ability anyway: for the year following our twins' birth, we survived solely on pasta which bubbled merrily for at least an hour and a half, and felt like a mouthful of wet Sellotape.

Maybe now that they're older it's safe to invite friends round for food and loads of wine (which doesn't constitute a dinner party). However, J doesn't fancy this; he still feels fragile after an office party and is, in fact, 'poisoned'.

It seems we won't be over-indulging tonight. So, what *are* we doing?

Please excuse me for a moment while (after extensive talks with every woman-with-child that I know) I slip in this list of . . .

What a mother really wants for her birthday . . .

. . . is the right kind of gift. This is very, very important. It says: How Things Are Between Us. Presents track the peaks and troughs of a relationship. I still recall the birthday morning when I woke up next to my long-term ex to discover zero presents.

Blissfully unaware of his monumental faux pas, he yawned and said, 'I'll pop out to get you something at lunchtime.'

What a mother wants is: *not* something that has been 'popped out' for. A panic-bought feeling decreases one's pleasure by at least fifty per cent. We want something that's been carefully selected from some obscure shop that he's had to look up on the web – and nothing practical, of course. My friend Jane recalls being given an enormous gift from her beloved (most of the women I know still get all panty on receiving Really Big Parcels), only to plummet into a deep depression on discovering it was a tool box. She rummaged through the individual presents stashed in its little compartments, expecting to unearth her 'real' gift. What was this – earrings? Perfume? No, a wrench. A set of drill bits. Her wretched gift completely blighted her thirty-fifth birthday.

Likewise, a relationship of mine was obviously in decline when I bought him a juicer. It was used once, never cleaned quite thoroughly enough and, when we parted, given back to me with a 'This is yours, I think.' That same year, I received a flying lesson from my then-partner; by the time I'd trekked to a little airfield on the outskirts of Watford, we'd broken up. I flew around miserably for half an hour, staring down at flat fields, and hurried home to tell my empty, boyfriend-less flat that it had been 'really great and exciting'.

These days, I love being bought non-practical underwear. J always heads for the same shop; the staff bend over backwards to help him select just the right garment. There are no frosty stares, as if to say: 'We know why you're here, pervo – *and we're calling the police.*' In fact, the first time J went in, the assistants were so charming and attentive – 'and drop-dead gorgeous,' he added – that he said he'd be happy to shop there any time at all. Which was very helpful of him, I thought.

you're still a couple, honest

I started to unwrap this enormous present from Mark. I was so excited until I discovered it was . . . a dustbin. Yes, it was full of champagne – which, as I was pregnant, I couldn't drink – but no amount of goodies stashed inside could take away from the fact that it was a bloody dustbin.
Misha, database analyst and mother to Tasha, five, and Lauren, fourteen months

When you become a parent there's a tendency for your in-laws to buy you practical gifts. Last birthday, three months after I'd given birth to our second child, my mother-in-law gave me a frying pan. I was devastated. My husband told me to forget it and shove it away in a cupboard, but I couldn't get over the fact that I'd become a frying-pan-for-birthday kind of person.
June, full-time mother to Louis, four, and Charlotte, eighteen months

The quality of your present has a direct effect on your sex drive. If he's been really thoughtful, you feel pampered and good about yourself. If my partner gave me some money and told me to go out and buy my own present, I fear that we'd never do it again.
Kim, part-time teacher and mother to Emily, seven

Sex: should you keep doing it, or just not bother?

Reasons to do it:

☆ According to Edinburgh-based neuropsychologist David Weeks, having regular sex can take up to seven years off your appearance.

☆ It's one way of enjoying ourselves without hiring a babysitter.

☆ We're supposed to enjoy sex *more* once we've produced children. Something to do with the heightened blood supply brought to the lower pelvic floor during pregnancy.

☆ We'll sleep better.

☆ Being married or living with a long-term partner, and having children, can all cause a decrease in sex drive. So we have good reason to feel proud if we manage to do it.

Reasons to just go to sleep:

☆ Parents spend large portions of their lives looking for things (car keys, purse, TV remote) and don't have time to figure out where our sex drive's gone.

☆ We learn that, post-childbirth, we can avoid putting pressure on a 'tender perineum' by placing a pillow beneath the bottom during lovemaking. Such nuggets of info hardly have us simmering with desire.

We might wake up the kids. Tabloid headline: 'Children left sobbing while parents romped.'

There's no time. Morning sex is out when your kids wake at six-thirty am. As for sex in the day – yes, babies and toddlers take naps, but are programmed to wake up and start roaring the instant your start having lewd thoughts. In the evenings most parents are too fagged out to expend unnecessary energy. They are certainly not slathering each other with sandalwood or ylang ylang oils.

If you're breastfeeding, the same hormone which floods the body during orgasm also causes your milk to eject. So climax is accompanied by a kind of dual fountain effect.

What happens to long-term couples

Alice, Maggie, Sara and I met as single, badly-behaved flatmates two decades ago. Recently we indulged in a weekend at a swanky Glasgow hotel. In the old days, we would have wrung the mini bar dry and howled over our sexual exploits. This time around, with eight children between us (but not, thankfully, *with* us), we're extremely aroused over the quality of the hotel's complimentary toiletries.

'How often do you and Adam have sex these days?' I ask Maggie.

'Wow, here's a *full-sized* Molton Brown body lotion. It smells delicious. Maybe twice,' she adds, slathering it all over her shoulders.

'Twice?' Sara asks. 'I don't know how you find the time.'

243.

'Or can be bothered,' says Alice, who is reluctant to waste perfectly good bed time for any activity other than viewing American sitcoms or reading interiors magazines.

'No, no,' says Maggie, aghast. 'Twice a *year*.'

'You're joking,' I say.

'Well, it's more often on holiday. Then we might manage it four or five times in a fortnight, which is fun, but I couldn't live like that all year round.'

I'm sure Maggie isn't so unusual. In fact a major survey published by the *Journal of American Medicine* revealed that forty per cent of men and over thirty per cent of women have zero interest in sex. So-called sexperts offer advice such as: 'Set aside a whole evening' for erotic massage. (A whole evening? I hardly think so.) All those gung-ho headlines in women's mags – 'Rekindle that passion!' 'Put sex back on the map!' – sound pretty drastic and, frankly, exhausting.

But does it have to be so bleak? Couples with busier lives than ours enjoy lovely, fulfilling sex and not just on their birthdays. As an eminent psychologist once told me: 'Sexuality is not about youth or the width of your hips; it's about seeing ourselves and each other as sexual creatures, not merely as providers, parents or housekeepers.'

How I tried to rev up our sex life

A review copy of a new sex manual pops through my letterbox. Let's not be cynical and assume it's crammed with the usual creaky advice. The publishers claim that, in the US, this is 'the book that got more than a million couples back in the bedroom'.

It's packed with seduction techniques for both women and men to try – so many quirky ideas, in fact, that I fear J and I have become terribly humdrum in the bedroom. Is this a symptom of long-term relationships? Am I too old and wizened to enjoy being smeared with honey? And what would we say if one of the kids blundered into our bedroom – that I was pretending to be a slice of toast?

At first glance, certain seductions seem simple enough, though I cannot quite picture myself frolicking about our house, wearing only a towel, coaxing J into a chase-me game. Especially when I discover that he should yank off the towel to discover that . . . oh dear, I'm tightly bandaged in cling film. Don't fancy doing yourself up like a shrink-wrapped chicken portion? The author suggests you ask your lover to make a lasso – clearly, a woman is incapable of knotting a rope – and hand it to you so you can, well, lasso him. She suggests that you then set a cake timer – who has one of these? What do they look like? – for five minutes (your time limit for a quickie). If I behaved in this manner, J would gently suggest I've been working too hard, and should arrange a chat with my doctor. Or he'd just move out.

Other seduction techniques are utterly impractical unless you have acres of time (ie, no job or children). For instance: he places a personal ad in the paper, directing you to a florist's, where your blooms are presented to you with a note, asking you to hotfoot it to a lingerie store. Here, you are given a parcel of foxy fripperies, accompanied by a *second* note, inviting you to join him at a motel. What would our three children be up to, while all this was going on? Tied up (by the lasso) to the banisters? The author reckons you should *find* the time to have lots of interesting sex. Like it's that simple. She also believes that, if your offspring witness you and your beloved snuggling and snogging each other, then they'll grow into loving adults themselves. Sorry, but my kids cannot abide J and me kissing each other. Witnessing their parents so much as holding hands is our kids' signal to deliberately pierce themselves with kitchen implements, just to cause a diversion.

In desperation, I read all the women's *and* men's seduction tips, hoping to find a saucy idea that's reasonably unembarrassing, and won't require a complex back-up system involving overnight babysitters, or slapping. It's virtually impossible. Even the pretty humdrum tricks – those not requiring a cheerleader outfit – leave me cold, simply because, whatever I do, J will know it came from a book.

There's a massage technique that's intended for a man to perform on a woman, but I decide to give it whirl. The idea is, your hands merely hover over your partner's back, grazing the tiny hairs. Of course J enjoys it. I don't need a book to tell me than an adult male will enjoy thirty minutes of uninterrupted stroking while lying face down on a bed, dreaming of favourable Motherwell scores.

The following week, J goes away on a conference. The author is keen on dirty phone talk, which always makes me think of women in huge, gravy-stained housecoats, sawing at gnarled toenails with emery boards while gasping, 'Baby, you've got me so hot.' However, I'm pretty desperate by now – I've been instructed by a women's magazine to 'test several techniques' in the book – and call J's mobile. He's full of the joys – on his fourth pint, at a guess – at a picturesque Richmond pub. I'm in drizzly Scotland, shattered after shimmying three children bedwards and having several passers-by shove my broken-down car from its diagonal position across our High Street. 'Going back to your hotel room soon?' I ask in a casual manner.

'No,' he says. 'We'll be out for a few hours yet.' I can hear his colleagues, yacking, laughing and having a wonderful, infant-free time.

'Ring me later,' I say, in what I hope is a suggestive voice. By eleven pm, I've downed a bottle of wine (for Dutch courage) and tried to call his hotel room several times. The receptionist has never heard of him. Sometime at around one am, I'm vaguely aware of the distant peep of my mobile's ringtone. In a fit of pique, I leave it.

Two days later, he's back. I'm up for some special reunion scenario, and plunder the pages for ideas. But the author's over-reliance on props is quite off-putting: wigs, drinking straws, opera-length gloves, mentholated cough sweets, even a toy medical kit. The book's making me tense. I'm stuck, confused, robbed of libido. She's also big on teasing, which I'm all for in a spontaneous kind of way, but she spreads it over several days, suggesting that you leave naughty notes around the house and garage. The *garage?* I can't imagine doing anything remotely pleasurable surrounded by cans of Nitromorse stripper and our lawnmower, reminding us that the grass needs cutting.

By the time J comes home I've even gone off kissing. The problem, I think, lies mainly with the fact that, like every woman I know in her thirties or forties, I'm brim-full of sex advice. It's become as scintillating as the instructions on a bottle of Toilet Duck. Our lives are awash with instructions, the right way to do things; it's why I've never learned to programme our video, or set the central heating timer so it goes on and off when we want, rather than subjecting us to furnace-like, or Arctic conditions, twenty-four hours a day. The author is, of course, quite right in that variety is a wonderful thing. Who doesn't wish to be seduced in a highly erotic manner? I'd just rather he dreamed it up all by himself.

Kids can sabotage your sex life if you let them. Ours are old enough now to get up on their own on a Saturday morning, come downstairs, pour bowls of cereal and put on a video, while we stay in bed. The kitchen's a bombsite with milk and Cheerios sloshed everywhere, but it's worth it.
Jess, hair salon owner and mother to Caitlin, eight, and Ross, seven

Why I'm owed 378 lie-ins

After the birth of our twins I stumbled upon a new way of negotiating with J. It went this way: he had spent three baby-free
hours floating around Tower Records. Only fair, then, that I
should be allowed a night out with friends plus an opportunity
to recover the following morning, with infants removed from
the house.

This scoring system invaded our daily lives. I'd keep a mental
tally of J's lie-ins (380) versus mine (2). Such tactics were
tiresome – all that mental arithmetic – but appeared to be
the only way of wangling some personal space. In granting her
partner permission to go skiing with colleagues, my friend Jill
amassed 'around 360 points' which, in parenting currency, would
neatly convert into a girls' weekend in Dublin.

Before we had children, we simply chose to go out. There was
no negotiating, no need for a tit-for-tat system. And this gaining
and spending of points felt so petty and childish; the assumption
was that fun had to be 'earned' and paid for at a later date. I
once accused J of 'stealing' a Sunday when he somehow wound
up in licensed premises after escorting a friend to Edinburgh
Airport. And what about all those lunch breaks he had at work?
What did he do then? Amble around W.H. Smith, selecting
reading material to fill his copious free time?

Gradually, as the children became slightly more manageable,
our points system fell by the wayside. As one friend pointed out:
'It's a relief to stop all that nonsense. It just makes you feel lowly
and pathetic.'

I couldn't agree more. But I'm still owed 378 lie-ins.

12

how to be perfect

Never shouting, smoking, or being late for school: things
perfect parents do (that we can copy) • some lovely children's books • repetitive brain injury (or: my daughter's
obsession with *Green Eggs and Ham)*
• when you can't be fagged reading • how to look
perfect • my very imperfect day • the day I turned into
Nigella and practically ate myself

No one likes a perfect parent. Look at him – mulling over
which university his 'gifted' six-year-old might eventually go
to. Listen to her – bragging that her daughter, aged three, can
recite the months of the year in the right order (in Spanish).
Top of my hated phrase list are the words: 'Of course, we do a
lot with her,' which, in turn, implies: 'And, clearly, you don't.'
Perfect parents do little for one's self-esteem and are best avoided.

Sometimes, though, I experience an urge to *fake* perfection.
It's fun to at least pretend you're utterly sorted – that raising
small infants is no more taxing than nurturing a houseplant.
With this aim in mind, there follow a dozen things perfect
parents do which we blundering, shop-soiled, refreshingly flawed
individuals can copy.

1 Have spookily clean children . . .

I've never been a fan of immaculate kids. They make me feel nervous – how does he remain so pristine? What does he do all day? – and also pretty slobbish and incompetent, as my own children are usually splattered with some kind of foodstuff or dung. However, I do wish my children looked a little more ironed and groomed occasionally – when their auntie's visiting from Germany, or they're going to a birthday party. My sons tend to tumble straight from the garden, and their woodlouse-terrorising endeavours, to the party without changing or even washing their hands.

When children are filthy, you have three options: leave them in a vile and putrid state, which is absolutely fine as long as you're not expecting anyone to visit; order a complete change of attire, therefore doubling your wash load; or – my preferred method – simply pop another outfit on top of the mucky one, repeating as necessary until your child looks like Michelin man come bed time.

As for dirty faces, the obvious solution is to always carry tissues. But as my pal Helen said: 'Do I really want to be the kind of person who's always spitting on tissues?'

2 . . . who wear gorgeous clothes

Occasionally I yearn to bin the naff and horribly appliquéd clothes my kids love to wear, and to dress them in heart-melting outfits. Here are some sources of lovely kids' stuff.

♥ **Baby Planet** started as a Portobello Market stall and now runs a small site (*www.baby-planet.co.uk*) which sells summer basics from babies to around age six. Everything's very affordable and all tie-dyed using (if these things matter to you) phosphate-free permanent colours so you can feel kind of wholesome and a friend to our planet, while your kids look utterly cute in a Cornish coast kind of way.

♥ **Giant Peach** (*www.giantpeach.co.uk*) focuses on baby-wear (like soft leather Daisy Root shoes – perfect baby presents) plus toddler swimwear, cute printed T-shirts, plus pleasing wooden toys – alphabet letters and book-ends, the kind of bedroom accessories you imagined your kids would have, before you had children and discovered that they only like nasty, noisy plastic things from Woolies.

♥ Check out **Benetton** for bright, funky casual clothes for kids aged two to six. No online shopping, but for store locator visit *www.benetton.com*.

♥ **Monsoon** has the party frock market sewn up – gorgeous, girlie creations with abundant sequins and embroidery (my own daughter favours a more murky palette and would rather poke herself in the eyes than be bought a Monsoon dress. However I'm aware most girls go loopy for this sort of thing). Monsoon Boy is a more recent addition, offering beautifully-made trousers, printed shirts and hooded tops. A limited selection of the babies' and girls' ranges are available online (*www.monsoon.co.uk*). For branches call 08701 553553.

- What is it about the French and their funky, affordable kidswear? **Petit Bateau** (visit www.petit-bateau.com) focuses on lovely, easy-going clothes for romping about in; La Redoute (visit www.redoute.co.uk for a catalogue) offers brilliant value, fast delivery and acres of choice.

- Our supermarkets are not to be sniffed at. **George Jnr** at Asda is pretty speedy at picking up on wantable trends, and is cheap as chips.

3 Sew labels into their children's nursery/school clothes

I'm always so impressed when I glimpse the inside of a kid's sweatshirt and there's a carefully sewn-on label which reads: LYDIA MURPHY. What I tend to do is scrawl on the ordinary label with indelible pen, which creates a less pleasing effect. Either that, or I just don't bother, and we lose everything.

Far better to order sew-on name tapes from John Lewis or www.minilabels.co.uk, who also supply mightily impressive durable plastic labels for shoes, books and other items which tend to go walkies.

4 Keep a gigantic, well-maintained fruitbowl in a prominent position to impress visiting adults

I have been aiming to do the above since leaving the parental nest back in 1982. Tactics to ensure the consumption of five fruit/veg portions a day include hauling home ridiculous amounts of fresh produce from the supermarket, then watching with interest as oranges toughen into little grenades. The decomposition process can be accelerated by storing a selection of fruit in thecar 'for healthy snacks'. An innocuous morsel – a single grape, say – only has to be left in there overnight to acquire a blueish fuzz.

Since having children, I've gone to great lengths to ensure that they do consume some fruit most days; while they'll happily snack from the posh end of Fruit World (peaches, nectarines, strawberries, cherries), they're a little less enthusiastic when presented with an apple. (Reading this, my son shouts over my shoulder: 'I do like fruit! Fruit Winders!')

5 Never smoke fags

A perennial favourite of mine, and still top of the to-do list. Quitters report that the first two weeks are the worst; after fourteen nights of waking up bathed in your own sweat, you will be awash with cash and regain the ability to communicate with your family. You may also be divorced, but at least you won't have yellow teeth. These are mine and J's recent arguments caused by ciggie withdrawal:

Noisy typing
Me: What are you doing in here?
Him: Reading.
Me: But you lit a fire in the dining room . . .
Him: And you set up your laptop in there.
Me: Whoo, sorry! Does my typing disturb you?
Him: Look, if you're working, I'd rather get out of your –
Me: I'm not working, just making notes. Come back where the fire is.

Him: I am FINE right here.
Me: Forget it, I'll not bother working. I won't make any money at all.
Him: For God's sake!
Me: What? What? I'm not working. Happy now?

Turning into a medieval person

Me, to my son, who is whirling around kitchen in aimless fashion: Watch that cup of milk! It will surely spill.
J: You sound weird. Why do you talk funny whenever you stop smoking?
Me: What kind of funny?
Him: Like a medieval person. Verily, that cup will surely spilleth . . .
Me: I just said . . .
Him: Forsooth!
Me: *I'm* weird? What's up with you?
Him: Dunno. Just feel like the God of Hellfire, that's all.

Shoddy massage technique

Him: You know when you do a massage? Never, ever tamper with this bit [indicates back of neck].
Me: I didn't touch that bit.
Him: No, but you were heading towards it . . .
Me: I give you a massage and you criticise my technique?
Him: Yes. You could really injure a person, doing that.

It's the *Lanark Gazette* or me

Me: Did you ask for that fortnight's holiday at Easter?
Him: Yes.
Me: And did you get it?
J studies our local paper, the *Lanark Gazette*.
Me: If we want to go to Crieff, we'd better book it.

Him: Hmmm [still poring over newspaper].
Me: What's so interesting in the bloody *Lanark Gazette*?
Him: Umm.
Me: Do you want to go away at Easter or not?
Him, tossing down Lanark Gazette *in fit of pique*: Easter? Easter? How should I know what I want to do at Easter?

Cold pie

Him [lifting T-shirt to expose belly]: Look at me, I'm all bloated.
Me: So am I.
Him: Yeah, I just watched you eat all that cold steak pie.
Me: I just had a tiny bit. There's enough for the kids tomorrow if—
Him: There's nothing left of it! Look, you've dug a ruddy great hole in it.
Me [with flakes of puff pastry flying out of my mouth]: Are you policing my eating habits?
Him: Take a look at yourself with your gob stuffed with pie. It's not nice.

Ham salad

Him: This is a lovely ham salad.
Me: What do you mean, a lovely ham salad?
Him: I really mean it, this is—
Me: Don't be so bloody facetious.
Him: No, what I really mean is, one of my favourite meals in the whole wide world is a—
Me: !&£*!!

Ultimate Detoxifier Machine

Me: I'm not sure about this haircut.
Him: It'd look okay if you styled it.
Me: What do you mean, styled it?

Him: It looked great when you came back from the hairdresser.
Me: Of course it did. She moussed it, backcombed it, straightened it . . .
Him [triumphantly]: Well, there you go!
Me: You think I have time to—
J flicks his eyes towards the *Lanark Gazette*, settling on an article about the Ultimate Detoxifier Machine, 'an inter-cellular machine which taps away at calcified deposits in the abdominal area then stimulates the lymphatic system to remove those toxins'. The picture shows a bikini-clad girl with little pads stuck all over her body, even her skinny little ankles.
Me: Look, a detoxification course costs £500.
Him: That's a hundred packets of fags.

6 Never shout

After a whole hour of my sons bickering over who got to wear the school fleece, rather than the school sweatshirt, I blew a gasket at the school gate and threw down my daughter's shopping trolley. Dozens of teeny toys bounced on to the road. 'Ooh!' another mother said. 'I didn't know you were *like that*.'

Research indicates that yelling at children is just as damaging as smacking. A friend once suggested: 'When you feel like shouting, drop your voice to a whisper. They're more likely to hear you that way.' I have tried this; my children assumed I was ill, yawned in my face, and carried on constructing something called a tree-tent from a freshly-laundered duvet cover.

It's more realistic, I feel, to accept that we'll shout occasionally – but will always say sorry afterwards. This ensures a satisfyingly inconsistent message and the realisation that, if they goad you into bellowing at them, you'll feel so guilty afterwards that the chocs will soon come out.

7 Give beautiful birthday/Christmas presents to other children

Sorted parents keep a 'gift drawer' filled with lovely unisex presents which can be whipped out and wrapped at a second's notice. They also have the children make all birthday and Christmas cards and write personal thank you notes (not just 'Thank you for my prezant it was nise'). Gift-wise, you can't go far wrong with:

- Girlie trinkets from **Accessorize**. Pick from nail polish kits, glitzy bags, purses, gloves, notebooks and, for older girls, lovely photo frames (visit www.accessorize.co.uk for branches and online boutique).

- As a stationery addict I gain tons of pleasure from giving older children swanky notebooks and cuter-than-cute desk accessories from **Paperchase** (visit www.paperchase.co.uk for store guide).

- To zoom off the scale perfection-wise, give a present of year-long animal sponsorship at the child's nearest zoo (just go to the sponsorship section on the zoo's website). Gecko, anyone? Or a share of a white rhinoceros?

- My friend Kath swears by **www.letterbox.co.uk** for its brilliant selection of parent-pleasing gifts, including fabulous dressing-up outfits (my daughter's beloved paint-your-own teaset came from here).

- Visit **www.jojomamanbebe.co.uk** for a small but lovely and unusual selection of gifts for babies and younger children (but try not to be distracted by the wantable items in the family house section).

- ♥ For those eek! I forgot moments . . . **www.wheesh.com** has a gift-finder bar and vast stock ranging from the humdrum to pretty and tasteful. Better still, it can arrange next-day delivery in mainland UK, to save your blushes.

- ♥ Hand-made cards are always wildly impressive – but your child might not be in the creative mood when a friend's birthday approaches. A handy rainy-day activity is to get your kids to draw or paint a stack of cards so you can always yank one out of the drawer at short notice. Cue applause.

8 Make their own play doh

Aided by a recipe in a children's craft book, my kids and I mixed flour, baking powder and vinegar to make vile-smelling dough. I was so self-satisfied that I was actually starting to make myself feel quite nauseous. As a friend was popping around later – a friend who does so much crafty stuff that her TV's remote could go missing and no one would notice for a week – I left the dough out in a really prominent position on the kitchen worktop. In the meantime, my kids could shape it into animals, three-tier wedding cakes, a scale model of Welwyn Garden City – the possibilities were endless.

However, no one wanted to make anything. My sons had just lolled upside down on the sofa, sliding their mucky shoes up and down our newly-painted living room wall. My daughter, who has developed a Judas fixation since glimpsing a Peter Howson painting at the Rozelle Gallery in Ayr, kept wittering, 'Why did Judas have a sad face? Did he kill Jesus? What happens when somebody dies? Will you have a grave or be burned?'

It's disturbing to learn that your children would rather sprawl about, firing random questions, than do constructive activities with their mother. I don't devote every second of the day to arts and crafts; however, during those rare moments when I'm overwhelmed by the creative urge, I expect my kids to at least humour me by joining in.

FOOTNOTE: To experience that self-satisfied glow for yourself, put three tablespoons baking powder into a bowl, add half a cup of vinegar from a jar of pickled onions or gherkins, then mix in one cup of flour, half a cup of oil, and a few drops of kids' ready-mixed paint. Knead well, and pat yourself on the back (remembering to first wash your hands).

9 Belong to a gym

Just because you're a parent doesn't mean you have 'let yourself go', right? It's those gym accessories that have seduced me in the past: the cute body lotion dispensers, the lockers with nifty sliding card action. You forget that you'll have to acquaint yourself with those awful machines, or that, during a workout, an instructor will eye your tentative moves and bark a firm: 'No.'

Fortunately, the majority of us don't venture into these places after the first visit. But we do have a membership card in the wallet, and are therefore able to say, 'My gym.'

10 Display kids' artwork in a tasteful manner

This doesn't mean Blu-tacking dog-eared scrawlings on to every inch of wall space. According to my friend Jane Alexander, a health/well being/feng shui guru (and author of *Spirit of the*

Home, Thorsons): 'It looks far better if you mount a few really special drawings in clip frames than plaster them all over the walls.'

For a vast range of frames in all sizes – including cheapie clipframes – visit **www.fastframes.co.uk** and banish Blu-tack smears forever.

11 Be organised in the mornings

Children's school uniforms will be laid out the night before. My sons will never again suffer the humiliation of having to beg for scraps of other people's snacks because their mother has forgotten their playtime goodies. They will be greeted by a clean fragrant parent at the school gates, who is not panting.

All this will be achieved by creating a calm and tidy home environment, requiring the binning of all superfluous paperwork. This includes the kids' artwork which they proudly brought home from school/nursery: 'No, honey, I haven't seen your pasta picture – but I'm sure it'll turn up . . .'

12 Read bed-time stories every evening

'Where *is Green Eggs and Ham?*' My daughter is currently obsessed with the Dr Seuss classic which I found vaguely funny the first sixty-five times I read it, but am now starting to experience a violent jangling sensation in my brain whenever I glimpse its cover and even hear the words 'green' or 'ham'.

My child is tearing her room apart in an attempt to locate the story. Books are flung from her book basket: beautifully illustrated stories, which I would be happy to read, but which she rejects because they are not *Green Eggs and Ham*. I try to distract her with *Where The Wild Things Are* – also a favourite – but which is now dismissed as 'stupid'. Why do children crave the same thing over and over? They would happily consume a favourite meal every day for months at a stretch. They form crazed attachments to horrible orange nylon trousers which must be washed every night, so they are ready to be worn every morning.

However, parents are aware that reading to children is A Good Thing, and so we abide by their rules. We read when our eyelids are leaden and are reprimanded for yawning or 'reading in a sleepy voice'. A parent quickly discovers that a major design fault of the bed-time story is that it happens at around eight pm – precisely when Reading Parent is knackered, and can hear Non-Reading Parent uncorking wine in the kitchen. Once a child reaches the age of two, they are primed to detect when Reading Parent, perhaps imagining how that first glass of wine will taste, skips a bit of the story in order to hurry downstairs before Non-Reading Parent has drained the bottle. 'You missed a bit,' they bark, becoming so het up and furious that you're forced to start at the beginning again, then start *again* as child two appears in the bedroom, when you're one page from the end.

My daughter is now refusing to go to bed without *Green Eggs and Ham*. 'It's lost,' I tell her, 'we'll find it tomorrow.' I choose another book and start reading to an invisible child. Daughter stomps out of her room in disgust. Sons dive into bed with me; daughter thunders back in, appalled that her brothers are fouling her pristine bed linen with their filthy feet.

It's tricky, having three children who all wish to be read to, yet have wildly varying tastes (one benefit of triplets, I guess). My daughter is now doing forward rolls on her bed. The boys have slithered underneath to drag out the five sleeping bags for which we paid around £97, yet have slept in only once.

'Where's *Green Eggs and Ham*?' my daughter bellows. As we search and search for the dratted thing, it strikes me that vast portions of a parent's life are spent hunting for things which really shouldn't matter.

The hunt is called off. *Green Eggs* appears to have melted away. Surely it can't have been stashed where a four-year-old will never find it? No – we must have been burgled.

Some beautiful books we've read over and over and over

Toddler territory

- *Miffy* series by Dick Bruna: pleasingly simple. My daughter has outgrown the stories but loves to trace the clearly outlined illustrations.

- *Tom and Pippo* series by Helen Oxenbury. Gentle in tone and, with thick board pages, pretty chewable too.

- *1001 words* – anything, in fact, by Jan Picnkowski: for poring over and naming things when your child's leaning to talk.

Picture books

- *The Gruffalo, Room on the Broom, The Snail and the Whale* and *The Smartest Giant In Town*, all by Julia Donaldson and Axel Scheffler. Fantastic rhyming text, fragments of which lodge themselves firmly in the head, to be chanted years later (a bit like the best bits of *Withnail and I*).

- *Leon and Bob* by Simon James. Just perfect. The last page makes my vision blur every time.

♡ *Albie* and *Albie and the Space Rocket* by Andy Cutbill. The latter also features a toilet, used as part of a spacecraft, which perhaps explains its enduring appeal to my bog-obsessed children.

♡ *Don't Put Your Finger in the Jelly, Nelly!* by Nick Sharratt. Fabulously realistic pictures, and wonderful for pokey fingers.

♡ *Where the Wild Things Are* and *In The Night Kitchen* by Maurice Sendak. Surreal and wonderful – our all-time faves.

♡ Also loved by my children but are repetitive enough to cause meltdown in parental brain: *Cat in the Hat, Fox in Socks, I Wish That I Had Duck Feet* and – mercy – *Green Eggs and Ham,* all by Dr Seuss.

Poetry books

♡ For younger children *My Very First Mother Goose* by Iona Opie and Rosemary Wells, and Edward Lear's *Nonsense Songs,* illustrated by Bee Willey, have provided a welcome breather from Green Eggs and Ruddy Ham.

♡ My boys can't resist snorting over the bonkers rhymes in *The Day I Fell Down the Toilet and Other Poems* by Steve Turner (yes, toilets again).

The classics (How blinking perfect do you feel, reading these to your children?)

♡ *The Water Babies* by Charles Kingsley. Hearing about a poor, ill-treated chimney sweep shows your own children how very pampered and over-indulged they really are.

♥ *Peter Pan* by J.M. Barrie. After being read this, my son purchased a plastic 'hook' which he refused to take off for weeks on end, even for bed.

♥ *Stig of the Dump* by Clive King. Wild and mysterious – a classic adventure.

Some books for older children which helped to cure my sons' reluctance to read

At around six years old, my sons were beginning to read by themselves, but losing interest in books. We flailed around, never choosing quite the right book until a teacher friend recommended non-fiction paperbacks on boy-pleasing subjects like wild animals, outer space and sea creatures. I also found that DC Comic books (*Batman*, *Superman*, all the superhero stuff) appealed; little chunks of text in speech balloons were more digestible than great wodges of text. These led on to a lengthy obsession with *Asterix* and especially *Tin Tin*, which threw up interesting questions about opium dens. Other sure-fire hits:

♥ *Danny Champion of the World, Charlie and the Chocolate Factory, The BFG, Fantastic Mr Fox*, all by – in fact anything by – Roald Dahl (not forgetting the hilarious *The Twits*).

♥ *Little Red Riding Wolf* and *Cinderboy* by Laurence Anholt (chuckly takes on traditional tales).

♥ The *Horrible Histories* series. Pleasingly bitty and very gruesome.

When you really can't be fagged reading

If I'm really bushed I just paraphrase the story to get through it as quickly as possible. Most children's stories still hang together if you just read the first sentence of each page.
Ruth, make-up artist and mother to Lara, five, and Emma, two

Once the children could read for themselves, we let them have quiet time in the evenings with their books, or listening to a storytape. I'm sad that we didn't read to them for longer but they started to prefer storytapes to us droning on and yawning all over their books.
Matthew, care assistant and father to Connor, ten, and Ben, seven

If you're pushed for time, books of poems with colourful pictures are a good story substitute. Reading a couple of poems takes no time and feels longer as each is an event in its own right. My three-year-old also likes comic-style books – she happily 'reads' one for ages as the frames make it easy to follow the story. While she reads to her teddies, feeling very grown-up, I settle her little sister to sleep.
Sue, mother to three-year-old Erin and Jessica, twenty months

I explain that my contact lenses are tired and aren't working properly.
Rosie, mother of boys aged five and six

Trying to *look* perfect

Call me shallow, but I do feel that a mother's state of mind can be at least partially determined by her outward appearance. During grim, stressful times, I've gone for months without coming into direct contact with mascara. As my children's demands have eased slightly, I feel perfectly entitled to make my sons late for school by applying at least powder, eye shadow and lipstick before leaving the house. It makes me feel halfway human in the mornings.

However, certain former colleagues clearly have me down as an old no-make-up plain-face. The commissioning editor of a women's glossy magazine sent me an email along the lines of: 'We're doing a life swap feature – want to take part? We've found this woman who uses an amazing range of products and spends hours pampering herself – it's quite incredible. As a contrast, we need someone completely low-maintenance who hardly does anything nice to herself. We thought of you.'

Thus flattered to pieces, and with ego threatening to burst out of the top of my head, I agreed to adopt the mysterious Peta's beauty routine for three days.

My so-called 'routine'

Shower: any old soap, any old shampoo (no conditioner).

After shower: Clinique Dramatically Different Moisturising Lotion (also at night), deodorant (any with a working ball).

Evening: twenty-minute soak with Crabtree & Evelyn bath foam followed by Clinique on face.

Other bits:

Clean teeth morning and night with whatever's going.

Shave legs and underarms once a week with Bic disposable.

Have hair cut every 2–3 months and chop own fringe which J says makes me look 'a bit deranged'.

Pluck brows when they bush out.

Peta's routine

In shower: Aveda Camomile Shampoo, Aveda Camomile Color Conditioner, Clarins Eau Dynamisante Shower Gel.

After shower: Cleanse and moisturise with Eve Lom products. Caudalie Eye Contour Cream, Vaseline Intensive Care Deodorant, The Sanctuary Mande Lular Body Soufflé.

Teeth: cleaned up to five times a day with Braun electric toothbrush and Denblan toothpaste, followed by flossing and mouthwash.

Evening: Bath for up to an hour with Space NK Bath Oil (Stillness); shave legs and bikini line with Gillette Venus razor.

Once a week: scrub with Clarins Foaming Body Exfoliator or Origins Salt Rub. Apply Clarins Self Tanning Instant Spray. Treat feet with Origins Soothing Foot Scrub and Energising Foot Cream, plus polish (Chanel Rouge Noir in winter, Kabuki in summer).

If going out: Mac Strobe Cream, YSL Touch Eclat, Estee Lauder Eye Defining Pencil, Mac eye shadow, Bobbi Brown blusher, Laura Mercier lipgloss.

Peta also has a weekly sports massage, facial, manicure and pedicure and has her hair cut every four weeks.

At this point I'd like to mention that, at the tender age of twenty, I blagged my way into a job as Beauty Editor on a magazine. I boned up on techniques such as eyebrow plucking and exfoliation (although I was more interested in rubbing my copious free lipstick on to the faces of boys). So how has my beauty routine dwindled to practically zilch? I blame it on the children (of course), working from home (resulting in minimal contact with fellow human beings) and living in rural Scotland, which is so windy and rainy that you look pretty ravaged whatever you slap on your face.

Day one. It's with a mixture of heady excitement (so many goodies!) and trepidation (so much to bloody remember) that I commence Peta's regime. And I fall at the first hurdle. So many products burst forth from Peta's box of tricks – and I have nowhere to put them. Peta's bathroom is no doubt a tranquil space with glass shelves, a vase of lilies and a candle labelled 'Serenity'. Every surface of our bathroom is jammed with sailing boats and plastic zoo animals and miniature watering cans.

My mood fails to improve as I commence Peta's routine. It's been so long since I used conditioner that I'm forced to study the bottle to see how long to leave it on. Two to five minutes? What am I supposed to do during this time? I shower, leave the conditioner on, and tackle my teeth, beating off my children as they clamour for 'just a wee shot' of the fancy electric toothbrush. My kids have never seen anyone flossing before. 'There's blood coming out,' my son whimpers. All three kids teeter back, horrified that I appear to be sawing my own gums.

We're about to set off for school when I realise that my hair's still gunked up with conditioner and I haven't cleansed or moisturised yet. I hurry up the street with dripping (but divinely marzipan-smelling) hair. Back home with my daughter I tackle cleansing . . . after a shower? How clean can a person be? There's worse to come: Eve Lom products come with *instructions*. The regime appears terribly faffy, involving repeatedly pressing a wet muslin cloth on to the face – but afterwards, my skin feels pleasantly springy. I slather Mande Lular on to exposed areas, aided by my daughter, and ignoring the guilt about all the things I should be doing.

I collect the boys after school – amid comments from other mothers that I am looking very 'done up' – and we head for the park. It's been raining heavily. Instead of haring about with the kids and having a laugh, I'm hung up about muddy splodges on my freshly-painted toes, as if I'm some rarified creature who should be at home, rubbing in lotions. By nightfall I am anxious that I forgot the eye cream, have only cleaned my teeth once and feel peculiar wearing someone else's choice of perfume. Feeling downhearted – I can't even pamper myself properly – I splosh a little Stillness from Space NK into the bath.

Day two. I wake up feeling anxious that, as well as adhering to Peta's usual routine, I need to incorporate the weekly stuff (tanning spray, salt scrub, grainy stuff for feet etc). I'm sure I look wonderful already – although J has yet to try to ravage me, or swoon with desire – but it's all so ruddy time-consuming. I get through the day but forget conditioner, soufflé and, more worryingly, teeth. Spend entire evening shaving, slathering and salt scrubbing. My legs are so excited, a rash springs up.

Day three. It is apparent that I cannot keep up Peta's routine without lashing my children to the water tank in the attic. Peta and I have never met but I find myself obsessing over her lifestyle. As I bung Wee Willie Winkie sausages from the grill on to plastic plates, I picture her, groomed and souffled, nibbling on a wild mushroom and pumpkin risotto at the Ivy.

But the day improves. We visit my friend Sue who says, 'You're looking well. Have you been having beauty treatments or something?'

'Me?' I splutter. 'Are you kidding?'

The highly organised mother

J says, 'You're obsessive.' I say that, really, my habit is the one thing that's holding this family together. In fact, I'm so hooked that a lovely lady from Radio Scotland once came to interview me about it.

You see, I make lists. Nothing sets me a-tingling like seeing words stacked on top of each other, written neatly on Post-It notes. Crossing things off feels marvellous. Serious list-makers are known to write things down that they've already done, purely for the joy of scoring them off. These days I maintain a hierarchy of lists: everyday stuff on Post-Its or clipboard. Potentially life-changing tasks in a padded notebook impregnated with a secret substance formulated to repel anyone under the age of fifteen. I keep health lists: 'Drink two litres water per day. Eat fruit. Don't have any more children.'

J regards my list-making as faintly amusing, forgetting that, if I were to stop, we would be starving and wearing filthy clothing, or stark naked. He doesn't realise the joy to be had from lists – other people's lists, I mean. Way back in the Edwardian era, when I had an office job, I would while away tedious meetings by furtively scanning my colleague Natalie's notebook (fuchsia mock snakeskin, probably Paperchase) and read: 'Collect dress. Try hair serum. Be nicer to Adrian.'

Another colleague kept a list on her pinboard which read, 'Learn Spanish. Book Guatemala. Flying lessons.' I knew she was showing off, that her real list would read, 'polish shoes' and 'buy soap powder'. But – let's be honest here – the real function of lists is not to act as memory joggers, but to kid ourselves that we are wildly busy, highly efficient, all-round wonderful human beings.

I have to be organised – it's just too stressful if I'm not. Lunchboxes and school uniforms are all ready the night before, evening meals are planned for the week – I'm a list obsessive, and have figured out the perfect way of storing my lists. I've bought one of those clear plastic hanging things with lots of pockets which are meant for displaying photos. With this, I can view

all my lists – family, work, personal, urgent, etc – all
at once.
Felicity, mother to Tom, seven, and Adam, three, who says her
list-making is 'like a sickness'

The day I felt very imperfect

Ever noticed how a single sentence can make, or ruin, your day?
Like: 'Mum, I've got an itchy head.' Or, 'It just broke!' Such a
thing happened one morning when I'd just deposited the boys
at that fabulous virtually free institution (school) and overheard
another mother say: 'No, I'll skip coffee, thanks. I'm just going
home to make a mousse cake.'

What was this thing, a mousse cake? A mousse? Or a cake?
Or something in between? A scarily high proportion of the
people around rural South Lanarkshire are highly talented in
the home baking arena, making their own biscuits, scones, cakes
– you name it. The week we moved here, a neighbour popped
by to ask for donations for the baking stall at a cancer fund-
raising event. At ten pm I was still slogging over these wretched
biscuits, trying to figure out whether they were irreparably
burned, or just 'highly fired' in a rustic sort of way. My old friend
Marie phoned and snorted when I told her what I was doing.
'For Christ's sake,' she spluttered. 'Why don't you just give them
five quid?'

So I don't need to hear strangers bragging about 'just' popping
home to make mousse cakes. In my experience, there's no 'just'
about it.

271

And the day I became sickeningly perfect (well, nearly)

Nigella Lawson has been voted top role model for British mothers. Nigella herself admits, 'I'm hopelessly negligent and never actually do much with my children other than cook.' However, always aiming to do better at this parenting lark, I decide to give Nigella-style mothering a whirl for one day. Maybe, with enough luscious images of the woman herself about my kitchen, some of her fabulousness might rub off on me.

Nigella day

7.45 am. Rather than eyeballing a fantastically wealthy advertising bigshot/Britart collector, I wake up with J, who is snoring throatily and owns a faded Captain Beefheart print. He's neither posh, nor rich; a good thing, perhaps, as I've never been able to fancy posh/rich men with their bad dancing and love of Dire Straits. However, we do own a messy, crumb-infested bed, not unlike the Emin installation Charles Saatchi paid £150,000 for.

8.45 am. Still lazing on rumpled Britart which feels appropriately Nigella-ish – she admits to eating spaghetti in bed. Nigella's children are probably capable of making their own toast or even their mother's soft-set peach and redcurrant jam. Unfortunately, my own children require assistance especially as we are having American Pancakes (from Nigella's book *Nigella Bites*) but without the maple syrup as our small town (pop: 1,900) doesn't appear to sell it. Ah well, on to the pancakes. I'm so busy sweating over the pan than I manage to eat only one. Nor have I managed to get dressed yet, let alone unearth a Nigella-style cashmere sweater or sexy, slithery dress.

9.30 am. Daughter's nursery is having a fund-raiser in the park. My contribution to such events is usually a bottle of nasty sweet German wine that's been kicking around our pantry for seventeen years but this time, flushed with creativity and goodness, I make Nigella's Easter Nests, not because it's Easter, but due to the fact that any idiot can bash up Shredded Wheat and chocolate. We carry the nests to the park uncovered so our neighbours can bestow praise and kiss my feet. My children buy two nests each at 20p. Nigella herself admits: 'Can't say I'm absolutely mad about eating them.' Ditto, Nige.

12 noon. Home to batter-splattered kitchen, mounds of washing up, and another damn meal to prepare. I'm making Golden Jubilee Chicken (from Nigella's *Forever Summer*), a recipe she intends to use up 'a piece of cold chicken leftover in the fridge'. We never have anything so useful lying about. Any leftovers tend to be of the cold sausage type, slumped under foil and causing J to observe, 'I think something's rotting in here.' Fortunately, I stocked up in ingredients yesterday: mango, spring onion, limes, coriander and little gem lettuce. J pronounces the dish 'light and refreshing'.

1.15 pm. J wants to know if I'm planning to bake a cake, as 'baking is Nigella's thing, really.' He glances at her photo adoringly, and flushes pink.

2.15 pm. Exhausted from watching me cooking so much, J falls asleep on the sofa for two hours. I take the kids back to the park and run into a friend who offers my sons red Cola. Feel Nigella-ness ebbing away. That blasted woman makes her own Elder and Passionfruit Cooler.

4.15 pm. Back home, I think about calling my dad, the former Tory Chancellor, but remember he's plain old Keith, a retired photographer, who tells me he's pouring concrete into some crevice in his kitchen. I inform him that major improvements are happening in our kitchen too.

4.45 pm. I am experiencing over-familiarity with chopping boards and the cooker. Tea is Linguine with Garlic Oil and Pancetta (from *Nigella Bites*) except there's no pancetta, only bacon. It slithers down nicely. My park pal has popped round with his red Cola and two daughters, so they all have a taste. It feels pleasingly spontaneous – a true Nigella moment.

5.45 pm. Dime Bar Ice-Cream (from *Forever Summer*) for pud. I had planned to make my own ice-cream – I've borrowed my friend Adele's ice-cream-maker and bought cream, sugar and eggs – but cannot be buggered with any more faffing about. My sons pulverise Dime Bars in the food processor until a 'glassy sand' texture is achieved, and stir the caramel grains into shop-bought ice-cream. Everyone wolfs it.

6.30 pm. Check my face in the mirror. Rather than being alabaster skinned, like Nigella, I look knackered and hot. Not hot in a ravish-me way – just hot.

9.30 pm. With the kids in bed, I whip up a jug of Fragonard: fizzy wine with pulped strawberries. Wash the food processor jug for the third time.

11.45 pm. Still don't have Nigella's swoonsome breasts but, as a pretty rubbish cook, I'm proud of my achievements today. I drift into sleep, mildly sloshed on Fragonard, truly believing that I have reached the epitome of good-mother-ness – that my children are blessed human beings, and I'm doing a remarkable job.

And then I wake up.

13

things i wish my mother had told me (before i became a mother myself)

There's no point in trying to **potty train** by force, unless you actively enjoy catching the unsavoury missiles which roll out of your child's trouser leg. Children only get their act together when they're ready. Odds are that your kid will not commence primary school encased in gigantic Pampers.

Working parents might feel guilty but, according to Jennifer Smith, Childhood Educational Psychologist at Middlesex University: 'Children are naturally sociable, and it's good for them to encounter a **wide circle of people of all ages**. What they do need is consistency; if they're presented with a succession of carers, they have to start all over each time. But with consistency of care, and as long as your child sees you every day – to hug, kiss and cuddle – she'll still form her primary bond with you, the parent.'

Only celebrities wear **heels during pregnancy**.

Children are actually pretty handy to have around sometimes, their sudden 'illnesses' providing the perfect excuse to **duck out of tedious dinner parties** hosted by people you don't really like.

Compared to pristine firstborn, subsequent children are usually pretty **grubby around the edges**. It's not that we care for them any less. We're just less hung up on outward appearance and, yes, knackered.

No matter how spruced-up your child may appear to you, a fellow parent will always point out that something is oozing behind an ear, or **a nostril requires urgent attention**.

While we try to do a decent job of parenting purely for our kids' sake – to help them grow into happy, bright and well-formed adults, just like ourselves – a tiny part of us cares desperately that **other people think we're doing an excellent job**. It's why we crumble on hearing the mildest criticism of our children, and virtually explode with pride and delight when they're praised or admired.

Whilst children can tolerate the sight of us fully clothed, going about our domestic activities, they soon become repulsed by our naked bodies and the sight of **two adults kissing**. Recently, spotting a snogging scenario going on in our kitchen, our four-year-old thundered in and stamped on J's foot.

Just because your child falls about laughing (or screws up the face in disgust) when **glimpsing your naked body** it does not mean that you require cosmetic surgery. They think *all* adult bodies are weird.

Shoving the kids in front of a full-length video, then sneaking upstairs with your partner for a bit of a play about, does not count as **leaving children unattended**. Sometimes it's the only way to do it.

Taking the kids to a **car boot sale**, armed with a couple of quid each, is a fun way to spend a weekend morning. But you're also giving them licence to bring piles of malfunctioning Furbees and other assorted crap into the house.

You can help your child to **learn left from right** by stretching the thumb and forefinger of the left hand to form a capital 'L' shape.

Glimpsing your child's devastated bedroom, and roaring, 'Look at the state of this room! Clear it up – do you here me?' is a sure sign that you are **turning into your mother**. Nothing can be done to halt this process, so don't fight it.

Dressing **twins in identical outfits** might look cute, but be prepared to have strangers and even close friends referring to them not by name, but 'this one' and 'that one' or their two names joined together with an 'or' in the middle – ie, 'Toby-or-Ben.'

No matter how abominably your child has behaved during the day, he will still appear **utterly angelic** when he's asleep.

An appropriate book or video can sometimes help to **alleviate a child's fears**. *Owl Babies* (Martin Waddell and Patrick Benson) deals with separation anxiety; my sons' irrational fear of Santa diminished after several viewings of Raymond Briggs' delightful vid, *Father Christmas*.

Children can take an instant dislike to **people we love** or who are regular visitors to the home. One friend reports that, between the ages of one and two and a half, her daughter was terrified of kind Auntie Myra because she didn't have any top teeth.

Whatever anyone tells you, **pets' cages or hutches do not self-cleanse**.

It's tempting, when you're pregnant, to share with friends your **preferred baby names**. I told one friend that we liked Babette for a girl. Her reaction – 'Oh for Christ's sake!' – rendered it unusable.

Allowing children to **dress themselves** might take nearly two hours and result in their wearing four inside-out T-shirts on top of each other, but is a valuable skill and should be encouraged.

No one can underestimate the sheer deliciousness of **cold fish fingers** and oven chips left on a child's plate.

There's not a child on this earth who likes **Brussels sprouts**.

Falling into the habit of lying down with your child in order to **lull him to sleep** will result in you waking up at three-thirty am with a cricked neck and a kid who refuses to nod off without you being there.

Sleep training our children was hellish for two nights, but ultimately one of the most sanity-saving things we ever did.

Children may exhibit appalling taste in clothes, toys and bedroom décor, but their **musical preferences** can be influenced from a very early age.

However kid-friendly they may be, it's a terrible idea to persuade child-free friends to **come on holiday with you**.

Kids only ever throw up while wearing **hideously expensive clothes**. Anything from Adams or Woolworth's Ladybird range will remain unmarred and offer many years of faithful service.

It is possible to have a swanky night away with your children in tow. Some hotels provide nannies who'll whisk your infants away in the morning so you can enjoy a **long lie-in**. Try www.parentsneedpampering.co.uk.

When **travelling by plane**, it's a good idea to dress children in light layers which can be peeled off or bundled back on as the temperature fluctuates. They'll be thrilled by their in-flight meal – the plastic cutlery, little sachets of pepper and salt – and may request that their food is presented in a similar manner at home.

Travelling with children might be a hassle but you can at least console yourself that, when they reach the age of sixteen, they **won't want to go on holiday** with you any more.

No matter how much you adore your children, some days you're just not in the mood to have them **clambering all over you**. This is perfectly natural. Personally, I cannot abide them wrapping their arms around my legs, causing me to do a weird kind of shuffle-walk.

Most children reach a stage at which they're not too bad to have around. Rumour has it that, at some point, they disappear with an Interrail ticket for weeks on end and return home willing to undertake a wide array of tasks from cleaning the oven to **repointing the house**.

By the age of around five, children are hugely **motivated by money**. Threatening to dock their pocket money if they won't settle to sleep by a respectable hour is an effective way of grabbing back your evenings.

Children cannot resist **drawing on themselves** with felt pen, or rubbing an ink pad all over their arms.

It is perfectly normal to realise that, although it's nearly Christmas, there's still **sand on the floor** of the car from your summer holiday.

A child will only squeal, **'Yaaahh! My shoes are too small!'** in the presence of other parents.

While **firstborn is used to being King Pin**, kicking up a storm if his apple has not been peeled and neatly sliced into segments of equal thickness, younger sibling spies a fragment of discarded peel stuck to someone's heel, and nabs it.

Despite the fact that you have dutifully tripped along to several hundred school-related events – plays, concerts, sports days – your child will only ever refer to the one occasion when **'you didn't come'**.

Some of us go to great lengths – like moving to the country – in order to raise our children in a **safe, yet stimulating environment**. We forget that some urban kids are terrified of farm animals and just don't know what to do with all that grass and space.

If second children are easy going, the third takes care of himself virtually from birth. This is, of course, Mother Nature's way of tricking us into having **just one more baby**. What difference would it make? All the furniture's trashed anyway.

A parent is so **thrilled to be in the pub** that they can take up to twenty-five minutes trying to decide what they'd like to drink.

Life isn't fair. For instance, children are often blessed with the **most lustrous of eyelashes**, yet couldn't care less about such matters.

Children will argue about the tiniest thing. My sons have had a full-blown scuffle over a **cracked plastic beaker**.

Unless you're prepared to agree that three Jammy Dodgers constitute a perfectly acceptable breakfast, **tantrums are inevitable**.

It's good for children to see us **reading grown-up material**. One of my sons once declared, in an accusing tone, 'You never read books!' It occurred to me that he'd never seen me turning the pages of anything other than a picture book, or slim paperback with Captain Underpants on the jacket. We owe it to our children to show them that we read for fun too. Even if it is just a mangled copy of *Heat*.

A hideous, fighty day can be salvaged by **heading for water**: the beach, if you live by the coast; a river to throw sticks and pebbles into; even puddles to splash in (and, yes, roll about in).

Your children can make you feel **very decrepit**. My daughter is under the impression that I'm at least ninety-seven years old, and refers to my childhood as 'the olden days', as in: 'Did you have toys in the olden days?'

In photos taken just before we became parents, most of us **look about thirteen years old**.

Children are thrilled by the **glamorous world of the child-free adult**. When my old flatmate Eva came to stay, my kids spent the entire weekend examining her mysterious possessions: hair mousse, a Revlon Hot Air Styler, a black plastic object which they assumed was some sort of weapon, but turned out to be a hair dryer.

In the presence of such a rarified creature, **your own appearance deteriorates**. You might find that your children shun your attentions altogether, far preferring the visitor who possesses toe separators and a whizzy toothbrush which blasts off gunk with 'sonic waves'.

Every parent should know the opening hours of their **local off-licence**.

Nothing thrills a toddler more than opening and shutting the **little CD drawer** several thousand times. His fun is curtailed when the stereo is sent away for repair at great expense.

Once you've had kids, you can bid a sorry farewell to your shelves of CDs **all arranged in alphabetical order**.

And your **dressing gown cord**, which is now used to tie up 'naughty' toys.

You might think that children get sick of the same old dreary adult faces. Not so. Any efforts made to **improve our appearance** are greeted with suspicion or even hostility. When I started to wear my hair 'up', instead of leaving it drooping miserably around my face, one son announced that he didn't like 'bunned hair' and that I looked like a witch.

Children's bellies are designed for **blowing raspberries on**.

Sometimes you might tell yourself: **'I really must be so much nicer to my beloved.'** This can backfire. Whenever I've tried to be extra-courteous to J – bringing him hot drinks, enquiring about his hectic day at the office – he's assumed I've done something bad, like sat on his glasses.

In the early days of parenthood, I would arrange our offspring to form a charming tableau, ready to **greet Daddy on his return from work**. However, I quickly cottoned on that such a spectacle – baby snoozing, toddlers quietly colouring in – presented an utterly false picture of motherhood, and might lead him to conclude that I spent my days pushing back my cuticles and napping. These days I invite other people's kids for tea to ensure that the house ricochets with unrecognisable faces which lurch towards J and force him to hurry out to the back yard and smoke fags until they've all gone away.

Our children still love us, even when we've just **shouted at them**.

Many happy hours can be spent **snipping out pictures from the Argos catalogue** and announcing, 'I want this.' Sometimes your children might even want to join in.

It's not unusual for a kid to decide he's going to exist on nothing but **plain pasta and pretzels** for six months.

Like most things in life – abandoning a bottle or dummy, sucking on a bit of old blanket – a child will learn to **ride a bike** when he's ready, and not due to your exhausting efforts.

Every neighbourhood boasts one clever tyke who learned to ride his bike without stabilisers at **two years old.**

The very fact that you have produced children means that, at some point, you will be required to chair the toddler group, raise PTA funds, or **provide scrumptious home-made goodies for the baking stall.** The only way to duck out of such duties is to return to full-time employment very soon after each child's birth.

Most people would rather stick pins in their eyes than go to a **toddler group's fund-raising disco.**

No one should attempt to **cut their child's hair** unless they're a trained hairdresser.

Compared to a house where young people reside, the average workplace is a **haven of tranquillity.** Lunchbreaks, clutter-free desk, ample supply of other adults to talk to – what's not to like?

It's virtually impossible not to blub at your **child's school concert.**

Almost everyone thinks that they **know more about child-raising** than you do. They are wrong. There is nothing for it but to turn a deaf ear to the barrage of advice, and pick the brains of friends whom you trust.

Friends with older children sometimes tell me: 'It doesn't get any easier, you know. It's just *different*.' While I'm sure this is true, I refuse to believe that the whole parenting deal doesn't become less stressful and more pleasurable and that, as our offspring grow older, we adults **start to feel more human again.** For instance, at age three, one of my sons decided that it would be a great idea to hammer a nail into our new £950 fireplace, 'to hang things on'. He's now fully aware that such a reckless act would result in his PS2 being offered on eBay.

All children leave home eventually. When they do, we'll be able to go out when we want to and stay up as late as we like without a niggling fear of being woken at five-thirty am. We'll have manicured nails, fish finger-less fridges, and be able to watch TV without fighting our way through a mound of scattered PlayStation games. No one will demand that we switch over from the programme we're watching, just because *Scooby Doo*'s on.

When we invite friends round for dinner, no one will charge downstairs and announce that they like 'trying on Mum's pants'. When we're chatting to a faraway friend we won't be interrupted by someone shouting, 'Give me the phone! I want to speak!' and grappling for the receiver. No one will demand to climb on our backs, and ride us like a pony, unless we ask them to.

We will go on holiday during term time, read seven novels in a fortnight, and inhabit a sun-lounger all by ourselves rather than sharing with our children and their dripping inflatable boats and snorkel gear. We will never again visit soft play centres or children's farms. In time, we will forget that these places even exist.

We'll pass on the toys, books and battered doll's house to friends' children. We will never again read *The Gruffalo*. When shopping we will linger at the Clinique counter without worrying that our companions might topple the display stand over, or grind their nails into the pressed powder testers. We'll stop for lunch. When a friend says, 'Let's have another glass of wine,' we won't reply, 'Better not,' and bolt out of the restaurant, leaving a blizzard of scribbled-on napkins.

We may still wander through parks, but we won't loiter for ninety-five minutes at the swings, with a small person bellowing,

'Higher!' We'll be calmer, cleaner and, if we look knackered, we'll only have ourselves to blame. Our lives will become ours again.

And we won't know what to do with ourselves.

a directory
of places and stuff

Places

Almond Valley Heritage Centre, Livingston, West Lothian
   www.almondvalley.co.uk
Blackpool Zoo www.blackpoolzoo.org.uk
Colchester Zoo www.colchester-zoo.co.uk
Deep Sea World, North Queensferry, Fife
   www.deepseaworld. com
Eureka, Halifax www.eureka.org.uk
Ffestiniog Railway, Snowdonia www.festrail.co.uk
Glasgow Science Centre www.glasgowsciencecentre.org
Harewood House, near Leeds, West Yorkshire www.harewood.org
Jorvik Viking Centre, York www.jorvik-viking-centre.co.uk
Keighley and Worth Valley Railway, West Yorkshire
   www.kwvr.co.uk
Leeds Castle, Kent www.leeds-castle.com
Museum of Transport, Glasgow www.glasgowmuseums.com
National Maritime Museum, Falmouth, Cornwall
   www.nmmc.co.uk
National Railway Museum, York www.nrm.org.uk
Noah's Ark Zoo Farm, near Bristol
   www.noahsarkzoofarm.co.uk
North York Moors Railway, Pickering www.nymr.demon.co.uk
Observatory Science Centre, Herstmonceux
   www.the-observatory.org
Paignton Zoo www.paignton.org

www.parentsneedpampering.co.uk Heavenly hotel breaks for
harassed parents
River Dart Adventures, South Devon www.riverdart.co.uk
Warwick Castle www.warwick-castle.co.uk
Whipsnade Zoo www.whipsnade.co.uk

Stuff

www.accessorize.co.uk Girlie trinkets a-plenty
www.baby-planet.co.uk Eco-friendly kidswear
www.beds2go.co.uk Toy chests and ottomans
www.benetton.com For colourful kids
www.fastframes.co.uk Frame your offspring's creations
www.giantpeach.co.uk Cute clothes for babies and toddlers
www.theholdingcompany.co.uk Slick storage
www.ikea.com Fab kids' furniture, weird ice-cream
www.johnlewis.com For just about everything
www.jojomamanbebe.co.uk Gifts for babies and younger
children
www.just4kids.co.uk Zany toy boxes
www.letterbox.co.uk Wondrous gift selection
www.littledreamers.co.uk Bedroom furniture for nippers
www.minilabels.co.uk Label your kids' school clothes – like
proper mothers do
www.monsoon.co.uk Party dress heaven
www.muddypuddles.com Splosh-proof rainwear
www.muji.com Gifts, storage, smart lunchboxes
www.next.co.uk Eye-pleasing kids' furniture
www.paperchase.co.uk Highly desirable stationery (too lovely
for kids)
www.partybox.co.uk and www.partytreasures.co.uk For the
whole birthday party caboodle
www.petit-bateau.com Kids' casuals
www.pier.co.uk Tons of toy storage

www.redoute.co.uk Affordable French chic
www.wheesh.com Last-minute gifts
www.woolworths.co.uk School uniforms, stationery, lunch-boxes, vids – all cheap as chips

Three invaluable sites for when you're losing your noddle

www.babycentre.co.uk
www.ivillage.co.uk
www.mumsnet.com

Fiona Gibson

Babyface

Mum's the word . . .

When journalist Nina places a lonely hearts ad, she doesn't expect it to lead to an unplanned baby, gossipy coffee mornings and a dull-as-ditchwater partner.

Trapped at home with nappy-changing L-plates, she craves a little glamour and the odd free lunch. And that's when her fashion editor friend spots her new talent – and baby Ben's career as a model is launched.

Nina intends to tell her partner – but the time is never quite right. And exposure of her secret is only a photographic assignment away . . .

'Warm, compelling . . . hilarious to singletons
and mothers alike' *Marie Claire*

'A fantastic debut. More than funny, it's true'
Louise Bagshawe

HODDER

Fiona Gibson

Wonderboy

What happens when a couple downshifts to the country with a child who is scared of any animal bigger than a hamster and has developed a strange obsession with mazes?

Ro and Marcus have swapped London life for a cottage in a peaceful country village. When a newcomer threatens the 'best-kept' village status by allowing his garden to grow wild, Marcus starts a log of the lawn's height and condition. As the newcomer becomes the first friend her son has ever had, Ro is faced with a life-changing decision . . .

'Fans of rueful social comedy will chortle over the escapades of Ro, who heads to the country with her husband, Marcus, and their son, Tod, in search of a more laid-back lifestyle . . . witty exposé of the perils and pitfalls of relocation.' *Elle*

'Addictive.' *Company*

HODDER